BASIC WRITINGS
IN CHRISTIAN
EDUCATION

BASIC WRITINGS IN CHRISTIAN EDUCATION

Edited by KENDIG BRUBAKER CULLY

THE WESTMINSTER PRESS
Philadelphia

PRINTED IN THE UNITED STATES OF AMERICA

For
my wife,
Iris V. Cully,
Companion in Love and in Study

CONTENTS

PREFACE   9

PART I: THE EARLIER CENTURIES

  1. Clement of Alexandria:
     Christ the Educator   15

  2. Gregory Thaumaturgus:
     Address to Origen   25

  3. Cyril of Jerusalem: *The Catechetical
     Lectures — the Procatechesis*   32

  4. Jerome: *Letter to Pacatula*   41

  5. John Chrysostom: *The Right Way for
     Parents to Bring Up Their Children*   49

  6. Aurelius Augustine: *The Catechizing
     of the Uninstructed*   62

  7. *Constitutions of the Holy Apostles*   74

PART II: THE MIDDLE CENTURIES

  8. Alcuin: *Letter to Charlemagne*   83

  9. Charlemagne:
     Educational Proclamations   88

10. Rabanus Maurus:
    Education of the Clergy   93

11. Thomas Aquinas:
    How to Study and *The Teacher*   102

12. Jean Gerson:
    On Leading Children to Christ   119

PART III: THE REFORMATION AND AFTER

13. Martin Luther: *To the Councilmen of
    All Cities in Germany that They
    Establish and Maintain Christian
    Schools*   135

14. Ulrich Zwingli: *Of the Upbringing
    and Education of Youth in Good
    Manners and Christian Discipline*   150

15. John Calvin: *The Catechism of the
    Church of Geneva*   162

16. Roger Ascham: *The Schoolmaster*   170

17. John Amos Comenius:
    The Great Didactic   177

18. Thomas Fuller:
    The Good Schoolmaster   185

19. John Milton: *On Education*   192

20. John Locke: *Some Thoughts Con-
    cerning Education*   205

21. Jean Baptiste de la Salle:
    The Conduct of the Schools   216

22. August Hermann Francke:
    Thoughts on Teaching   224

23. Cotton Mather: *A Brief Essay to Direct and Excite Family Religion*   229

24. Isaac Watts: *Christian Discipline: or the Character of a Polite Young Gentleman*   238

PART IV: THE EIGHTEENTH CENTURY AND BEYOND

25. Johann Heinrich Pestalozzi: *Leonard and Gertrude*   253

26. Johann Friedrich Herbart: *Outlines of Educational Doctrine*   265

27. Friedrich Froebel: *The Education of Man*   275

28. Horace Mann: *American Free Schools*   287

29. Horace Bushnell: *What Christian Nurture Is*   295

30. John Dewey: *My Pedagogic Creed*   310

31. George Albert Coe: *The Starting Point of a Solution* and *Coda*   325

BIBLIOGRAPHY

General Works on Historical Backgrounds of Education   339

Works Illustrative of Trends and Developments in Christian Education Since George Albert Coe   342

INDEX   343

PREFACE

The educational task of the Christian church began simultaneously with the emergence of the church itself. As soon as converts were won to the fellowship of Christ's flock, some means had to be used to nurture them in the faith. From the first century to the present, the church has had to be concerned with the teaching aspects of its corporate existence. That it has taken this responsibility seriously is evident from the abundance of material from practically every century testifying to a concern with the what and the how of education.

Unfortunately, too often the cumulative heritage of educational wisdom from the Christian past has been overlooked in our necessary involvement with the insistently present situation. Yet the present moment is richly illuminated whenever we see it through the ongoing experience of the Christian believers across the years. We discover with happy surprise that problems we have thought peculiar to our own time were equally pressing, though in different guise, to our forerunners. Not infrequently, too, we find that their way of meeting those problems was insightful in a way that can help us with our own.

All theological disciplines in recent years have been recognizing the importance of a historical stance from which to view the present confrontation of the church and the world. But it must be admitted that Christian educators have been less eager to acquire such a historical perspective within their own discipline than have their colleagues in related fields.

This anthology is designed as a contribution to the reorientation of Christian education which is now emerging. It is hoped that the variety of types of writing on a wide range of pedagogical matters with which these writers deal will open new vistas for many, whether they be students, professors, clergymen, practitioners of Christian education in parishes, or laymen eager to enlarge their perspective. It is even to be expected that classes in universities and teachers colleges might welcome an opportunity to see how much concerned with educational theory and methodology Christian writers have been across many centuries. They will see also how deeply interwoven with secular education the whole enterprise of Christian education necessarily has been. Pestalozzi was animated by a deeply Christian concern, and his methods strongly influenced cultural schools. John Dewey preferred " the religious " to commitment to any specific religion, yet his pragmatic insights helped to alter the teaching methods of the church's schools as well as those of the community's schools.

Here, then, are thirty-one writings, each of which has some distinctive orientation. From the thought-world of Clement of Alexandria in the second century to that of George Albert Coe in the early part of the twentieth there is a considerable change in climate; or, one should say, there are manifold changes of climate. Yet the continuity of Christian concern is evident, in one form or another, in each of these selections.

The reason for ending the anthology with George Albert Coe is that he was, in a sense, the zenith of one type of Christian education orientation in the modern period, an architect of the liberal religious education movement, certainly in the United States of America. Since his major writings of the nineteen twenties and thirties, the climate has undergone another remarkable change. The influence of the ecumenical movement, the newer Biblical theology, the insights of depth psychology, not to mention the soberer feeling tone of a world that has suffered through two wars and still does not see the emergence of anything like the order Herbert Spencer and his descendants fondly anticipated — these facts have produced different dimensions of concern with which Christian theorists and practitioners recently have been coming to grips. For that reason we have appended at the end of this work a list of books illustrative of trends and developments since Coe. He himself, during his lifetime, saw the changing intellectual and theological climate and publicly lamented all forms of neo-orthodoxy that seemed to him to be a reversion to past and inferior goals. Already we can see Coe in retrospect: that is the reason he seemed to be the logical " giant " with whom to conclude our readings.

I wish to thank the publishers who have given gracious permission to make use of copyrighted materials. Also, the libraries that have lent their materials freely, particularly the libraries of Seabury-Western Theological Seminary, Garrett Biblical Institute and Union Theological Seminary (New York), the Congregational Library of Boston, the General Theological Library of Boston, the library of Northwestern University, the library of the Divinity School of Harvard University, and the Free Library of Rutland, Vermont. Also, my wife, Iris V. Cully, and our daughter

Melissa, who helped me very much in preparing the manuscript, and who, with our other daughter, Patience, gave me freedom for the completion of this work during a supposed " holiday " at our farm in the Green Mountains of Vermont.

KENDIG BRUBAKER CULLY

Evanston, Illinois

PART I

The Earlier Centuries

1

CLEMENT OF ALEXANDRIA
(ca. 150–ca. 215)

Clement, a father of the Greek Church, was probably born in Athens. He died in Palestine. About 180 he went to study under Pantaenus, head of the catechetical school at Alexandria. Later, Clement succeeded his teacher, presiding over the school and teaching from ca. 190 to ca. 203. Among his pupils was Origen, who in turn succeeded him. Clement sought to relate Christian thinking to Greek thought as represented in the dramatists, Homer, Plato, and the Stoic philosophers. He encouraged his students to see that the fullness of knowledge lies in Christ.

In Christ the Educator, *a translation of the* Paidagogos, *we can see one of the earliest efforts in the church to develop a theory of pedagogy for Christian leaders, faced with the necessity of providing a nurture for their community in Christ. It is refreshing to find thus early in Christian education a clear awareness as to the difference between mere knowledge and authentic spiritual cultivation, and a vital analysis of the relation between teacher and pupil.*

Christ the Educator *is the second part of a three-part work, of which the first part is the* Protreptikos (The Exhortation to the Greeks) *and the third, the* Stromateis (the Miscellanies). The Writings of Clement of Alexandria, *tr.*

by William Wilson, are available in the Ante-Nicene Christian Library, Vols. IV, XII (Edinburgh, 1867–1869). The Exhortation to the Greeks, The Rich Man's Salvation, Fragment of an Address Entitled " To the Newly Baptized," *tr. by G. W. Butterworth, are available in The Loeb Classical Library (Harvard University Press, 1919). The introduction to Vol. 23 of The Fathers of the Church: A New Translation, tr. by Simon P. Wood, C.P., contains valuable biographical and bibliographical information concerning Clement, as well as a fine introduction to* Christ the Educator; *it is published by Fathers of the Church, Inc. (1954). A fragment of Clement's entitled* St. John and the Young Man He Loved, *tr. by Walter Lowrie, was published in* The Church Review, *Vol. VII, No. 4, Dec., 1946, pp. 1 f. (Church Society for College Work of the Protestant Episcopal Church).*

CLEMENT OF ALEXANDRIA . . .

Christ the Educator

O you who are children! An indestructible cornerstone
of knowledge, holy temple of the great God, has been hewn
out especially for us as a foundation for the truth. This cornerstone is noble persuasion, or the desire for eternal life
aroused by an intelligent response to it, laid in the ground
of our minds.

For, be it noted, there are these three things in man:
habits, deeds, and passions. Of these, habits come under
the influence of the word of persuasion, the guide to godliness. This is the word that underlies and supports, like the
keel of a ship, the whole structure of the faith. Under its
spell, we surrender, even cheerfully, our old ideas, become
young again to gain salvation, and sing in the inspired
words of the psalm: " How good is God to Israel, to those
who are upright of heart." As for deeds, they are affected
by the word of counsel, and passions are healed by that of
consolation.

Clement of Alexandria, *Christ the Educator,* tr. by Simon P. Wood, C.P.
(Vol. 23, The Fathers of the Church: A New Translation, founded by
Ludwig Schopp; Roy Joseph Deferrari, Editorial Director). Fathers of
the Church, Inc., 1954. Used by permission. Selections here from Book I,
passim.

These three words, however, are but one: the self-same
Word who forcibly draws men from their natural, worldly
way of life and educates them to the only true salvation:
faith in God. That is to say, the Heavenly Guide, the Word,
once he begins to call men to salvation, takes to himself the
name of persuasion (this sort of appeal, although only one
type, is properly given the name of the whole, that is, word,
since the whole service of God has a persuasive appeal, instilling in a receptive mind the desire for life now and for
the life to come); but the Word also heals and counsels,
all at the same time. In fact, he follows up his own activity
by encouraging the one he has already persuaded, and particularly by offering a cure for his passions.

Let us call him, then, by the one title: Educator of little
ones, an Educator who does not simply follow behind,
but who leads the way, for his aim is to improve the soul,
not just to instruct it; to guide to a life of virtue, not
merely to one of knowledge. Yet, that same word does
teach. It is simply that in this work, we are not considering him in that light. As Teacher, he explains and reveals
through instruction, but as Educator he is practical. First
he persuades men to form habits of life, then he encourages them to fulfill their duties by laying down clear-cut
counsels and by holding up, for us to follow, examples of
those who have erred in the past. Both are most useful: the
advice, that it may be obeyed; the other, given in the form
of example, has a twofold object — either that we may
choose the good and imitate it or condemn and avoid the
bad.

Healing of the passions follows as a consequence. The
Educator strengthens souls with the persuasion implied in
these examples, and then he gives the nourishing, mild
medicine, so to speak, of his loving counsels to the sick

man that he may come to a full knowledge of the truth. Health and knowledge are not the same; one is a result of study, the other of healing. In fact, if a person is sick, he cannot master any of the things taught him until he is first completely cured. We give instructions to someone who is sick for an entirely different reason than we do to someone who is learning; the latter, we instruct that he may acquire knowledge, the first, that he may regain health. Just as our body needs a physician when it is sick, so, too, when we are weak, our soul needs the Educator to cure its ills. Only then does it need the Teacher to guide it and develop its capacity to know, once it is made pure and capable of retaining the revelation of the Word.

Therefore, the all-loving Word, anxious to perfect us in a way that leads progressively to salvation, makes effective use of an order well adapted to our development; at first he persuades, then he educates, and after all this he teaches. . . . (I:1,2,3.)

That education is the training given children is evident from the very name. It remains for us to consider who the children are as explained by the Scriptures and, from the same Scriptural passages, to understand the Educator.

We are the children. Scripture mentions us very often and in many different ways, and refers to us under different titles, thereby introducing variety in the simple language of the faith. For example, in the Gospel, it says: " And the Lord, standing on the shore, said to his disciples [they were fishing], ' Children, do you have no fish? ' " Those who already had the position of disciples he now calls ' children.' . . .

Does it surprise you to hear that full-grown men of all nations are children in God's eyes? Then you do not know much about the Greek language, I think, where we can see that a beautiful and attractive young woman who is more-over also freeborn, is to this day called " child," and slaves are called " little children," although both are young women. They are complimented by such pet names because of the flower of their youth. . . .

There can be no doubt that we also call the most excellent and perfect possessions in life by names derived from the word " child," that is, education and culture. We define education as a sound training from childhood in the path of virtue. Be that as it may, the Lord once very clearly revealed what he means by the name " little child." A dispute having arisen among the apostles as to which of them was greater, Jesus made a little child stand among them, saying, " If anyone will humble himself as this little child, he is greater in the kingdom of heaven." Therefore, he does not mean by " little child " one who has not yet reached the use of reason because of his immaturity, as some have thought. When he says, " Unless you become as these children, you shall not enter the kingdom of heaven," we must not foolishly mistake his meaning. We are not little ones in the sense that we roll on the floor or crawl on the ground as snakes do. That is to grovel in unreasoning desires with our whole body prostrate. We strain upward with our minds, we have given up sin and the world, we tread the earth, although with light foot, only to the degree that appearances demand, that we may be in this world. We, indeed, cultivate holy wisdom, which seems foolishness to those bent on evil.

Really, then, children are those who look upon God alone as their father, who are simple, little ones, uncontaminated, who are lovers of the horn of the unicorn. To these, surely, who have matured in the Word, he has proclaimed his message, bidding them not to be concerned with the affairs of this life and encouraging them to imitate children and devote themselves to the Father alone. . . .

Now, if there is, as the Scripture says, but " one teacher, in heaven," then, surely, all who are on earth can with good reason be called disciples. The plain truth is that what is perfect belongs to the Lord, who is ever teaching, while the role of child and little one belongs to us, who are ever learning. . . . (I:12,14,16,17.)

It is possible, too, for us to make a completely adequate answer to any carping critics. We are children and little ones, but certainly not because the learning we acquire is puerile or rudimentary, as those puffed up in their own knowledge falsely charge. On the contrary, when we were reborn, we straightway received the perfection for which we strive. For we were enlightened, that is, we came to the knowledge of God. Certainly, he who possesses knowledge of the Perfect Being is not imperfect. . . .

When we are baptized, we are enlightened; being enlightened, we become adopted sons; becoming adopted sons, we are made perfect; and becoming perfect, we are made divine. " I have said," it is written, " you are gods and all of you the sons of the Most High " (Ps. 81:6). . . .

In the same way that inexperience yields to experience, and impossibility to possibility, so darkness is completely dispelled by light. Darkness is ignorance, for it makes us fall into sin and lose the ability to see the truth clearly. But knowledge is light, for it dispels the darkness of ignorance and endows us with keenness of vision. The very act of expelling things that are bad reveals what is good. To be sure, the things that ignorance restricts, to our harm, knowledge sets free, for our good. The quickest way to loose those bonds is to make use of man's faith, and God's grace, for sins are forgiven through the one divine remedy, baptism in the Word. . . . (I:25,26,29.)

We have now shown that not only does Scripture call all of us children, but also it figuratively calls us who follow Christ, little ones, and that the only perfect being is the Father of all (in fact, the Son is in him, and the Father is in the Son). If we would follow right order, we should now speak of the Educator of little ones and explain who he is.

He is called Jesus. On occasion, he speaks of himself as a shepherd, as when he says, " I am the good shepherd." In keeping with this metaphor of shepherds leading their sheep, he leads his children, the shepherd with the care of his little ones. The little ones, in their simplicity, are given the figurative name of sheep: " And there shall be one sheepfold," he says, " and one shepherd."

Therefore, the Word who leads his children to salvation is unquestionably an Educator of little ones. In fact, through Osee (Hosea), the Word says plainly of himself, " I am your Educator." The material he educates us in is fear of God, for this fear instructs us in the service of God, educates to the knowledge of truth, and guides by a path leading straight up to heaven.

Education is a word used in many different senses. There is education in the sense of the one who is being led and instructed; there is that of the one who leads and gives instruction; and thirdly, there is education in the sense of the guidance itself; and finally, the things that are taught, such as precepts. The education that God gives is the imparting of the truth that will guide us correctly to the contemplation of God, and a description of holy deeds that endure forever. . . . (I:53,54.)

Truly, the Educator of mankind, the divine Word of

ours, has devoted himself with all his strength to save his little ones by all the means at the disposal of his wisdom: warning, blaming, rebuking, correcting, threatening, healing, promising, bestowing favors — in a word, " binding as if with many bits " the unreasonable impulses of human nature. In fact, the Lord acts toward us just as we do toward our children. " Hast thou children? Chastise them," Wisdom advises, " and hast thou daughters? Have a care of their body and show not thy countenance gay toward them." Yet we have a great love for our children, sons or daughters, more than that we have for anything else. Indeed, those who are very affable in their relations with others really show less love simply because they never become provoked, while those who administer rebuke for the good of someone else, although they are disagreeable at the moment, render a service that affects the life after the grave. So, too, the Lord is interested, not in promoting our present pleasure, but the happiness that is to come. . . . (I:75.)

From the subjects that we have already discussed, it must be concluded that Jesus, our Educator, has outlined for us the true life, and that he educates the man who abides in Christ. His character is not excessively fear-inspiring, yet neither is it overindulgent in its kindness. He imposes commands, but at the same time expresses them in such a way that we can fulfill them. . . .

His main concern is to consider the way and the means by which the life of man might be made more conformable to salvation. He does truly make this his concern. He seeks to train us to the condition of a wayfarer, that is, to make us well girded and unimpeded by provisions, that we might be self-sufficient of life and practise a moderate frugality in our journey toward the good life of eternity, telling us that each one of us is to be his own storehouse: " Do not be anxious about tomorrow." He means to say that he who has dedicated himself to Christ ought to be self-sufficient and his own servant, and, besides, live his life from day to day. (I:98.)

2

GREGORY THAUMATURGUS
(ca. 210–ca. 270)

Originally named Theodorus, Gregory Thaumaturgus ("the Wonder-worker") was born at Neocaesarea, Pontus, Asia Minor, and died during the reign of Aurelian. His nickname was given him by followers who were convinced he had performed many miracles. He and his brother were drawn to Caesarea, where they studied under the famous Origen until they returned to Pontus and founded the Christian church in their native country (according to Eusebius). Gregory became the first bishop in Pontus. The tradition is that when he began his evangelistic work in Pontus there were only seventeen Christians; at the time of his death only seventeen heathen remained.

The Address to Origen *is a tribute from a pupil to that teacher who served notably in the catechetical schools at Caesarea and Alexandria. In the collection of essays entitled* Great Teachers Portrayed by Those Who Studied Under Them, *ed. by Houston Peterson (Rutgers University Press, 1946), writers of the nineteenth and twentieth centuries describe some of the great persons who were their instructors in very recent times. The desire to capture in words the particular quality that makes a teacher significant existed as long ago as Gregory's time. Here we see set forth, sometimes almost more eulogistically than mod-*

ern taste would dictate, those attributes of personality and concerns for the pupil which certainly must in some measure characterize the Christian teacher at his best and greatest in any century, whether he functions in a university or in a Sunday church school in some local parish.

Gregory also wrote an Epistle *and a* Paraphrase of Ecclesiastes. *For background information on Gregory and Origen, see the introduction in the edition of the* Address to Origen *from which our translation is taken, W. Metcalfe,* Translations of Christian Literature, *Series I, Greek Texts (S.P.C.K., London; The Macmillan Company, New York, 1920), pp. 7–41. Additional useful information is contained in E. de Faye,* Origen and His Work (*tr. by F. Rothwell, George Allen and Unwin, Ltd., London, 1926.*)

GREGORY THAUMATURGUS . . .

Address to Origen

And he took us over, from the first day, veritably the
first day, the most precious of all days — if I may say so —
when first the true light began to rise upon me, began by
using every device to bind us firmly, us who were like some
wild beasts, or fishes, or birds, fallen into snares or nets,
trying to struggle out and escape away, and wishful to
depart from him to Berytus or our fatherland. He used
every turn of language, pulled every string, as they say,
employed every resource of his abilities, praised philosophy and those enamored of philosophy in long numerous
and apt eulogies, insisting that they only lived the life be-
fitting the reasonable beings who studied to live rightly,
who "knew themselves," first their own nature, and secondly, the things essentially good which a human being
ought to follow after, and the really evil things which he
ought to avoid. He reproached ignorance and all the ignorant, and they are many, who, like younglings blind of
intellect, knowing not even what they are, erring like ir-

Gregory Thaumaturgus, *Address to Origen*, tr. by W. Metcalfe in *Translations of Christian Literature*, Series I, Greek Texts, pp. 57–88, *passim*.
S.P.C.K., London; The Macmillan Company, New York, 1920. Used by
permission of S.P.C.K.

rational creatures, utterly ignorant and unwilling to learn what good or evil is, rush and fly as if after good things, after the possessions and opinions and esteem of the multitude, and after bodily comforts, reckoning these things of much, nay, the utmost value, and after such of the arts as can furnish these forth, and after such callings as can provide them, military service, the civil service and the practice of law. He laid special stress on the things which were exciting us, while — said he — we were neglecting the chief of our endowments, namely, reason. I cannot now tell how many sayings of this sort he was wont to utter forth urging us to philosophize, and not one day only, but all those early days when we first resorted to him transfixed by his word as by a dart, and in our new youth (for he was compounded of a certain sweet grace and persuasiveness and a certain cogency) while we were still casting about and considering and essaying to philosophize, but not yet fully decided, yet withal somehow unable to draw back, and attracted to him by some constraining power greater than his words. One could by no means reverence the Lord of all — this faculty of which man alone of all things living on the earth has received the privilege and honor; probably everyone, whether wise or simple, possesses it, who has not utterly lost his understanding through some infatuation — he used to declare, and that truly, that true religion was utterly impossible to one who did not philosophize. Heaping such sayings one upon another in great number, he would carry us away like enchanted creatures finally rendered completely motionless by his arts, and settle us, I know not where, by his arguments, with a power which was divine.

Furthermore, something else was striking the goad of friendship into us, no easily resisted thing; that was the

keenness and great urgency of his ability and good disposition, which shone so benevolently upon us in his very tones
as he discoursed or talked, trying not to get an easy victory
over us in argument, but by his able and kindly and genuine ability to save us and render us partakers of the benefits of philosophy, and especially of those which the Deity
had granted to him particularly in greater measure than to
most men, perhaps than to any of the present day, having
granted to him of religion the saving Word who visits many
and operates in all as many as He may approach (for there
is none who can resist Him who is and is to be King of all),
yet is hidden and not comprehended easily, nor even with
effort, by the many, so that when questioned they can
state aught clearly about Him. Like some spark kindled
within my soul there was kindled and blazed forth my love
both toward Him, most desirable of all for his beauty unspeakable, the Word holy and altogether lovely, and toward this man his friend and prophet. Deeply stricken by
it, I was led to neglect all that seemed to concern me: affairs, studies, even my favorite law, home and kindred
there, no less than those among whom I was sojourning.
One thing only was dear and affected by me: philosophy
and its teacher, this divine man — and the soul of Jonathan
was knit with David. . . . By some such constraints, this
David having enlaced us has held us from that day until
now, unable, even if we would, to loose ourselves from his
bonds. Even if we depart abroad, he will not cease to hold
our soul thus knit according to the divine saying.

Origen's Dialectic

Thus taking us from the first and encompassing us about
on every hand, when he had toiled much, and seemed to
have come to a standstill, then he treated us as a skilled

farmer would some field, wild and either nowise good soil, but salt and parched, shallow and sandy; or else not utterly fruitless or unfertile, but though rich, yet dry and untended, rough and encumbered with thorns and wild bushes; or as a vinedresser would some stock, either wild and devoid of fruit, yet not wholly useless, if one by the vinedresser's art should take a cultivated shoot to engraft, slitting it in the middle, and inserting the graft, and binding it fast and should then tend them till both shot together as one (for you may see a tree mixed and bastard, fruitful out of barren, bearing the fruit of the good olive on wild roots); or as a wild tree, yet not useless to the skilled nurseryman; or a tree cultivated, but uselessly luxuriant, or leafless and sapless and dry from want of attention, choked by the excessive growth of superfluous shoots, hindered from shooting to perfection and bearing fruit by its neighbors. He found us in somewhat the same condition, and with his husbandman's skill surveyed us, and not only observed the faults beheld of all and openly to be seen, but dug down and searched to the inmost recesses, asking and propounding and hearing us answer. When he perceived anything that was not useless and unprofitable and ineffectual in us, he broke the ground, turned it over, watered it, used every device, applied all his skill and care, and wrought us into shape. The "thorns and thistles," and all the tribe of wild grasses and herbs which our mad and startled soul had sent forth and thrown up (for it was disordered and hasty) he cut out and pulled up with his inquiries and restraint, grappling with us in argument, and sometimes overthrowing us in true Socratic fashion if he espied us rushing off in all directions like wild horses, plunging out of the track and running aimlessly about, until by persuasion and compulsion, as if by the bit of reason in our mouth, he rendered us quiet to his hand. It was difficult and not without discomfort to us at first, as he produced his reasons to us unaccustomed and not as yet practised in following the argument as he produced it; yet he reformed us. When in any respect he had made us fit, and prepared us well for the reception of the words of truth, then, as in ground well wrought and softened, ready to foster the proffered seed, he brought it on without stint, making his sowing in due season, and in due season all the rest of his attentions, performing each in the appropriate way and with the appropriate instruments of reason. Whatever was dulled or spurious in the soul, whether it was so constitutionally or had become gross from excessive bodily nurture, he quickened or restrained with the fine reasonings and turns of the reasonable affections, which from the simplest beginnings twine round one another, until they result in a web from which there is no means of escape. These roused us like sleepers, and taught us to adhere constantly to the tasks set before us, and not to weary because of their length or their minuteness. What part was uncritical and hasty in us, as when we agreed with whatever presented itself, even though it happened to be false, or often contradicted, even though true statements were made, he educated with arguments such as those above mentioned and various others, for this part of philosophy is many-sided. . . . Well he taught us to consider not only obvious and evident, but sometimes erroneous and sophisticated arguments, to probe each and sound it to see whether it gave any echo of unsoundness; and to have grounds first for our confidence in ourselves, and so to have grounds for our agreement with others or for our own utterances. In this manner he gave us a reasonable training for the critical part of our soul — as regards words and arguments. . . .

3

CYRIL OF JERUSALEM
(ca. 310–386)

Cyril was born at (or near) Jerusalem. Prior to his election as bishop of Jerusalem in 350, he had hesitated between Arianism and orthodoxy. Once having accepted a bishopric, however, he became an astute defender of the orthodox faith against the Arians. His special adversary was Acacius, the Arian bishop of Caesarea, who was able to force Cyril's deposition in 357, though Cyril resumed his see in 381. One of his contributions to the life of the early church was his success in establishing the ordered rhythm of the Christian year as the normal pattern in the Jerusalem church.

It was customary for catechetical lectures to be delivered during Lent, leading up to the baptism of catechumens at Easter. In The Catechetical Lectures *we have a brilliant example of this form of lecture-discourse, which was a paramount teaching method in the early church. Note that the " catechism," the question-and-answer form we usually associate with that term, came into full development during the Reformation period. In the early centuries the catechesis was a form of introduction to the total basic beliefs of the church.*

We have reproduced only the Introductory Lecture, called the Procatechesis. *Succeeding lectures take up such*

32

subjects as Baptism, repentance, the remission of sins, faith, and the Son of God. See the general introduction to Vol. IV of The Library of Christian Classics, Cyril of Jerusalem and Nemesius of Emesa, ed. by William Telfer (The Westminster Press, 1955), for a good summary of Cyril's life and influence, as well as details concerning the cate-chetical methods employed in his time.

CYRIL OF JERUSALEM . . .

The Catechetical Lectures

THE INTRODUCTORY LECTURE, OR PROCATECHESIS

Already the savour of bliss is upon you, who have come to be enlightened; you have begun to pluck spiritual flowers with which to weave you heavenly crowns. Already you are redolent of the fragrance of the Holy Spirit. You have reached the royal vestibule. O may the King himself conduct you within!

Lo, now the trees are in blossom; and grant the fruit be duly gathered!

So far, your names have been enrolled, and you have been called up for service. The lamps have been kindled for the wedding procession. There is longing for the citizenship of heaven. There is good intention, with hope, to back it up. . . . If your intention is worthy, that it is that sets you among these " called." For though you be present here in the body, that is no use if your heart be not here as well. . . .

Cyril of Jerusalem, *Procatechesis* (Introductory Lecture) of *The Catechetical Lectures,* in *Cyril of Jerusalem and Nemesius of Emesa,* ed. by William Telfer, Vol. IV, pp. 64–76, *passim.* The Library of Christian Classics. The Westminster Press, Philadelphia; S. C. M. Press, London, 1955. Used by permission.

For we, Christ's ministers, have received each one of you. If you think of us as, figuratively, his doorkeepers, then we have left the door unfastened. There has been nothing to stop you coming here with your soul covered in the mire of sins, with purpose anything but pure. And in you have come, been passed as fit, and your name inscribed on the roll. Look, I ask you, at this solemn setting of the church. Give heed to the order and thought-out arranging of it, the Scripture lessons, the attendance of the entire ecclesiastical body, the arrangements for teaching. Let the very place put you in awe, and be admonished by what you behold. Be glad to make your escape now, so as to return tomorrow in a better disposition. Let us say that your soul is wrapped in avarice. When you come back, let it wear a different dress: I do not mean on top of the old one, but with the old one taken off. Strip off, I beg, fornication and uncleanness and put on that brilliant robe, self-discipline. Off with the former habit, I charge you, e'er Jesus, bridegroom of souls, comes to view your array! You have a long period of grace, forty days for repentance. You have plenty of time to discard and wash thoroughly your soul's apparel, and so to clothe yourself and come back. But if you just continue in your evil disposition, I have cleared myself by telling you, but you cannot expect to receive God's grace. For though the water will receive you, the Holy Spirit will not. . . .

Perhaps you had a different reason for coming. For it is quite what might happen, that a man should be wanting to advance his suit with a Christian woman, and to that end has come here. And there is the like possibility the other way round. Or often it may be a slave that wanted to please his master, or a person that comes for the sake of his friend. I accept this as bait for the hook, and I welcome you as one who shall be saved, by a good hope, in spite of having come with an unsound intention. It may well be that you did not know where you were coming or what sort of a net it is that is taking you. And now you are inside the ecclesiastical fish nets. Let yourself be taken, do not take off, for Jesus is angling for you, not to make you die, but by his having died, to make you live. For die you must, and rise again, as you heard how the apostle says, " Dead indeed unto sin, but alive " unto righteousness. Die to your sins and live unto righteousness. As from today, I say, live.

Look, I ask you, and see with how great a dignity Jesus favors you. You were called catechumen, which means one into whom something is dinned from without. You heard of some hope, but you did not know what. You heard mysteries without understanding anything. You heard Scriptures without plumbing their depth. It is not dinned in, any more, but whispered. For the indwelling Spirit is fashioning your mind into mansions for God. When you hear, in future, Scriptures concerning mysteries, you will understand things you knew nothing of. And do not esteem it a trifle what you are receiving. Being but a wretched man, you are recipient of a divine title. For listen to Paul, " God is faithful," or to another text in Scripture, " God is faithful and just." It was as foreseeing that a divine title would come to be applied to men that the psalmist, speaking in the Person of God, said, " I have said, ye are gods, and are all children of the Most High." But see that when the title is faithful, the purpose is not faithless. You have entered the contest, run your course steadfastly. No other chance like this will come your way. . . .

So persevere with the catechizings. If we prolong our discourse, never let your mind relax, seeing that what you are being provided with is your arms against the operations of your foe. . . . Your weapons are all ready, and readiest of all is the sword of the Spirit. You must hold out your right hands for them, that is, have a right intention to fight the Lord's battle, to overcome the operations of your foe, and not be worsted in any heretic encounter.

Let this be your solemn charge; learn the things that are told you, and keep them forever. Do not think of them as on a par with ordinary sermons. Sermons are good things and should evoke your faith. But, suppose we neglected to-day's sermon; we attend to tomorrow's. In the sequence of carefully prepared instructions for baptismal regeneration, if today's lecture be neglected, when will the matter be put right? Think of this as being the season for planting young trees. If we do not now dig and set them deep in the earth, when can we find another opportunity for planting well what has been once planted badly? Or think of cate-chesis as like a building. We get no profit from toil ex-pended, unless we dig deep to lay the foundations, unless we mortar together the successive courses of the building so as to compact our house in one, with not a crack to be found, nor the structure unsound in any way. Stone must follow stone in the appointed order, and corners be turned in each successive course. Unevennesses must be leveled off, so that the building may rise without fault. So we are proffering to you, as it were, building stones of knowledge. You have to be told about the living God, you have to be told about the judgment, you have to be told about Christ, you have to be told about the resurrection. There are many things to be said, and in their proper order. As they are be-ing said, they appear casual, but afterward they present themselves as all connected together. Now if you do not do the joining of them in one, if you do not remember what went before and what came after, the builder builds his house, but the building you will have will be unsound.

So when the instruction is over, if any catechumen tries to get out of you what your teachers told you, tell nothing, for he is outside the mystery that we have delivered to you, with its hope of the age to come. Guard the mystery for his sake from whom you look for reward. . . .

You who have been enrolled here become sons and daughters of one Mother. When you arrive before the time for exorcising, let each of you speak only what helps to godliness. If any of the class does not arrive, go seek him. If you were asked out to dinner, would you not wait for a fellow guest? If you had a brother, would you not seek that brother's good? Whatever you do, do not start unprofitable gossip; about what has been happening in the city, or your village, or what the emperor has done, or the bishop, or your presbyter. Lift your eyes to God. It is the time for you to need him. " Be still and know that I am God." If you see the believers who are assisting in the church quite at their ease, remember that they have reason to be. They know what they have received, and they are in a state of grace. You, on the other hand, are just in the balance to decide whether you shall be received or not. Do not ape those who have reached security, but make it your aim to be in fear. . . .

I shall see each man's earnestness. I shall see each woman's devotion. Burn out impiety from your mind, put your soul on the anvil, and your stubborn infidelity under the hammer. Let the loose scales fall from the iron and leave pure metal. Let the iron rust fall off and leave clean iron. And may God at length grant you to see that night when darkness is turned into day, of which it was said, " The darkness hideth not from thee, but the night shall shine as the day." Then let the gate of paradise be opened to each

man and each woman among you. Then may you enjoy waters that bear Christ and have his sweet savour. Then may
you receive his name of Christian, and the capacity for
heavenly things. And even now, I pray you, lift up the eyes
of your mind: take thought now of angelic choirs, and God,
the master of the universe enthroned, with his only-begotten Son sitting on his right hand, and his Spirit with him,
while thrones and dominations do him service, and likewise each man and woman of you as being in a state of
salvation. Even now imagine that your ears catch those
lovely strains wherewith the angels acclaim you saved.
" Blessed are those whose transgressions are forgiven and
whose sins are covered " when, as stars of the church, you
enter paradise with glorious body and radiant soul.

Great is the baptism to which you are coming: It is ran-
som to captives and remission of sins. It is the death of sin
and the soul's regeneration. It is a garment of light and a
holy seal that can never be dissolved. It is a chariot to heav-
en, the delights of paradise, the pledge of the Kingdom,
the gift of sonship. But a dragon is keeping watch beside
the road you are walking. Take care lest he bite you with
unbelief. He sees so many on the road to being saved, and
seeks whom he may devour. The end of your journey is
the Father of Spirits, but the way lies past that dragon.
How, then, shall you get past him? By having " your feet
shod with the preparation of the gospel of peace " so as
to take no hurt, though he do bite. Let faith dwell in your
heart, have a strong hope, and be strongly shod, to get by
the enemy and reach the Master's presence. Prepare your
heart to receive instruction, and enter into holy mysteries.
Pray yet more often that God will judge you worthy of
heavenly and immortal mysteries. Cease not day or night,
but when sleep falls from your eyes, then let your mind

free itself to pray. Should you see some unbecoming thought rising into consciousness, take the remembrance of judgment as means of safety. Devote your mind to study, and evil concerns will slip from it. If you meet someone who says: " Are you getting ready to plunge in the water? Are there no city baths any more "? then know that the dragon of the sea got ready these temptations for you. Mind not the lips that speak but the God that works. Guard your soul, that you be not caught, and persevering in hope may be heir to eternal salvation.

We are but human, who declare and teach these things. Do not you make of our building " hay, stubble," and chaff, so that we suffer loss, in our work being burnt up. But make our work " gold, silver, precious stones." It is my part to tell you, yours to carry it forward, but God's to bring it to completion. Let us brace our minds, concentrate our souls, prepare our hearts. The race is run in matters of soul, and the prize consists of rewards in heaven. And God, who knows your hearts and can tell who is genuine and who but feigns, is able to keep the former steadfast and bring the latter to a state of faith. For God can turn an infidel into a believer, if he will but surrender to him his heart. May God " blot out the handwriting that is against you," wink at your transgressions heretofore, plant you in his church, en- roll you in his own host, and equip you with the arms of righteousness. May he will you with the heavenly guerdons of the New Testament, and give you the seal of the Holy Spirit, that cannot be removed forevermore, in Jesus Christ our Lord, to whom be glory, world without end. Amen.

4

JEROME

(ca. 345–420)

Jerome (Eusebius Sophronius Hieronymus) was born in Stridon, Pannonia (now part of Yugoslavia), and died at Bethlehem, Palestine. As a youth he studied rhetoric in Rome under the famous grammarians Aelius Donatus and Victorinus. During a trip through the Orient in 373 he became ill. While convalescing, he began the study of Greek and the Bible. For several years he lived in the desert as a hermit, finally going to Antioch, where he was ordained in 379 by Bishop Paulinus. With Paulinus he went to the Second General Council at Constantinople and to the Council at Rome in 382. He remained in Rome for three years, during which time he became an adviser to Pope Damasus I and began his work on the revision of the Latin Bible. This version, the Vulgate, was to be made the official Roman Catholic text of the Bible at the Council of Trent. He became popular as an instructor in the ascetic life for a group of young women, leaving Rome only when popular prejudice was aroused against the monks under a new Pope, Siricius, after the death of Damasus. Taking two of his female disciples with him, he went to Palestine, where, at Bethlehem, he founded a monastery and a convent, as well as a hospice for visiting pilgrims from many parts of the world. At his death he was still working on a commen-

tary on Jeremiah, even though he had become blind and weakened through age.

The Letters of Jerome are considered to be one of the four greatest collections of letters in Latin literature, the others being those of Cicero, Seneca, and Pliny. We have chosen to reproduce the Letter to Pacatula as an illustration of the views of an ascetic on child training. It may be assumed that such views were to a considerable extent current among many Christian leaders of his time. Whatever we may think today of some of his views, the fact remains that a genuine concern for the young was prevalent in one who took the trouble in his advanced age to " write a letter to an infant."

The Principal Works of St. Jerome, *tr. by W. H. Fremantle, is Vol. 6 in Series II of the Select Library of Nicene and Post-Nicene Fathers (Charles Scribner's Sons, 1893). Books about Jerome include the following:* St. Jerome: the Early Years, *tr. by F. J. Sheed (Sheed & Ward, Inc., 1933);* E. L. Cutts, Saint Jerome *(E. and J. B. Young and Co., London, 1897);* A Monument to Saint Jerome: Essays on Some Aspects of His Life, Works and Influence, *ed. by Francis X. Murphy (Sheed & Ward, Inc., 1952).*

JEROME . . .

Letter to Pacatula

FEMININE TRAINING

It is a difficult matter to write to a little girl who will not
understand what you say, of whose mind you know nothing, and whose inclinations it would be dangerous to warrant. To use the words of a famous orator's preface — " in
her case praise is based on expectation rather than accomplishment." How can you urge self-control on a child who
still craves after cakes, who babbles softly in her mother's
arms, and finds honey sweeter than words? Can she pay
attention to the deep sayings of the apostle, when she takes
more pleasure in old wives' tales than in them? Can she
heed the dark riddles of the prophets when her nurse's
frown is sufficient to frighten her? Can she appreciate the
majesty of the gospel when its lightnings dazzle all men's
senses? How can I bid her to be obedient to her parents,
this child who beats her mother with baby hand? So my
little Pacatula must read this letter herself in days to come;
and in the meantime learn her alphabet, spelling, gram-

Jerome, "Letter to Pacatula" (413), tr. by F. A. Wright, in *Select
Letters of St. Jerome*, Letter CXXVIII, pp. 467–481, *passim*. G. P. Put-
nam's Sons, Inc., 1933. Reprinted by permission of Harvard University
Press and The Loeb Classical Library.

mar, and syntax. To get her to repeat her lessons in her little shrill voice, she must have a prize of a honey cake offered to her. She will do her work quickly if she is going to receive as reward some sweetmeat, or bright flower, or glittering bauble, or pretty doll. Meanwhile, too, she must learn to spin, drawing down the threads with tender fingers; and though at first she may often break the yarn, she will one day cease to do so. Then, when work is over, she may indulge in play, hanging on her mother's neck and snatching kisses from her relations. Let her be rewarded for singing the psalms aloud, so that she may love what she is forced to do, and it be not work but pleasure, not a matter of necessity but one of free will.

Some mothers, when they have vowed a daughter to virginity, are wont to dress her in dark clothes, to wrap her up in a little black cloak, and to let her wear no gold ornaments on her head and neck. In reality this method is a wise one, for the child does not then become accustomed to things which afterward she must lay aside. Other mothers think differently. " What is the use," they say, " of her not having pretty things? Will she not see other girls having them? The toilette appeals to all women, and we know that many whose chastity is beyond reproach take pleasure in dressing not for men but for themselves. Nay, rather, let her grow sated with having, and let her see that others are praised, who have not. And it is better that she should despise through being sated, than that by not having she should want to have." " This," they argue, " is the plan that the Lord used with the people of Israel. They craved after the fleshpots of Egypt, and so he sent them swarms of quails until they gorged themselves and were sick. Many worldlings who have tried all the pleasures of the senses find it easier to give them up than do those who from youth

have known nothing of desire. The one tread underfoot
what they know, the others are attracted by what is unknown. The one penitently avoid the snares of pleasure
from which they have escaped, the others are allured by
the delights of the body and the titillation of the flesh until
they find that what they thought was honey is really deadly
poison. For we know that "the lips of a strange woman
drop as an honeycomb, which for the moment is as
oil in the eater's mouth, but is afterward found more bitter
than gall." Therefore it is that honey is never offered in the
sacrifices of the Lord, that the wax in which honey is
stored is held in contempt, and that oil expressed from the
bitter olive is burned in God's temple. Moreover, the Pass-
over is eaten with bitter herbs and with "the unleavened
bread of sincerity and truth." Those who take thereof shall
suffer persecution in this world. Wherefore the prophet
sings symbolically, "I sat alone, because I was filled with
bitterness." . . .

Other people's conduct has made me wander somewhat
from my path, and in instructing, or rather nursing, the
baby Pacatula, I have in a moment incurred the enmity of
many ladies who will be hard to pacify. I will now return
to my subject. Females should only mix with their own sex;
they should not know how to play with boys, nay, they
should be afraid to do so. A girl should have no acquaintance with lewd talk, and if amidst the noisy bustle of a
household she hears an unclean word, she should not understand it. Her mother's nod should be as good as speech,
her mother's advice equivalent to a command. She should
love her as her parent, obey her as her mistress, fear her
as her teacher. At first she will be but a shy little maid without all her teeth, but as soon as she has reached her seventh
year and has learned to blush, knowing what she should

not say, and doubting what she should say, she should commit the Psalter to memory, and until she is grown up she should make the books of Solomon, the Gospels, the apostles, and the prophets the treasure of her heart. She should not appear in public too freely nor always seek a crowded church. Let her find all her pleasure in her own room. She must never look at foppish youths or curled coxcombs, who wound the soul through the ears with their honeyed talk. She must be protected also from the wantonness of other girls. The more freedom of access such persons have, the more difficult they are to shake off; the knowledge they have acquired, they impart in secret and corrupt a secluded Danaë with vulgar gossip. Let her teacher be her companion, her attendant her guardian, and let her be a woman not given to much wine, one who, as the apostle says, is not idle nor a tattler, but sober, grave, skilled in spinning, saying only such words as will train a girl's mind in virtue. For as water follows behind a finger in the sand, so soft and tender youth is pliable for good or evil, and can be drawn wherever you guide it. Spruce gallants often try the effect of soft words, affable manners, and trifling gifts upon a nurse in order to win access to her charge. After succeeding in a gentle approach, they blow the spark into a flame and become gradually more and more shameless. It is then impossible to stop them, and they prove the truth of the line, " You can hardly blame a habit which yourself you have allowed."

I am ashamed to say it, and yet I must: women of rank who could have suitors of even higher station cohabit with men of the lowest class and even with slaves. Sometimes in the name of religion and under a cloak of continence they desert their husbands, and like another Helen follow their Paris without any fear of Menelaus. Such things are seen and lamented, but they are not punished, for the multitude of sinners give license to sin.

Shame on us, the world is falling in ruins, but our sins still flourish. The glorious city that was the head of the Roman Empire has been engulfed in one terrific blaze. There is no part of the earth where exiles from Rome are not to be found. Churches once held sacred have fallen into dust and ashes, and still we set our hearts greedily on money. We live as though we were doomed to death on the morrow, but we build houses as though we were going to live forever in this world. Our walls glitter with gold, gold gleams upon our ceilings and upon the capitals of our pillars: yet Christ is dying at our doors in the persons of his poor, naked, and hungry. We read that Aaron, the high priest, faced the furious flames and with his burning censer stayed God's wrath. In the might of his priesthood he stood between life and death, and the fire did not dare to pass his feet. God said to Moses, " Let me alone and I will consume this people," showing by the words " let me alone " that he can be stayed from carrying out his threat; for the prayers of his servant hindered God's power. Who, think you, is there now under heaven able to face God's wrath, to meet the flames, and to say with the apostle, " I could wish that I myself were accursed for my brethren "? Flocks and shepherds perish together, because the priest is now even as the people. Moses in his compassionate love said, " Yet now if thou wilt, forgive their sin; and if not, blot me, I pray thee, out of thy book." He wished to perish with the perishing, and was not content to win salvation for himself; for indeed " in the multitude of people is the king's honor."

Such are the times into which our Pacatula has been born, these are the rattles of her infancy. She will know of tears before laughter, she will feel sorrow sooner than joy. Scarcely has she trod the stage before the curtain falls. She thinks that the world was ever thus, she knows not of the past, she shrinks from the present, she fixes her desires on what is to come. After mourning incessantly for my dead friends, I have at length recovered composure, and my affection for you, brother Gaudentius, has induced me to dictate this rough discourse and in my old age write a letter to an infant. I preferred to answer your request inadequately rather than not to answer it at all. As it is, my own inclinations have been paralyzed by my grief; in the other case, you might have doubted the sincerity of my friendship.

5

JOHN CHRYSOSTOM
(ca. 347–407)

John Chrysostom was born at Antioch in Syria and died near Comana in Cappadocia. He served as bishop of Antioch and later as Patriarch of Constantinople from 398 to 404. He is remembered as the greatest preacher in the early Greek Church. So great was his reputation that it is said that more than five hundred sermons were even ascribed to him erroneously. He was deeply interested in rhetoric as it applied to both preaching and Biblical interpretation.

The work here reproduced follows an address on vainglory and is intended to serve as a guide to parents in bringing up their children in such a way as to avoid the bitter fruits of the life of vanity. Like Jerome, John Chrysostom is somewhat on the ascetic side, but it is noteworthy that he mingled with his severity a profound recognition of the manner of a child's learning through the senses. He was aware of parental responsibility for child nurture, so often abrogated in our recent decades by parents who have turned over to the church and school functions that only the home can really guide and supervise. Long before Freudian discoveries about the importance of the child's earliest years in relation to his later life, this church father warned his hearers to " make use of the beginning of [the

49

child's] life as thou shouldest."

Chrysostom's Commentary on the Epistle to the Galatians *and* Homilies on the Epistle to the Ephesians *are translated in Vol. V of A Library of the Fathers of the Holy Catholic Church (Oxford University Press, 1840). The* Homilies on Galatians, Ephesians, Philippians, Colossians, Thessalonians, Timothy, Titus, and Philemon *are in Vol. XIII of the Select Library of Nicene and Post-Nicene Fathers (Charles Scribner's Sons, 1886–1890). Oxford University Press published an edition of* The Homilies on the Epistles of St. Paul the Apostle to the Philippians, Colossians, and Thessalonians *in 1848. Robert Wheeler Bush,* The Life and Times of Chrysostom *(London, 1858), contains biographical data. Chrysostomus Baur,* John Chrysostom and His Time, *tr. by Sister M. Gonzaga, R. S. M. (Sands and Company, London, 1959), is a comprehensive study of his life and works.*

JOHN CHRYSOSTOM . . .

The Right Way for Parents to Bring Up Their Children

The man-child has lately been born. His father thinks of every means, not whereby he may direct the child's life wisely, but whereby he may adorn it and clothe it in fine raiment and golden ornaments. Why dost thou this, O man? Granted that thou dost thyself wear these, why dost thou rear in this luxury thy son who is as yet still ignorant of this folly? For what purpose dost thou put a necklet about his throat? There is need for a strict tutor to direct the boy, no need for gold. . . .

Many may laugh at what I am saying on the ground that these things are trifles. They are not trifles but of the first importance. The girl who has been reared in her mother's quarters to be excited by female ornaments, when she leaves her father's house will be a sore vexation to her bridegroom and a greater burden to him than the tax collectors. I have told you already that vice is hard to drive

Chrysostom, John, *Address on Vainglory and the Right Way for Parents to Bring Up Their Children*, in Laistner, M. L. W., *Christianity and Pagan Culture in the Later Roman Empire*, pp. 93–122, *passim*. Cornell University Press, 1951. Used by permission.

away for this reason, that no one takes thought for his children, no one discourses to them about virginity and sobriety or about contempt of wealth and fame, or of the precepts laid down in the Scriptures.

What will become of boys when from earliest youth they are without teachers? If grown men, after being nurtured from the womb and continuing their education to old age, still do not live righteously, what wrong will not children, accustomed from the threshold of life to empty words, commit? In our own day every man takes the greatest pains to train his boy in the arts and in literature and speech. But to exercise this child's soul in virtue, to that no man any longer pays heed.

I shall not cease exhorting and begging and supplicating you before all else to discipline your sons from the first. If thou dost care for thy son, show it thus, and in other ways too thou wilt have thy reward. Hearken to the words of Paul, " If they continue in faith and charity and holiness with sobriety " (I Tim. 2:15). And even if thou art conscious of a myriad vices within thyself, nevertheless devise some compensation for thy vices. Raise up an athlete for Christ! I do not mean by this, hold him back from wedlock and send him to desert regions and prepare him to assume the monastic life. It is not this that I mean. I wish for this and used to pray that all might embrace it; but as it seems to be too heavy a burden, I do not insist upon it. Raise up an athlete for Christ, and teach him though he is living in the world to be reverent from his earliest youth.

If good precepts are impressed on the soul while it is yet tender, no man will be able to destroy them when they have set firm, even as does a waxen seal. The child is still trembling and fearful and afraid in look and speech and in all else. Make use of the beginning of his life as thou shouldst. Thou wilt be the first to benefit, if thou hast a good son, and then God. Thou dost labor for thyself.

They say that pearls when first they are collected are but water. But if he that receives them is skilled in his craft, he places the drop on his hand; and, moving it with a gentle rotating movement as it lies on the palm of his upturned hand, he shapes it skillfully and renders it perfectly round. Then, when it has received its form, he can no longer mold it; for that which is soft and with its proper shape not yet set firm is in every way adaptable and therefore is easily suited to every purpose. But that which is hard, having acquired a certain material outline, can be deprived of its hardness only with difficulty and is not changed into another shape.

To each of you fathers and mothers I say, just as we see artists fashioning their paintings and statues with great precision, so we must care for these wondrous statues of ours. Painters when they have set the canvas on the easel paint on it day by day to accomplish their purpose. Sculptors too, working in marble, proceed in a similar manner; they remove what is superfluous and add what is lacking. Even so you must proceed. Like the creator of statues do you give all your leisure to fashioning these wondrous statues for God. And, as you remove what is superfluous and add what is lacking, inspect them day by day, to see what good qualities nature has supplied so that you will increase them, and what faults so that you will eradicate them. And first of all, take the greatest care to banish licentious speech; for love of this above all frets the souls of the young. Before he is of an age to try it, teach thy son to be sober and vigilant and to shorten sleep for the sake of prayer, and with every word and deed to set upon himself the seal of the faith.

Regard thyself as a king ruling over a city, which is the soul of thy son; for the soul is in truth a city. And, even as in a city some are thieves and some are honest men, some work steadily and some transact their business fitfully, so it is with the thoughts and reasoning in the soul. Some make war on wrongdoers, like soldiers in a city; others take thought for everything, both the welfare of the body and of the home, like those who carry on the government in cities. Some give orders, like the magistrates; some again counsel lewdness, like profligates; others reverence, like the virtuous. And some are effeminate, even as are women among us; others speak folly, like children. And some again receive orders as slaves, like servants in the city, while others are wellborn, like free men.

Hence we need laws to banish evildoers and admit the good and prevent the evildoers from rising up against the good. And, just as in a city, if laws are passed which permit thieves great license, the general welfare is undermined, and if the soldiers do not devote their ardor to its proper use, they ruin the body politic, and if each citizen abandons his own household affairs and busies himself with another's, he destroys good order by his greed and ambition — so it is also in the case of the child.

The child's soul then is a city, a city but lately founded and built, a city containing citizens who are strangers with no experience as yet, such as it is very easy to direct; for men who have been reared and have grown old under a bad constitution it would be difficult to reform, though not impossible. Even they can be reformed if they be willing. But those who are quite without experience would readily accept the laws that thou givest them.

Draw up laws then for this city and its citizens, laws that inspire fear and are strong, and uphold them if they are being transgressed; for it is useless to draw up laws, if their enforcement does not follow.

Draw up laws, and do you pay close attention; for our legislation is for the world and today we are founding a city. Suppose that the outer walls and four gates, the senses, are built. The whole body shall be the wall, as it were, the gates are the eyes, the tongue, the hearing, the sense of smell, and, if you will, the sense of touch. It is through these gates that the citizens of the city go in and out; that is to say, it is through these gates that thoughts are corrupted or rightly guided.

Well, now, let us first of all approach the gate of the tongue, seeing that this is the busiest of all, and let us, to begin with and before all the other gates, provide this one with doors and bolts, not of wood or iron but of gold. Verily the city that is thus equipped is golden; for it is not any mortal but the King of the universe who intends to dwell in this city, if it has been well built. . . . But when we have fashioned the gates massive and golden and have fixed on the bolt, we must fashion the citizens also to be worthy of the city. Of what character shall these citizens be? We must train the child to utter grave and reverent words. . . . Let their words be giving thanks, solemn hymns; let their discourse ever be about God, about heavenly philosophy.

How shall this be? And in what manner shall we train them? . . .

Make a law straightway that he use no one in dispute, that he speak ill of no man, that he swear not, that he be not contentious. If thou shouldest see him transgressing this law, punish him, now with a stern look, now with incisive, now with reproachful, words; at other times win him with gentleness and promises. Have not recourse to

blows constantly and accustom him not to be trained by
the rod; for if he feel it constantly as he is being trained,
he will learn to despise it. And when he has learned to despise it, he has reduced thy system to nought. . . .

Teach him to be fair and courteous. If thou dost see a
servant ill-used by him, do not overlook it, but punish him
who is free; for if he knows that he may not ill use even a
slave, he will abstain all the more from insulting or slander-
ing one who is free and of his class. Stop his mouth from
speaking evil. If thou didst see him traducing another,
curb him and direct his tongue toward his own faults. . . .

Thus this gate will have been made worthy of the Lord,
when no word that is shameful or flippant or foolish or the
like is spoken, but all beseems the Master. . . .

Now let us pass to another gate. Which is that? One that
lies close by the first and resembles it greatly, I mean, the
sense of hearing. . . .

Let children then hear nothing harmful from servants
or tutors or nurses. But, even as plants need the greatest
amount of care when they are tender shoots, so also do
children; and so let us take thought for good nurses that a
fair foundation from the ground up be laid for the young
and that from the beginning they may receive nought that
is evil.

Therefore let them not hear frivolous and old wives'
tales: "This youth kissed that maiden. The king's son and
the younger daughter have done this." Do not let them
hear these stories, but let them hear others simply told
with no elaboration. . . . But when the boy takes relaxation from his studies — for the soul delights to dwell on
stories of eld — speak to him, drawing him away from all
childish folly; for thou art raising a philosopher and athlete and citizen of heaven. Speak to him and tell him this

story: "Once upon a time there were two sons of one father, even two brothers." Then after a pause continue: "And they were the children of the same mother, one being the elder, the other the younger son. The elder was a tiller of the ground, the younger a shepherd; and he led out his flocks to woodland and lake." Make thy stories agreeable that they may give the child pleasure and his soul may not grow weary. . . .

And let the child's mother sit by while his soul is being formed thus by such tales, so that she too may take part and praise the story. . . . Tell him this story one evening at supper. Let his mother repeat the same tale; then, when he has heard it often, ask him too, saying, "Tell me the story" so that he may be eager to imitate you. And when he has memorized it thou wilt also tell him how it profits him. The soul indeed, as it receives the story within itself before thou hast elaborated it, is aware that it will benefit. . . .

This is not all. Go leading him by the hand in church and pay heed particularly when this tale is real aloud. Thou wilt see him rejoice and leap with pleasure because he knows what the other children do not know, as he anticipates the story, recognizes it, and derives great gain from it. And hereafter the episode is fixed in his memory. . . .

Let us afford our children from the first an incentive to goodness from the name that we give them. Let none of us hasten to call his child after his forebears, his father and mother and grandsire and great-grandsire, but rather after the righteous — martyrs, bishops, apostles. Let this be an incentive to the children. Let one be called Peter, another John, another bear the name of one of the saints. . . .

Next, when he has grown older, tell him also more fearful tales; for thou shouldst not impose so great a burden on his understanding while he is still tender, lest thou dismay him. But when he is fifteen years old or more, let him hear of hell. Nay, when he is ten or eight or even younger, let him hear in full detail the story of the Flood, the destruction of Sodom, the descent into Egypt — whatever stories are full of divine punishment. When he is older let him hear also the deeds of the New Testament — deeds of grace and deeds of hell. With these stories and ten thousand others fortify his hearing, as thou dost offer him also examples drawn from his home. . . .

Let us pass on, if thou wilt, to another gate, the sense of smell. This gate too admits much that is harmful if it be not kept barred — I mean fragrant scents and herbs. Nothing weakens, nothing relaxes the right tension of the soul as a pleasure in sweet odors. " How then," says someone, "must one take pleasure in filth?" That is not my meaning, but that one should not take pleasure either in the one or in the other. Let no one bring him perfume; for, as soon as it penetrates to the brain, the whole body is relaxed. Thereby pleasures are fanned into flame and great schemes for their attainment. So bar this gate, for its function is to breathe the air, not to receive sweet odors. It may be that some laugh at us for troubling about trifles if we discourse about such a commonwealth. These are no trifles; nay, if we carry out our plan, our concern is with the origin and rhythmical education of the world.

Then there is yet another gate, fairer than those others but difficult to guard, the gate of the eyes; difficult for this reason, that it lies high up and is beautiful. It has many little postern gates and not only sees but is seen if well-fashioned.

Here strict laws are needed, the first being: Never send

thy son to the theater that he may not suffer utter corruption through his ears and eyes. And when he is abroad in the open squares, his attendant must be especially watchful as he passes through the alleys and must warn the boy of this so that he may never suffer this corruption. . . .

In this matter the tutor and attendant must exercise the greatest care. Show the boy other fair sights, and thou wilt steer his eyes away from those others. Show him the sky, the sun, the flowers of the earth, meadows, and fair books. Let these give pleasure to his eyes; and there are many others that are harmless.

This gate is difficult to guard, since there burns a fire within, and, so to speak, a natural compulsion. Let him learn hymns. If he is not inwardly aroused, he will not wish to see outwardly. . . .

There is yet another gateway, unlike the others because it extends through the whole body. We call it touch. It appears to be closed, yet it is, as it were, open and sends within whatever comes. Let us not allow it to have any truck with soft raiment or bodies. Let us make it austere. We are raising an athlete, let us concentrate our thought on that. And so let him not use soft couches or raiment. Let these be our ordinances.

Come now, when we have entered this city, let us write down and ordain laws, seeing that our arrangement of the gates is so fair. . . .

There is something more. Let us go to the master principle which keeps everything under control. To what do I allude? I mean wisdom. How great labor is needed to render him sagacious and to banish all folly. This is the great and wondrous function of philosophy, that he may know God and all the treasure laid up in heaven, and hell and the kingdom of the other world. " Fear of the Lord is the beginning of wisdom." (Prov. 1:7.)

Let us then implant in him this wisdom and let us exercise him therein that he may know the meaning of human desires, wealth, reputation, power, and may disdain these and strive after the highest. And let us bring words of exhortation to his mind: " My child, fear God alone and fear none other but him."

By this means he will be a man of good understanding and charm; for nothing is as productive of folly as those passions. The fear of God and the power of forming such a judgment of human affairs as it behooves us to have are sufficient for wisdom. The summit of wisdom is refusal to be excited at childish things. So let him be taught to think nothing of wealth or worldly reputation or power or death or the present life on earth. So will he be sagacious. If we lead him to the bridal chamber with a training such as this, consider how great a gift he will be to the bride.

Let us celebrate the marriage without flutes or harp or dancing; for a groom like ours is ashamed of such absurd customs. Nay, let us invite Christ there, for the bridegroom is worthy of him. Let us invite his disciples; all things shall be of the best for the groom. And he himself will learn to train his own sons in this way, and they theirs in turn, and the result will be a golden cord.

Let us teach him to attend to political affairs such as are within his capacity and free from sin. If he serves as a soldier, let him learn to shun base gain; and so too, if he defend the cause of those who have suffered wrong or in any other circumstance.

Let his mother learn to train her daughter by these precepts, to guide her away from extravagance and personal adornment and all other such vanities that are the mark of harlots. Let the mother act by this ordinance at all times and guide the youth and the maiden away from luxury and drunkenness. This also contributes greatly to virtue. Young men are troubled by desire, women by love of finery and excitement. Let us therefore repress all these tendencies. Thus we shall be able to please God by rearing such athletes for him that we and our children may light on the blessings that are promised to them that love him (cf. I Cor. 2:9), by the grace and mercy of our Lord Jesus Christ, to whom with the Father and the Holy Spirit be ascribed glory, power, and honor, now and forevermore. Amen.

6

AURELIUS AUGUSTINE
(354–430)

Although geographically circumscribed, Augustine's life reached spiritual and intellectual heights and depths. He was born at Tagaste in Numidia. He died at Hippo, his episcopal see, when that city was besieged by the Vandals. In 370 he went to Carthage as a student of rhetoric, a field in which he lectured in the same city from 374 until he went to Rome in 383. For about a decade he was a follower of the Manichaean movement, but had abandoned that persuasion when he arrived in Milan as a public rhetorician. Largely through the influence of his mother, Monica, and Bishop Ambrose, he was converted to Christianity in 386, after which he retired to Cassiciacum to write his first treatises. At his birthplace he established a monastery. The congregation in nearby Hippo persuaded him to be ordained to the priesthood, and in 396 he was made a bishop there. His celebrated treatise, City of God, was composed during the years 413 to 426, directly following the sacking of Rome by the Goths. Augustine's influence has been pervasive across all succeeding centuries and has been evident in thinkers as widely separated philosophically as Calvin and Descartes.

Augustine wrote a short treatise, De magistro (The Teacher), which consists of a dialogue between himself *and his son, Adeodatus. His longer work,* The Catechizing of the Uninstructed, *from which we reproduce selections here, is relevant for present-day reading in that it highlights the necessity for a method and a procedure in reaching today's religiously illiterate with sound teaching of the faith, even as it was necessary to do in Augustine's own time. His words of counsel to " Brother Deogratias " still have something to say to those today who are struggling with similar problems of teaching the untaught.*

Augustine's extensive writings are available in many editions. A good source book for Augustinian materials, including many bibliographical suggestions, is A Companion to the Study of St. Augustine, *ed. by Roy W. Battenhouse (Oxford University Press, 1955). Among his important treatises are the following:* Divine Providence and the Problem of Evil (De ordine), The Immortality of the Soul (De immortalitate animae), Freedom of the Will (De libero arbitrio), Christian Instruction (De doctrina christiana), Concerning Baptism (De Baptismo), On the Trinity (De Trinitate), Confessions. *Among the many books about Augustine we might cite Vernon J. Bourke,* Augustine's Quest of Wisdom *(Bruce Publishing Company, 1945); Charles N. Cochrane,* Christianity and Classical Culture *(which treats Augustine as well as a broader canvas of ideas) (Oxford University Press, 1940); John J. O'Meara,* The Young Augustine *(Longmans, Green & Co., Inc., 1954). Howard Grimes has a perceptive article, " St. Augustine on Teaching," in* Religious Education, *Vol. LIV, No. 2, March–April, 1959, pp. 171–176.*

AURELIUS AUGUSTINE . . .

The Catechizing of the Uninstructed

You have asked me, Brother Deogratias, to set down and
send to you something on the catechizing of the uninstructed, which may prove of use to you. For you tell me
that at Carthage, where you are a deacon, persons are often brought to you to be grounded in the first elements
of the Christian faith, because you are esteemed to possess
the gift of catechizing in ample measure by reason both of
your learning in the faith and of the graces of your exposition: you, however, are nearly always in straits to discover
how the truths by belief in which we are Christians may
be fittingly imparted; from what point our account should
begin, to what point it should be brought down, and
whether at its conclusion we ought to use some form of
exhortation, or precepts only, in the observance of which
he to whom we are speaking may know that the Christian
life and profession are ensured. Furthermore, you admit
and complain that in the course of a long and lukewarm exposition it has often befallen you to become petty and

Aurelius Augustine, *The Catechizing of the Uninstructed*, tr. by E. Phil-
lips Barker, in *A Treatise of Saint Aurelius Augustine, Bishop of Hippo,
on the Catechizing of the Uninstructed*. Methuen & Co., Ltd., London,
1912. Used by permission.

tedious even to yourself, not to mention the learner whom
you were trying to inform by your address and the other
persons present as listeners: so under stress of such feelings
you have been forced to adjure me, by the affection I owe
you, not to consider it burdensome amid my engagements
to set down for you something on this subject. . . .

But as touching your reflections on your own case, I
would not have you be uneasy because you have often
thought you were delivering a sorry and wearisome address. Possibly it did not seem so to the person whom you
were instructing, but your own words sounded to you unworthy of others' ears only because you were longing to
give your hearers something better. For my part, I am
nearly always dissatisfied with my own discourse, for I
hunger for that more excellent discourse which I often enjoy inwardly before I begin to unfold my thought aloud in
words: but when I find myself powerless to express my
conception worthily, I am saddened by the thought that
my tongue has failed to do my heart justice. For I wish my
hearer to grasp fully what I myself am grasping; and I feel
that I am not speaking in a manner to achieve that aim.
Mainly this is so because cognition floods the mind as it
were with a sudden blaze of light: speech, on the contrary,
is a slow, long-drawn, and very different process. While the
latter rolls on its way, the former has already darted into
hiding: yet because by some marvelous process it has
stamped on the memory certain imprints of itself, these last
during the momentary checks caused by the utterance of
the syllables. . . .

But the eagerness of those who desire to hear me often
lets me know that my delivery is not so chilly as it seems
to myself, and I gather from the pleasure they show that
they are receiving some benefit from it; and so I constantly

make it a point with myself not to fail in rendering a service in which I see they take in good part whatever is rendered. So you also ought to understand, by the very fact
that persons are so often brought to you to be instructed
in the faith, that your exposition is not so unsatisfactory to
others as to yourself, nor ought you to reckon yourself barren, because you fail to expound what you see in such a
fashion as you desire, since peradventure you are too weak
even to see as clearly as you desire. Indeed, in this life who
sees but in a glass darkly? Nor is love itself so mighty as
to break through the murky darkness of the flesh and
pierce to the eternal sunshine, from which even the things
that pass away derive such radiance as they possess.

But because the good advance from day to day toward
the vision of that day which knows no rolling of the sky
nor onset of the night, which eye hath not seen nor ear
heard, nor hath it entered into the heart of man, there is no
greater reason why our discourse should be cheapened in
our esteem, while we inform the uninstructed, than that
we find pleasure in discerning in an extraordinary way and
ordinary exposition becomes a wearisome task. Indeed, our
hearers really listen to us with far greater satisfaction when
we also feel a simultaneous delight, for the texture of our
discourse is affected by our own pleasure, and leaving us
with greater ease, finds a readier welcome.

Therefore it is no hard task to give guidance concerning
the point from which our account of the truths which are
instilled as necessary objects of belief must begin, and the
point at which it must end; how this account should be
varied so as to be shorter at one time, at another longer,
yet always full and perfect, and on what occasions the
longer and the shorter forms respectively should be used;
but our main anxiety must be how to secure the joy of the

teacher in his work: for the more fully he attains this, the more winning will he prove. And on this point there is a precept ready to hand. For if in the case of bodily currency, how much more in that of the spirit does God love a cheerful giver? But the presence of this cheerfulness in its proper hour depends on the mercy of him who has given precepts of that tenor. And so, in accordance with your wishes as I divine them, we will treat, in such fashion as God shall suggest, first of the fashion of our narrative, then of the delivering of precept and encouragement, and afterward of the means of securing the cheerfulness in question. . . .

A narration is full when each learner is instructed from the text " In the beginning God made the heaven and the earth " down to the present times of the church. Nevertheless we ought not for this reason either to repeat from memory (if we have learned them by heart) the whole Pentateuch, the whole of the books of Judges, Kings, and Esdras, the whole Gospel and Acts of the Apostles, or in the course of our narrative to reproduce and set forth in our own words all the contents of these books. Time does not allow this method, nor does any need enforce it; but we should rather summarize and classify the whole, choosing some of the more striking occurrences, which are heard with pleasure, and have taken a standing as cardinal points of the history, so that we must not display them as it were in their wrappings and immediately hurry them out of sight, but by dwelling upon them at some length, untie, so to speak, and unwrap them, and proffer them to the minds of our hearers to examine and admire, while the rest we only weave into our account in a rapid and sweeping survey. Thus the points we would have specially emphasized take prominence by the due subordination of others, and the person whom we wish to stir by our narrative reaches

them unwearied, nor is the memory of the learner whom
we sought to instruct by our teaching thrown into confusion. . . .

. . . If anyone comes to you for instruction well versed
in the liberal branches of study, who has already determined to be a Christian, and has come with the express
intent of becoming one, it is scarcely possible that he
should not be familiar with a great part of our Scriptures
and literature, and thus equipped already, must have come
only to be made a partaker in the sacraments. For it is the
way of such men thoroughly to sift the whole subject, not
in the same hour in which they become Christians, but beforehand, and to impart to such others as they may the
state of their own feelings and discuss them. Accordingly,
with these we must deal briefly, not wearisomely driving
home what they know, but touching upon it with discretion, so far as to say that we believe they are familiar with
this point or that; and in this manner we may enumerate in
passing all that has to be impressed upon the uninstructed
and unlearned; so that even if the man of education is
familiar with any point, he may not hear it as from a
teacher; while if he is still ignorant of anything, he may
learn it as we run over the points we think he knows already.

Undoubtedly he may also be asked with advantage what
motives stirred him to become a Christian, so that if you
see his conviction is derived from books, whether those of
the canon or of serviceable commentators, you may say
something about these at the outset, giving them the credit
due to their diverse excellencies, whether in respect of
canonical authority, or of the industry and fine subtlety of
the several exponents; commending especially in the canonical Scriptures that saving lowliness in which their ad-

mirable sublimity consists, but in other works the style
adapted so far as each author was able, to prouder and
therefore weaker minds, and displaying an eloquence more
sonorous and, as it were, more deftly fashioned on the
lathe.

We must also induce him to inform us by reading what
writer mainly, and by making what books his closest
friends, he was persuaded to desire to join the church.
When he has told us this, then, if those books are known to
us or we have at least heard by common report in the
church that they were written by some catholic of note, let
us joyfully approve them. But if he has stumbled upon the
volumes of some heretic, and through ignorance has perhaps laid up in his mind, believing it to be catholic, some
principle condemned by the true faith, we must earnestly
teach him, setting before him the authority of the universal church and men of the greatest learning besides, who
stand high for their disputations and writings concerning
her truth.

Notwithstanding even those who have passed from this
life as true catholics and have left some Christian literature
to posterity, in certain passages of their works, either because they have not been understood or (such is human
weakness) because they were not strong enough to pierce
with the gaze of the spirit into things more deeply hidden,
but strayed from the truth after a phantom of the true,
have proved an occasion for presumptuous and reckless
persons to devise and beget some heresy. And this is no
marvel, when on the ground of the canonical writings
themselves, in which is no unsound word, many have given
birth to a multitude of mischievous dogmas, dismembering
the oneness of our communion, not merely by understanding certain passages in a sense at variance with the writers'

meaning, or with the truth itself (for if this were all who would not cheerfully forgive human weakness that was ready to suffer correction?), but by championing with the fiercest animosity and stubborn arrogance their own perverse and distorted opinions.

All these subjects you must discuss in a discreet conference with him who draws near to the fellowship of the Christian people, not as a layman (as men say) but with all the polish and education derived from the books of learned men, taking on yourself authority only as far as to bid him beware of errors of presumption, as far as the humble mind which led him to approach you is still found to offer it a foothold. But all other things according to the rules of salutary doctrine, which you must set forth or discuss, whether concerning faith, or morals, or temptations, must one and all, in the course of a rapid treatment such as I have described, be referred to that more excellent way (i.e., I Cor. 12:31).

There are, moreover, certain persons who come from such grammarians' and rhetoricians' schools as are of the greatest resort — men whom you cannot be bold to number among mere laymen, nor yet among those men of deep learning whose wits are trained by inquiries of serious import. Accordingly when men such as these, possessing, it would seem, a pre-eminence in oratory above their fellows, come to be made Christians, we are bound to impart to them this further principle, beyond those impressed upon the unlettered — a principle of which they must be sedulously reminded — namely, that they should clothe themselves in Christian humility and learn not to despise those whom they see avoiding moral blemishes with more care than faults of style; and should not venture even to compare with the pure heart the trained tongue which they had grown accustomed even to honor more highly.

Further, they must be taught above all to listen to the
divine Scriptures, that a solid style may not fall meanly on
their ears because it is unpretentious, and that they may
not imagine that the words and actions which are read in
these books, swathed and covered as they are with fleshly
veils, are not to be unwrapped and laid open to the intelligence, but are to be taken literally: moreover, concerning
the actual value of a hidden meaning (through the presence of which they are also called mysteries) such men
must test by actual experience the power of an enigmatical
disguise in sharpening the desire for truth, and shaking off
the lethargy induced by surfeit, when some subject which
failed to stir them when it was set undisguised to their
hand is enucleated by the unraveling of some allegory.
For to these men it is specially advantageous to know that
thoughts must be reckoned superior to words, as the mind
is reckoned superior to the body.

It follows that they are bound to prefer to listen to discourses true rather than eloquent, as they are bound to prefer the possession of wise rather than handsome friends.
Let them also be assured that there is no voice to reach
the ears of God except the spiritual mood: thus they will
not mock if peradventure they observe that some bishops
and ministers of the church call upon God with barbarisms
and solecisms, or fail to understand the words they are ut-
tering and punctuate them amiss. Not that these faults
should go uncorrected, so that the people may say " Amen "
to what they plainly understand: but these things must be
piously endured by those who have learned that as in the
courts it is the ringing voice, so in a church it is the yearn-
ing heart that is eloquent. Godly oratory, the language of
the courts, may sometimes perhaps be called, but never

godly orison. Concerning the sacrament they are about to receive, it is enough for persons of insight to hear what it means: with those who are slower of understanding we must proceed by way of considerably more words and similitudes, that they may not despise what they see. . . .

. . . It cannot fail to be the case that different persons will affect the intending speaker in different ways, and that the discourse which is delivered will bear, as it were, a kind of outward countenance disclosing the mood of the mind from which it springs, and will influence the hearers diversely according to that same diversity of mood, and the hearers will mutually influence each other by their mere presence. But as we are at this moment dealing with training of the uninstructed, I bear witness to you of myself that I am differently stirred according as I see set before me for instruction a cultivated man, a dullard, a fellow countryman, a foreigner, a rich man, a poor man, a private citizen, a public man, a man set in some authority, a person of this or that nation, of this age or that, of one sex or the other, a man representing this or that philosophical school, this popular and erroneous persuasion or the other; and in sympathy with my own varying emotions my discourse itself starts, proceeds, and ends.

And since, though the same love is owed to all, the same remedy is not to be applied to all, in like manner love itself travails with some, is made weak with others; some it is at pains to edify, others it trembles to offend; bows down to some, before others stands upright; is mild to some, stern to others, an enemy to none, a mother to all. And when someone who has not made trial of the way whereof I speak, in the same spirit of love, sees us, because some gift bestowed upon us has the power to charm, growing in praise and in repute upon the lips of the many, he deems us therefore happy: but may God, into whose sight enters the sighing of the prisoner, look upon our affliction and our travail and forgive us all our sins. Wherefore if anything in us has so well pleased you, that you seek to hear from us some account of the form to be observed in your discourse, you would learn this better, by watching us and listening to us when busied with the work itself, than by reading when we do but dictate.

7

CONSTITUTIONS OF THE HOLY APOSTLES

(ca. 375)

Here we deal with a writing that has no known author. It is thought that it dates ca. 375, and that its sources include earlier documents, including the Didache, *Hippolytus' Tradition, and Barnabas.*

This work abounds in directions for the conduct of the church's life in its manifold details and growing complexity. The brief sections reproduced here indicate attitudes in the church toward pagan literature as well as toward the Biblical materials. The aim of the instruction of the catechumens was to "strengthen them in piety, unite them to and number them with his holy flock." The congregation are bidden to pray for the catechumens: "Let us still earnestly put up our supplications for them, that they may obtain the forgiveness of their transgressions by their admission, and so may be thought worthy of the holy mysteries, and a constant communion with the saints." These responsibilities perennially have been assumed by the members of the church — the older in the faith who nurture the younger.

For a survey of recent developments in thought about

the Constitutions of the Holy Apostles, *see the article
"Apostolic Constitutions" (as it is frequently called), by
Noah Edward Fehl in Vol. I,* Twentieth Century Encyclo-
pedia of Religious Knowledge, *ed. by Lefferts A. Loetscher
(Baker Book House, 1955), pp. 55 f.*

CONSTITUTIONS OF THE HOLY APOSTLES . . .

WHAT BOOKS OF SCRIPTURE WE OUGHT TO READ

If thou stayest at home, read the books of the Law, of
the Kings, with the Prophets; sing the hymns of David;
and peruse diligently the Gospel, which is the completion
of the other. (I. ii. v.)

THAT WE OUGHT TO ABSTAIN FROM ALL THE BOOKS OF THOSE THAT ARE OUT OF THE CHURCH

Abstain from all the heathen books. For what hast thou
to do with such foreign discourses, or laws, or false prophets, which subvert the faith of the unstable? For what
defect dost thou find in the law of God, that thou shouldest
have recourse to those heathenish fables? For if thou hast
a mind to read history, thou hast the books of the Kings;
if books of wisdom or poetry, thou hast those of the Prophets, of Job, and the Proverbs, in which thou wilt find
greater depth of sagacity than in all the heathen poets and
sophisters, because these are the words of the Lord, the
only wise God. If thou desirest something to sing, thou

Constitutions of the Holy Apostles, in *The Ante-Nicene Fathers:* Translations of the Fathers down to A.D. 325, ed. by Alexander Roberts and
James Donaldson, Vol. VII, pp. 391 ff. The Christian Literature Company, 1886.

hast the Psalms; if the origin of things, thou hast Genesis; if laws and statutes, thou hast the glorious law of the Lord God. Do thou therefore utterly abstain from all strange and diabolical books. Nay, when thou readest the law, think not thyself bound to observe the additional precepts; though not all of them, yet some of them. Read those barely for the sake of history, in order to the knowledge of them, and to glorify God that he has delivered thee from such great and so many bonds. Propose to thyself to distinguish what rules were from the law of nature, and what were added afterward, or were such additional rules as were introduced and given in the wilderness to the Israelites after the making of the calf; for the law contains those precepts which were spoken by the Lord God before the people fell into idolatry, and made a calf like the Egyptian Apis; that is, the Ten Commandments.

But as to those bonds which were further laid upon them after they had sinned, do not draw them upon thyself: for our Saviour came for no other reason but that *he might deliver those that were obnoxious thereto from the wrath which was reserved for them,* that he might fulfill the Law and the Prophets, and that he might abrogate or change those secondary bonds which were superadded to the rest of the law. For therefore did he call to us, and say, " *Come unto me,* all ye that labor and are heavy laden, and I will give you rest."

When, therefore, thou hast read the Law, which is agreeable to the Gospel and to the Prophets, read also the books of the Kings, that thou mayest thereby learn which of the kings were righteous, and how they were prospered by God, and how the promise of eternal life continued with them from him; but those kings which went a-whoring

from God did soon perish in their apostasy by the righteous
judgment of God, and were deprived of his life, inheriting,
instead of rest, eternal punishment. Wherefore by reading
these books thou wilt be mightily strengthened in the
faith, and edified in Christ, whose body and member thou
art. (I. ii. vi.)

Of Parents and Children

Ye fathers, educate your children in the Lord, bringing
them up in the nurture and admonition of the Lord; and
teach them such trades as are agreeable and suitable to
the word, lest they by such opportunity become extrava-
gant, and continue without punishment from their parents,
and so get relaxation before their time, and go astray from
that which is good. Wherefore be not afraid to reprove
them, and to teach them wisdom with severity. For your
corrections will not kill them, but rather preserve them. As
Solomon says somewhere in the Book of Wisdom: " Chas-
ten thy son, and he will refresh thee; so wilt thou have
good hope of him. Thou verily shalt smite him with the
rod, and shalt deliver his soul from death." And again,
says the same Solomon thus, " He that spareth his rod,
hateth his son "; and afterward, " Beat his sides whilst he
is an infant, lest he be hardened and disobey thee." He,
therefore, that neglects to admonish and instruct his own
son, hates his own child.

Do you therefore teach your children the word of the
Lord. Bring them under with cutting stripes, and make
them subject from their infancy, teaching them the Holy
Scriptures, which are Christian and divine, and delivering
to them ever sacred writing, " not giving them such liberty
that they get the mastery," and act against your opinion,
not permitting them to club together for a treat with their

equals. For so they will be turned to disorderly courses, and will fall into fornication; and if this happens by the carelessness of their parents, those that begat them will be guilty of their souls. For if the offending children get into the company of debauched persons by the negligence of those that begat them, they will not be punished alone by themselves; but their parents also will be condemned on their account. For this cause endeavor, at the time when they are of an age fit for marriage, to join them in wedlock, and settle them together, lest in the heat and fervor of their age their course of life become dissolute, and you be required to give an account by the Lord God in the Day of Judgment. (IV. ii. xi.)

How the Catechumens Are to Be Instructed in the Elements

Let him, therefore, who is to be taught the truth in regard to piety be instructed before his baptism in the knowledge of the unbegotten God, in the understanding of his only-begotten Son, in the assured acknowledgment of the Holy Ghost. Let him learn the order of the several parts of the Creation, the series of providence, the different dispensations of thy laws. Let him be instructed why the world was made, and why man was appointed to be a citizen therein; let him also know his own nature, of what sort it is; let him be taught how God punished the wicked with water and fire and did glorify the saints in every generation — I mean Seth, and Enos, and Enoch, and Noah, and Abraham and his posterity, and Melchizedek, and Job, and Moses, and Joshua, and Caleb, and Phineas the priest, and those that were holy in every generation; and how God still took care of and did not reject mankind, but called them from their error and vanity to the acknowledgement of the truth at various seasons, reducing them from bondage and impiety unto liberty and piety, from injustice to righteousness, from death eternal to everlasting life.

Let him that offers himself to baptism learn these and the like things during the time that he is a catechumen; and let him who lays his hands upon him adore God, the Lord of the whole world, and thank him for his creation, for his sending Christ his only-begotten Son, that he might save man by blotting out his transgressions, and that he might remit ungodliness and sins, and might " purify him from all filthiness of flesh and spirit," and sanctify man according to the good pleasure of his kindness, that he might inspire him with the knowledge of his will, and enlighten the eyes of his heart to consider of his wonderful works, and make known to him the judgments of righteousness, that so he might hate every way of iniquity, and walk in the way of truth, that he might be thought worthy of the laver of regeneration, to the adoption of sons, which is in Christ, that " being planted together in the likeness of the death of Christ," in hopes of a glorious communication, he may be mortified to sin, and may live to God, as to his mind, and word, and deed, and may be numbered together in the book of the living. And after this thanksgiving, let him instruct him in the doctrines concerning our Lord's incarnation, and in those concerning his Passion, and resurrection from the dead, and assumption. (VII. iii. xxxix.)

PART II

The Middle Centuries

8

ALCUIN

(735–804)

The Anglo-Saxon name of the famous Alcuin was Ealh-
wine. In Latin he is referred to as Albinus Flaccus. Born
at the ancient Eboracum (York), in England, he died at
Tours, France. Having achieved a notable eminence in
scholarly pursuits, he was invited by the Emperor Charlemagne to join the imperial court at Aachen (Aix-la-
Chapelle). He served as abbot of Ferrières and Troyes,
and headed the palace school. He had his share in theological disputation, having attended the Council of Frankfurt in 794, when he caused the adoptionist leader, Felix
of Urgel, to recant. Then he became abbot of Tours, where
he served from 796–804.

Alcuin will be remembered as having developed the
chief school in Carolingian Europe. More than anyone else
he brought a concern for cultural studies to the leaders of
the Frankish peoples. The Letter to Charlemagne, written
during his latter years, in the year 796, summarizes, in a
sense, Alcuin's lifelong devotion to the pursuit of wisdom
and portrays him in his unceasing role as advocate of the
highest spiritual and intellectual goals.

A purported dialogue between Alcuin and Charlemagne,
which ranges widely over basic intellectual and theological
matters, has been published under the title The Rhetoric

of Alcuin and Charlemagne, *tr. by Wilbur Samuel Howell* (*Princeton University Press, 1941*). *Here are a few books on Alcuin: Andrew Fleming West*, Alcuin and the Rise of the Christian Schools, *in The Great Educators Series* (*Charles Scribner's Sons, 1892*); *Eleanor Shipley Duckett*, Alcuin, Friend of Charlemagne: His World and His Work (*The Macmillan Company, 1951*); *Gerald Ellard*, Master Alcuin, Linguist: A Partner of Our Piety (*Jesuit Studies*) (*Loyola University Press, 1956*).

ALCUIN . . .

Letter to Charlemagne

But I, your Flaccus, am doing as you have urged and
wished. To some who are beneath the roof of St. Martin
I am striving to dispense the honey of Holy Scripture;
others I am eager to intoxicate with the old wine of ancient
learning; others again I am beginning to feed with the
apples of grammatical refinement; and there are some
whom I long to adorn with the knowledge of astronomy, as
a stately house is adorned with a painted roof. I am made
all things to all men that I may instruct many to the profit
of God's holy church and to the luster of your imperial
reign. So shall the grace of Almighty God toward me be
not in vain and the largess of your bounty be of no avail.
But I your servant lack in part the rarer books of scholastic
lore which in my native land I had, thanks to the unsparing
labor of my master and a little also to my own toil. This
I tell your excellency on the chance that in your boundless

"Alcuin to Charlemagne" (796), tr. by C. W. Colby, in Colby,
Charles W., ed., *Selections from the Sources of English History*, Being a
Supplement to Text-books of English History, 58 B.C.–A.D. 1832, pp.
17–19. Longmans, Green & Co., Inc., London, 1899. Used by permission.
Also in Cubberley, Ellwood P., ed., *Readings in the History of Educa-
tion*, pp. 92 f. Houghton Mifflin Company, 1920. Used by permission.

and beloved wisdom you may be pleased to have me send some of our youths to take thence what we need, and return to France with the flowers of Britain; that the garden may not be confined to York alone but may bear fruit in Tours, and that the south wind blowing over the gardens of the Loire may be charged with perfume. Then shall it be once more as is said in Solomon's Song from which I quote: " Let my beloved come into his garden and eat his pleasant fruits." And he shall say to his young men, " Eat, O friends; drink, yea, drink abundantly, O beloved. I sleep, but my heart waketh." Or that sentence of the prophet Isaiah which encourages us to learn wisdom, " Ho, every one that thirsteth, come ye to the waters, and he that hath no money; come ye, buy and eat; yea, come, buy wine and milk without money and without price."

This is a matter which has not escaped your most noble notice, how through all the pages of Holy Scripture we are urged to learn wisdom. In toiling toward the happy life nothing is more lofty, nothing more pleasant, nothing bolder against vices, nothing more praiseworthy in every place of dignity; and moreover, according to the words of philosophers, nothing is more essential to government, nothing more helpful to leading a moral life, than the beauty of wisdom, the praise of learning, and the advantages of scholarship. Whence also wisest Solomon exclaims in its praise " For wisdom is better than all things of price and no object of desire is to be compared with her. She exalts the meek; she brings honors to the great. Kings reign by her aid, and lawgivers decree justice. Happy are they who keep her ways, and happy are they who watch at her gates daily." O Lord King, exhort the youths who are in your excellency's palace to learn wisdom with all their might, and to gain it by daily toil while they are yet in the flush of youth, so that they may be deemed worthy to grow gray in honor, and by the help of wisdom may reach everlasting happiness. But I, according to the measure of my little talent, shall not be slothful to sow the seeds of wisdom among your servants in this region, mindful of the saying, " In the morning sow thy seed and in the evening withhold not thy hand: for thou knowest not whether shall prosper, either this or that, or whether they both alike shall be good."

In the morning I sowed in Britain studies which have flourished for a generation. Now as it were toward even I do not cease with blood grown cold to sow in France. And in both places I hope that by the grace of God the seed may spring. The solace of my broken strength is this saying of St. Jerome who in his letter to Nepotian has it: " Almost all the strength of an old man's body is changed and wisdom alone grows as the rest dwindles." And a little later, " The old age of those who have trained their youth in honest arts and have meditated in the law of the Lord day and night, becomes more learned with age, more polished by use, wiser by the lapse of time, and reaps the sweetest fruits of studies long grown old." In which letter whoever wishes may read much in praise of wisdom and the studies of the ancients, and may learn how the ancient sought to flourish in the beauty of wisdom. Ever advance toward this wisdom, beloved of God and praiseworthy on earth, and delight to recognize zeal; and adorn a nobility of worldly lineage with the greater nobility of the mind. In which may our Lord Jesus Christ, who is the virtue and wisdom of God, guard thee, exalt thee, and make thee enter the glory of his blessed and everlasting vision.

9

CHARLEMAGNE
(ca. 742–814)

The Emperor Charlemagne (Charles I), son of Pepin the Short, succeeded to the Frankish throne jointly with his brother Carloman in 768, but when Carloman died in 771, he took over the whole reign personally. The extension of his kingdom is a fascinating history of growing power and influence. One after another neighboring peoples were conquered, including the Saxons, the Lombards, the Arabs in Spain, the Bavarians, and the Danes, so that ultimately his reign extended over territories as far north as Schleswig-Holstein to as far south as a hundred miles below Rome, and east to west from Austria to northern Spain. On Christmas Day, 800, he was crowned emperor. In the sketch of Alcuin, above, we have seen how Charlemagne desired to extend learning in his realms. In addition to Alcuin other eminent scholars joined his court at Aachen.

Alcuin, who probably drafted the text of these proclamations on education in Charlemagne's behalf, wrote a life of the emperor entitled Vita Caroli Magni. *Because of the importance in educational history of these proclamations, we have included them in this collection. The one of 787 has been called " the first general charter of education for the Middle Ages."*

CHARLEMAGNE . . .

Educational Proclamations

A.D. 787

Charles, by the grace of God, King of the Franks and Lombards and Patrician of the Romans, to Abbot Baugulf and to all the congregation, also the faithful committed to you, we have directed a loving greeting by our ambassadors in the name of omnipotent God.

Be it known, therefore, to your devotion pleasing to God, that we, together with our faithful, have considered it to be useful that the bishoprics and monasteries entrusted by the favor of Christ to our control, in addition to the order of monastic life and the intercourse of holy religion, in the culture of letters also ought to be zealous in teaching those who by the grace of God are able to learn, according to the capacity of each individual, so that just as the observance of the rule imparts order and grace to honesty of morals, so also zeal in teaching and learning may do the same for sentences, so that those who desire to please God by living rightly should not neglect to please him also by

Charlemagne, *Educational Proclamations*, in Cubberley, Ellwood P., ed., *Readings in the History of Education*, pp. 90 f., tr. by D. C. Munro. Houghton Mifflin Company, 1920. Used by permission.

speaking correctly. For it is written, "Either from thy words thou shalt be justified or from thy words thou shalt be condemned" (Matt. 12:37). For although correct con- duct may be better than knowledge, nevertheless knowl- edge preceded conduct. Therefore, each one ought to study what he desires to accomplish, so that so much the more fully the mind may know what ought to be done, as the tongue hastens in the praises of omnipotent God with- out the hindrances of errors. For since errors should be shunned by all men, so much the more ought they to be avoided, as far as possible, by those who are chosen to this very purpose alone so that they ought to be the espe- cial servants of truth.

For when in the years just past, letters were often writ- ten to us from several monasteries in which it was stated that the brethren who dwelt there offered up on our be- half sacred and pious prayers, we have recognized in most of these letters correct thoughts and uncouth expressions; because what pious devotion dictated faithfully to the mind, the tongue, uneducated on account of the neglect of study, was not able to express in a letter without error. Whence it happened that we began to fear lest perchance, as the skill in writing was less, so also the wisdom for un- derstanding the Holy Scriptures might be much less than it rightly ought to be. And we all know well that, though errors of speech are dangerous, far more dangerous are er- rors of the understanding.

Therefore, we exhort you not only not to neglect the study of letters, but also with the most humble mind, pleas- ing to God, to study earnestly in order that you may be able more easily and more correctly to penetrate the mys- teries of the divine Scriptures, since, moreover, images, strophes, and similar figures are found in the sacred pages, no one doubts that each one in reading these will understand the spiritual sense more quickly if previously he shall have been fully instructed in the mastery of letters. Such men truly are to be chosen for this work as have both the will and the ability to learn and the desire to instruct others. And may this be done with a zeal as great as the earnestness with which we commend it. For we desire you to be, as it is fitting that soldiers of the church should be, devout in mind, learned in discourse, chaste in conduct, and eloquent in speech, so that whosoever shall seek to see you out of reverence for God, or on account of your reputation for holy conduct, just as he is edified by your appearance, may also be instructed by your wisdom, which he has learned from your reading or singing, and may go away joyfully giving thanks to omnipotent God. Do not neglect, therefore, if you wish to have our favor, to send copies of this letter to all your suffragans and fellow bishops and to all the monasteries. [And let no monk hold courts outside of his monastery or go to the judicial and other public assemblies. Farewell. (*Legens valeat.*)]

A.D. 789

And we also demand of your holiness that the ministers of the altar of God shall adorn their ministry by good manners, and likewise the other orders who observe a rule and the congregation of monks. We implore them to lead a just and fitting life just as God himself commanded in the gospel. " Let your light so shine before men that they may see your good works and glorify your Father which is in heaven," so that by their example many may be led to serve God; and let them join and associate to themselves not only children of servile condition, but also sons of free men. And let schools be established in which boys may learn to read. Correct carefully the psalms, the signs in writing *(notas)*, the songs, the calendar, the grammar, in each monastery or bishopric, and the catholic books; because often some desire to pray to God properly, but they pray badly because of the incorrect books. And do not permit your boys to corrupt them in reading or writing. If there is need of writing the gospel, psalter, and missal, let men of mature age do the writing with all diligence.

A.D. 802

(We will and command) that laymen shall learn thoroughly the Creed and the Lord's Prayer.

10

RABANUS MAURUS
(ca. 776–856)

Like Alcuin, of whom he was a kind of disciple, Rabanus
Maurus was deeply concerned with the transmission of
culture. He was born at Mainz, Germany, and died at
Winkel, in the same country. Before he became involved
in ecclesiastical administration, he taught theology and
rhetoric at a Parisian school conducted by Anglo-Saxon
missionaries. Later he was abbot of Fulda (822–840) and
archbishop of Mainz (consecrated, 847). To a large extent
he was responsible for the ninth-century revival of learning, and he has been called " the first teacher of Germany."
    Education of the Clergy ranks as one of the fullest dis-
cussions of the liberal arts from this period. Since the liberal arts had become the basis for advanced education, it
was important that the church should think through the
relation of the training of the professional clergy to the
classical disciplines, and in this respect Rabanus Maurus'
work is highly significant. Modern thoroughgoing studies
of theological education might well benefit from a backward glance at this man's thought concerning the need of
the clergy that they " should endeavor to grasp and include
in their knowledge" the broad foundations of education.

To some degree Rabanus Maurus was dependent on Isidore of Seville, from whose Etymologies *he derived much of his material. In time, however, Isidore's work tended to be supplanted by Rabanus Maurus' two treatises,* De rerum naturis *and* De Universo.

RABANUS MAURUS . . .

Education of the Clergy

An ecclesiastical education should qualify the sacred office of the ministry for divine service. It is fitting that those who from an exalted station undertake the direction of the life of the church should acquire fullness of knowledge, and that they further should strive after rectitude of life and perfection of development. They should not be allowed to remain in ignorance of anything that appears beneficial for their own information or for the instruction of those entrusted to their care. Therefore they should endeavor to grasp and include in their knowledge the following things: an acquaintance with Holy Scripture, the unadulterated truth of history, the derivative modes of speech, the mystical sense of words, the advantages growing out of the separate branches of knowledge, the integrity of life that manifests itself in good morals, delicacy and good taste in oral discourse, penetration in the explanation of doctrine, the different kinds of medicine, and the various forms of disease. Anyone to whom all this remains un-

Maurus, Rabanus, *Education of the Clergy*, Book III, in *Great Pedagogical Essays, Plato to Spencer*, ed. by F. V. N. Painter. American Book Company, 1905. Used by permission.

known is not able to care for his own welfare, let alone that of others. . . .

THE HOLY SCRIPTURE

The foundation, the content, and the perfection of all wisdom is Holy Scripture, which has taken its origin from that unchangeable and eternal Wisdom, which streams from the mouth of the Most High, which was begotten before every other creature through the Holy Spirit, which is a light incessantly beaming from the words of Holy Scripture. . . . Every truth, which is discovered by anyone, is recognized as true by the truth itself through the mediation of the truth; every good thing, which is in any way traced out, is recognized and determined as good by the good itself; all wisdom, which is brought to light by anyone, is found to be wisdom by wisdom itself. . . . Above all it is necessary that he who aims to attain the summit of wisdom should be converted to the fear of the Lord in order to know what the divine will bids us strive for and shun. . . . Therefore we are not to raise any objection to the Holy Scriptures, either when we understand them and feel ourselves smitten by their words, or when we do not understand them and give ourselves up to the thought that we can understand and grasp something better out of our own minds. . . .

THE LIBERAL ARTS

The first of the liberal arts is grammar, the second rhetoric, the third dialectic, the fourth arithmetic, the fifth geometry, the sixth music, and the seventh astronomy.

Grammar takes its name from the written character, as the derivation of the word indicates. The definition of grammar is this: Grammar is the science which teaches us to explain the poets and historians; it is the art which qualifies us to explain the poets and historians; it is the art which qualifies us to write and speak correctly. Grammar is the source and foundation of the liberal arts. It should be taught in every Christian school, since the art of writing and speaking correctly is attained through it. . . . All the forms of speech, of which secular science makes use in its writings, are found repeatedly employed in the Holy Scriptures. . . . Hence this art, though it may be secular, has nothing unworthy in itself; it should rather be learned as thoroughly as possible.

According to the statement of teachers, rhetoric is the art of using secular discourse effectively in the circumstances of daily life. From this definition rhetoric seems indeed to have reference merely to secular wisdom. Yet it is not foreign to ecclesiastical instruction. Whatever the preacher and herald of the divine law, in his instruction, brings forward in an eloquent and becoming manner, whatever in his written exposition he knows how to clothe in adequate and impressive language, he owes to his acquaintance with this art. Whoever at the proper time makes himself familiar with this art, and faithfully follows its rules in speaking and writing, needs not count it as something blameworthy. On the contrary, whoever thoroughly learns it so that he acquires the ability to proclaim God's word, performs a good work. . . .

Dialectic is the science of the understanding, which fits us for investigations and definitions, for explanations, and for distinguishing the true from the false. It is the science of sciences. It teaches how to teach others; it teaches learning itself; in it the reason marks and manifests itself according to its nature, efforts, and activities; it alone is capable of knowing; it not only will, but can lead others to knowledge; its conclusions lead us to an apprehension of our being and of our origin; through it we apprehend the origin and activity of the good, of Creator and creature; it teaches us to discover the truth and to unmask falsehood; it teaches us to draw conclusions; it shows us what is valid in argument and what is not; it teaches us to recognize what is contrary to the nature of things; it teaches us to distinguish in controversy the true, the probable, and the wholly false; by means of this science we are able to investigate everything with penetration, to determine its nature with certainty, and to discuss it with circumspection. Therefore the clergy must understand this excellent art and constantly reflect upon its laws in order that they may be able keenly to pierce the craftiness of errorists and to refute their fatal fallacies.

Arithmetic is the science of pure extension determinable by number; it is the science of numbers. Writers on secular science assign it, under the head of mathematics, to the first place, because it does not presuppose any of the other departments. Music, geometry, and astronomy, on the contrary, need the help of arithmetic; without it they cannot arise or exist. . . . The holy fathers were right in advising those eager for knowledge to cultivate arithmetic, because in large measure it turns the mind from fleshly desires, and furthermore awakens the wish to comprehend what with God's help we can merely receive with the heart. Therefore the significance of numbers is not to be underestimated. Its very great value for an interpretation of many passages of Holy Scriptures is manifest to all who exhibit zeal in their investigations. Not without good reason is it said in praise of God, " Thou hast ordained all things by measure, number, and weight " (Book of Wisdom 11:21). . . .

We now come to the discussion of geometry. It is an exposition of form proceeding from observation; it is also a very common means of demonstration among philosophers who, to adduce at once the most full-toned evidence, declare that their Jupiter made use of geometry in his works. I do not know indeed whether I should find praise or censure in this declaration of the philosophers that Jupiter engraved upon the vault of the skies precisely what they themselves draw in the sand of the earth. When this in a proper manner is transferred to God, the almighty Creator, this assumption may perhaps come near the truth. . . . The knowledge of all this brings to him, who is occupied with it, no small gain for his spiritual culture.

Music is the science of time intervals as they are perceived in tones. This science is as eminent as it is useful. He who is a stranger to it is not able to fulfill the duties of an ecclesiastical office in a suitable manner. A proper delivery in reading and a lovely rendering of the psalms in the church are regulated by a knowledge of this science. Yet it is not only good reading and beautiful psalmody that we owe to music; through it alone do we become capable of celebrating in the most solemn manner every divine service. Music penetrates all the activities of our life; in this sense, namely, that we above all carry out the commands of the Creator and bow with a pure heart to his commands; all that we speak, all that makes our heart beat faster, is shown through the rhythm of music united with the excellence of harmony; for music is the science which teaches us agreeably to change tones in duration and pitch. When we employ ourselves with good pursuits in life, we show ourselves thereby disciples of this art; so long as we do what is wrong, we do not feel ourselves drawn to music. Even heaven and earth, as everything that happens here through the arrangement of the Most High, is nothing but music, as Pythagoras testifies that this world was created by music and can be ruled by it. Even with the Christian religion music is most intimately united; thus it is possible that to him who does not know even a little music, many things remain closed and hidden.

There remains yet astronomy, which, as someone has said, is a weighty means of demonstration to the pious, and to the curious a grievous torment. If we seek to investigate it with a pure heart and an ample mind, then it fills us, as the ancients said, with great love for it. For what will it not signify, that we soar in spirit to the sky, that with penetration of mind we analyze that sublime structure, that we, in part at least, fathom with the keenness of our logical faculties what mighty space has enveloped in mystery! . . .

Astronomy, of which we now speak, teaches the laws of the stellar world. The stars can take their place or carry out their motion only in the manner established by the Creator, unless by the will of the Creator a miraculous change takes place. . . . That part of astronomy, which is built up on the investigation of natural phenomena, in order to determine the course of the sun, of the moon, and stars, and to effect a proper reckoning of time, the Christian clergy should seek to learn with the utmost diligence in order through the knowledge of laws brought to light and through the valid and convincing proof of the given means of evidence to place themselves in a position, not only to determine the course of past years according to truth and reality, but also for further times to draw confident conclusions, and to fix the time of Easter and all other festivals and holy days, and to announce to the congregation the proper celebration of them.

The seven liberal arts of the philosophers, which Christians should learn for their utility and advantage, we have, as I think, sufficiently discussed. We have this yet to add. When those, who are called philosophers, have in their expositions or in their writings uttered perchance some truth, which agrees with our faith, we should not handle it timidly, but rather take it as from its unlawful possessors and apply it to our own use. . . .

11

THOMAS AQUINAS
(ca. 1225–1274)

Thomas Aquinas, a native of Rocco Senna, Italy, came to be known as " The Angelic Doctor " or " The Father of Moral Philosophy," and is acknowledged as one of the most brilliant thinkers of his or any age. Educated at Monte Cassino and Naples, he became a Dominican in 1243. His scholarly interests led him to Paris, where he studied with Albertus Magnus, later accompanying his teacher to Köln in 1248. He himself taught at Köln, Paris, Rome, and elsewhere. His massive Summa Theologica *in three parts has had an enormous influence throughout the intellectual world, leading in modern times to a movement called Neo-Thomism. In his work Thomas attempted a synthesis of theology and philosophy according to Aristotelian foundations. His theology was made the official norm of Roman Catholic theology in 1879, having been so considered unofficially for many previous generations. A trip toward Lyons for a church council came to an untimely end, for en route he fell ill and died at a Cistercian monastery where he had stopped to rest. Tradition has it that he expounded the Song of Songs as he lay dying.*

How to Study *is simple and direct advice from the great thinker to a monastic brother who had inquired about a method of study. One might call it the precursor of in-*

numerable attempts to answer the same kind of question in succeeding centuries. De Magistro (The Teacher) *is cast in the formal style of a disputation. It is included here to illustrate the highly stylized analysis of an argument which was the basic teaching device in the medieval period. The defense of the " thesis " required of a present-day doctoral candidate dates back to this disputation method, although the mode of presentation and defense of a dissertation has been considerably altered in modern usage. It is also a fine example of Thomas' careful thought and his devotion to " principles " as the basis for action.*

The Everyman's Library has a Selected Writings, *ed. by M. C. D'Arcy (E. P. Dutton & Co., Inc., 1939). See also* Basic Writings of Saint Thomas Aquinas, *ed. by Anton C. Pegis (Random House, Inc., 1945). A foremost Thomistic scholar of the present, Étienne Gilson, has written* The Philosophy of St. Thomas Aquinas, *tr. by Edward Bullough (B. Herder Book Company, 1925). Other books: Martin Grabmann,* Thomas Aquinas: His Personality and Thought, *tr. by Virgil Michel (Longmans, Green & Co., Inc., 1928); John F. McCormick,* St. Thomas and the Life of Learning *(Marquette University Press, 1937); Gerald Vann,* St. Thomas Aquinas *(Benziger Brothers, 1941); F. C. Coplestone,* Aquinas *(Penguin Books, Inc., Harmondsworth, 1955) [Pelican Book]; Walz, Angela Maria,* Saint Thomas Aquinas, A Biographical Study, *tr. by Sebastian Bullough (The Newman Press, 1951).*

THOMAS AQUINAS . . .

How to Study

Brother John, most dear to me in Christ: Since you have asked me how one should set about to acquire the treasure of knowledge, this is my advice to you concerning it: namely, that you should choose to enter, not straightway into the ocean, but by way of the little streams; for difficult things ought to be reached by way of easy ones.

The following, therefore, is my advice to you concerning your way of living:

I urge you to hesitate before speaking, and to hesitate before visiting the common room.

Hold fast to the cleanness of your conscience.

Do not cease from devoting time to prayer.

Love your cell by making constant use of it, if you want to be admitted into the wine cellar.

Show yourself to be lovable to everybody, or at least try to do so; but be very familiar with nobody, for too

Aquinas, Thomas, *How to Study*, Being the Letter of St. Thomas to Brother John, *De Modo Studendi*; Latin Text with Translation and Exposition by Victor White, O.P. Blackfriars Publications, London, 1956 (6th ed.). Used by permission.

much familiarity breeds contempt and introduces factors which retard study.

Also, do not in any way get yourself involved in the doings and sayings of outsiders.

Avoid aimless meanderings above all things.

Do not fail to follow in the footsteps of the saints and of sound men.

Do not heed by *whom* a thing is said, but rather *what* is said you should commit to your memory.

What you read, set about to understand, verifying what is doubtful.

Strive to put whatsoever you can in the cupboard of your mind, as though you were wanting to fill a vessel to the brim.

" Seek not the things that are too high for thee."

Follow in the footsteps of that blessed Dominic, who, while he yet had life for his fellow traveler, brought forth and produced foliage, blossom, fruit — fruit both serviceable and astonishing — in the vineyard of the Lord of Hosts. If you shall have followed these steps, you will be able to attain to whatsoever you have a mind. Fare you well!

The Teacher

The four articles or divisions of the *De Magistro* deal with four points of inquiry, namely: (1) Whether man can teach and be called a teacher, or God alone? (2) Whether

Aquinas, Thomas, *De Magistro*, tr. by Mary Helen Mayer, in *The Philosophy of Teaching of St. Thomas Aquinas*, pp. 41–86. The Bruce Publishing Company, 1929. Articles III and IV are omitted here. Used by permission.

anyone can be called a teacher of himself? (3) Whether man can be taught by an angel? (4) Whether to teach is a function of the active or of the contemplative life?

Article 1

WHETHER MAN CAN TEACH ANOTHER AND BE CALLED A TEACHER, OR GOD ALONE? (Cf. *Summa Theol.* I, 117, A. 1.)

Objection 1. The question is on the teacher, and the first point of inquiry is whether man can teach and be called a teacher, or God alone; and it seems that God alone teaches and ought to be called a teacher (Matt. 23:8). "One is your master," and preceding this, "Be not you called Rabbi," on which the gloss says, "Lest you attribute divine honor to men, or usurp to yourselves what belongs to God." Therefore, to be a teacher or to teach seems to belong to God alone.

Objection 2. Further, if man teaches, he does so only through some symbols. For even if some things seem to be taught by themselves (for example, if when somebody asks what it is to walk, someone walks), yet this is not sufficient to teach him unless some symbol is added, as Augustine says in his book *De Magistro* (c. iii, *ad fin.*); and he explains why this is so, for this reason, that in the same thing there are many elements, so that it would not be known how far the demonstration held in regard to any aspect of that object, whether in regard to the substance of the object or in regard to some accident in it. But it is not possible to arrive at a knowledge of things through a symbol, because the knowledge of things is more potent than the knowledge of symbols, because the knowledge of symbols stands in relation to the knowledge of things as a means to an end. But an effect is not greater than its cause. Therefore, no one can give to another a knowledge of some things, and hence, cannot teach him.

Objection 3. Further, if the symbols of some things are proposed to someone by a man, either he to whom they are proposed knows those things of which they are the symbols, or he does not. If he knows them, he is not taught concerning them; but if he does not know them, then because the things are unknown, the meanings of the symbols cannot be known, for he who does not know this thing which is a rock, cannot know what this name " rock " signifies. When the signification of the symbols is unknown, we cannot learn anything through them. If, then, man does nothing more for instruction than propose symbols, it seems that man cannot be taught by man.

Objection 4. Further, to teach is nothing else than to cause knowledge in someone else. Now, the subject of knowledge is the intellect. But sensible symbols, through which alone it seems that man can be taught, are not received into the intellect but remain in the sensitive faculty. Therefore, man cannot be taught by man.

Objection 5. Further, if knowledge in one is caused by another, either the knowledge was in the one learning or it was not. If it was not in him and is caused in one by another, then one man causes knowledge in another, which is impossible. But if it was in him, it was either in perfect actuality and so cannot be caused, because what is does not become, or it was as a germ of knowledge. But germinal capacities cannot be reduced to actuality by any created power, but are planted in nature by God alone, as Augustine says *(Super Genes. ad Litt.)* Therefore, it remains that one man can in no way teach another.

Objection 6. Further, knowledge is a kind of accident. But an accident does not change from one subject to another. Hence, since teaching seems to be nothing else than a transfusion of knowledge from teacher to pupil, one cannot teach another.

Objection 7. Further (Rom., ch. 10), the gloss on " Faith cometh by hearing," says, " Though God teaches interiorly, yet the preacher proclaims from without." But knowledge is caused interiorly in the mind, not exteriorly in the sense. Therefore, man is taught by God alone and not by another man.

Objection 8. Further, Augustine says in the book *De Magistro,* " God alone has a teaching chair in heaven, who teaches truth interiorly, but another man stands in the same relation to the teaching chair as a farmer does to a tree." But the farmer is not the maker of the tree, but its cultivator. Therefore, man cannot be called the giver of knowledge, but the disposer to knowledge.

Objection 9. Further, if man is a true teacher, he must teach the truth. But whoever teaches the truth illumines the mind, since truth is the light of the mind. Therefore, man illumines the mind if he teaches. But this is false, since God is he " who enlighteneth every man that cometh into this world " (John 1:9). Therefore, one man cannot truly teach another.

Objection 10. Further, if one man teaches another, the teacher must change him from knowing potentially to knowing actually. Therefore, the pupil's knowledge must be reduced from potentiality to actuality. But what is reduced from potency to act must of necessity be changed. Therefore, knowledge or wisdom will be changed, which is contrary to Augustine [lib. 83, Quaest.), who says, " Wisdom coming to man is not itself changed but changes man."

Objection 11. Further, knowledge is a representation of

things in the mind, since knowledge is said to be an assimilation of the knower to the thing known. But one man cannot represent in another's mind the likenesses of things, for thus he would operate interiorly in him, which belongs to God alone. Therefore, one man cannot teach another.

Objection 12. Further, Boethius says in the book (*De Consol.* V), that through teaching, the mind of man is only stimulated to know. But he who stimulates the intellect to knowing does not make it know, just as one who stimulates another to seeing with his bodily sight does not make him see. Therefore, one man does not make another know and hence, cannot properly be said to teach him.

Objection 13. Further, there is required for knowledge a certitude of cognition; otherwise it would not be knowledge but opinion or belief, as Augustine says in the book *De Magistro.* But one man cannot cause certitude in another through the sensible symbols which he proposes, for what is in the sense is more oblique than what is in the intellect, and certitude is always produced in relation to something more direct. Therefore, one man cannot teach another.

Objection 14. Further, for knowledge there is needed only the intellective light and the species, but neither of these can be caused in one man by another; because this would necessitate that man create something, since it seems that simple forms of this kind cannot be produced except through creation. Therefore, man cannot cause knowledge in another, and hence, cannot teach him.

Objection 15. Further, nothing can form the mind of man except God alone, as Augustine says. But knowledge is a certain form of the mind. Therefore, God alone causes knowledge in the mind.

Objection 16. As guilt is in the mind, so is ignorance. But

God alone purges the mind of guilt. (Isa. 43:25.) "I am life that blot out thy iniquities for my own sake." Therefore, God alone purges the mind of ignorance, and he alone teaches.

Objection 17. Further, since knowledge is cognition with certitude, a man receives knowledge from that one through whose assertion he is made certain. But a man cannot be made certain by that which he hears another asserting; otherwise it would be necessary that whatever is said to anyone by a man should be held as certain. But a man is made certain only inasmuch as he hears truth speaking interiorly, to which truth he refers even about those things which he hears from man, so that he may be sure. Therefore, man does not teach, but truth which speaks interiorly, which is God.

Objection 18. Further, no one learns through the assertion of another what even before the assertion he could have answered if asked. But a disciple, even before the master speaks, could answer, if asked about those things which the master proposes. For he would not be taught by the assertion of the master unless he was confident that it was just as the master proposes. Therefore, one man is not taught by the assertion of another. . . .

Reply to Objection 1. Because the Lord prescribed that the disciples should not be called masters, it cannot be understood that this was prohibited absolutely; and the gloss explains how it is to be understood. We are forbidden to call man a teacher in the way that attributes to him the principal part of teaching which belongs to God, as it were putting our hope in the wisdom of men, and in regard to those things which we hear from men, not preferring them rather to the divine truth which speaks in us by the impression of his likeness, by which we are able to judge concerning all things.

Reply to Objection 2. The cognition of things is not brought about in us through a cognition of symbols but through a cognition of other more certain things, that is, of principles which are proposed to us through certain symbols and which are applied to other things previously unknown to us in the strict sense, although known after the fashion spoken of in the body of the article: for the cognition of principles, not the cognition of symbols causes in us a knowledge of conclusions.

Reply to Objection 3. Those things about which we are taught through symbols, we know to some degree, but to some degree we do not know. For example, if we are being taught what man is, we must know beforehand something about him, either the fact of his animality or of his substantiality, or at least of his existence, which cannot be unknown to us. In like manner, if we are being taught any conclusion, we must first know regarding the subject and its property, what they are, even though the principles from which the conclusion is being taught are known beforehand; for all learning comes about from pre-existing knowledge. . . . Hence, the reasoning in the third objection does not follow.

Reply to Objection 4. From the sensible symbols, which are received in the sense faculty, the intellect takes the essence which it uses in producing knowledge in itself, for the immediate, efficient cause of knowledge is not the symbols but the process of discursive reasoning from principles to conclusions, as was said in the body of the article.

Reply to Objection 5. In the one who is being taught, knowledge pre-exists not in complete actuality but, as it were, in germinal capacities, because the universal concept, the cognition of which is naturally implanted in us, are as seeds of all subsequent cognitions. Although germinal capacities are not educed to actuality through a created power as though they were infused by a created power, yet that which is in them originally and virtually can be educed to actuality by the action of a created power.

Reply to Objection 6. He who teaches is not said to transfer knowledge to the pupil, as though the same knowledge numerically which is in the teacher should be produced in the pupil; but through teaching there is produced in the pupil knowledge like that which is in the teacher, educed from potentiality to actuality, as was said in the body of the article.

Reply to Objection 7. Just as a doctor, although he works exteriorly while nature alone works interiorly, is said to cause healing, so man is said to teach, although he announces exteriorly while God teaches interiorly.

Reply to Objection 8. Augustine, in that he maintains in the *De Magistro* that God alone teaches, does not mean to deny that man teaches exteriorly, but to insist that God alone teaches interiorly.

Reply to Objection 9. Man can truly be called a true teacher teaching truth and enlightening the mind, not as though infusing the light of reason, but aiding the light of reason to the perfection of knowledge through those things which he proposes exteriorly according to the manner spoken of (Eph. 3:8-9): "To me, the least of all the saints, is given this grace, . . . to enlighten all men that they may see what is the dispensation of the mystery which hath been hidden from eternity in God."

Reply to Objection 10. Wisdom is twofold, created and uncreated. Both are infused in man. Because of the infusion of this wisdom, man can be changed for the better by developing. Uncreated wisdom cannot, indeed, be changed; created wisdom is changed in us *per accidens* but not per se; for wisdom itself may be considered in a twofold manner: on the one hand, in respect to the eternal things with which it is concerned, wisdom is entirely unchangeable; on the other hand, in respect to the existence which it has in the subject, it is changed *per accidens* when the subject is changed from having wisdom in potentiality to having it in actuality. For the intelligible forms, of which wisdom consists, are both likenesses of things and forms which perfect the intellect.

Reply to Objection 11. The intelligible forms, of which knowledge received from teaching is composed, are impressed in the pupil immediately through the active intellect but mediately through the teacher; for the teacher proposes the symbols of intelligible things from which the intellect takes the abstractions and impresses them on the passive intellect. Hence, the words of the teacher, heard or seen in writing, have the same relation to causing knowledge in the intellect as anything outside the mind has, because from both, the intellect takes the intelligible content (meaning); yet the words of the teacher have a closer relation to causing knowledge than have the mere perceivable things outside the mind, inasmuch as words are symbols of intelligible content.

Reply to Objection 12. The intellect and bodily vision are not the same, for bodily vision is not a logical power so that from certain of its objects it arrives at others; but all of its objects are visible to it as quickly as it is turned toward them. Hence, the one who has the power of sight has the same relation to looking toward all things visible as one having habitual knowledge has to directing attention toward what he habitually knows. Hence, the one looking does not need to be excited by another to see, except, inasmuch as his gaze may be directed by someone to something visible as with the pointing of the finger or something of that sort. But the intellective power, since it is discursive, does infer some things from others. Hence, it has not precisely an equal relation to all intelligible objects to be considered, but it sees certain things immediately, as those which are self-evident in which are contained implicitly other things which it cannot see except by making explicit through the office of reason that which is implicitly contained in these principles. Hence, before it has habitual knowledge, the intellect is not only in accidental potentiality to knowing things of this kind but even in essential potentiality, for it needs a mover which will lead it into actuality through teaching, as is said in VIII *Physics* (com. 32). He who knows something habitually, however, does not need this service of a mover. The teacher, then, excites the intellect to knowing those things which he is teaching as an essential mover, leading it from potentiality to actuality; but he who shows something to the bodily sight excites it as an accidental mover, according as one having habitual knowledge can be aroused to think about something.

Reply to Objection 13. The whole certitude of knowledge arises from the certitude of principles. Conclusions are then known to be valid when they are resolved into their principles. Therefore, the fact that anything is known with certitude is possible from the light of reason divinely implanted in us, by which God speaks in us. It does not arise from man's teaching from without, except inasmuch as in teaching he resolves conclusions into principles; from him, however, we could not reach a certitude of knowledge if there were not in us certitude of principles into which conclusions are resolved.

Reply to Objection 14. Man teaching exteriorly does not infuse the light of the intellect, but is, in some way, the cause of the intelligible species, inasmuch as he proposes to us certain symbols of intelligible content which the intellect receives from the symbols and stores in its very self.

Reply to Objection 15. When it is said that nothing can form the mind except God, its ultimate form is referred to, without which it is considered formless, whatever other form it may have. But this is that form by which it is turned to the Word and clings to it, through which alone the rational nature is said to be formed, as is evident in Augustine. (*Super Genes. ad Litt.*, lib. 1, c. 25, and lib. 83, Qq. Quaest. 5.)

Reply to Objection 16. Guilt is in the affective faculty, on which God alone can make an impression, as will be evident in the next article, but ignorance is in the intellect on which a created power can make an impression, since the active intellect impresses the intelligible species on the possible intellect, through the medium of which from sense impressions and man's instruction, knowledge is caused in our minds, as was said in the body of the article.

Reply to Objection 17. Certitude of knowledge, as was said, man has from God alone, who endowed us with the light of reason through which we know the principles from which certitude arises. And yet knowledge is caused in us by man in some sense way, as was said in the body of the article.

Reply to Objection 18. A pupil questioned by the teacher before instruction might answer regarding the principles through which he is being taught, but not regarding the conclusions which someone is teaching him. Therefore, he does not learn the principles from the teacher but only the conclusions.

Article 2

WHETHER ANYONE CAN BE CALLED A TEACHER OF HIMSELF

Objection 1. The second point of inquiry is whether anyone can be said to be a teacher of himself, and it seems that no one can; because an action ought to be attributed to a principal rather than to an instrumental cause. But the principal cause, as it were, of knowledge caused in us is the active intellect; and man who teaches exteriorly is a kind of instrumental cause, proposing to the active intellect the instruments by means of which it leads us to knowledge. Therefore, the active intellect teaches, rather than a man from without. If, therefore, on account of instruction from without the one who speaks is said to be the teacher of the one who hears, much more ought he who hears on account of the light of the active intellect, be called a teacher of himself.

Objection 2. Further, no one learns anything except as he comes to a certitude of knowledge. But certitude of knowledge is in us through principles naturally known by the light of the intellect. Therefore, it is particularly proper to the active intellect to teach, and hence, the same conclusion as before.

Objection 3. To teach is more proper to God than to man. Hence (Matt. 23:8), " One is your master." But God teaches us, inasmuch as he gives us the light of reason by which we can judge concerning all things. Therefore, the action of teaching ought to be attributed especially to that light.

Objection 4. To know something by discovery is more

perfect than to learn from another. . . . If, therefore, the name of teacher is assumed from that manner of acquiring knowledge by which one learns from another, so that one may be called a teacher of another, much more should the name of teacher be assumed from the way of learning by discovery so that one may be called his own teacher.

Objection 5. Just as one is led to virtue by himself and by others, so he is led to knowledge both by himself in discovery and by another in instruction. But those who arrive at the works of virtue without an extrinsic instructor are said to be a law unto themselves. (Rom. 2:14.) " When the Gentiles, who have not the law, do by nature those things that are of the law . . . [they] are a law to themselves." Therefore, he also who acquires knowledge through himself ought to be called a teacher of himself.

Objection 6. Further, the teacher is the cause of knowledge as the doctor is of health, as was said. But the doctor heals himself; therefore, man can teach himself.

On the contrary, the Philosopher says that it is impossible for the one teaching to learn because it is necessary for the teacher to have knowledge and for the learner not to have it. Therefore, man cannot teach himself nor be called his own teacher.

Further, teachership implies a relation of superordination and subordination, as lordship does. But relations of this kind cannot be of someone to himself, for one cannot be father of himself or lord of himself. Therefore, man cannot be called a teacher of himself. . . .

Reply to Objection 1. Although the active intellect is a more principal cause in some respects than is a man teaching extrinsically, yet complete knowledge does not pre-exist in it as in the teacher; hence, the reasoning does not follow.

Reply to Objection 2. The solution is evident from what has been said.

Reply to Objection 3. God knows explicitly everything which man is taught by him; hence, the function of teaching can be fittingly attributed to him. But it is otherwise with regard to the active intellect for the reason just given (Objection 1).

Reply to Objection 4. Although the mode of the acquisition of knowledge through discovery is more perfect on the part of the one receiving the knowledge, inasmuch as he is thereby distinguished as being more gifted for learning, nevertheless, on the part of what causes the knowledge, the more perfect mode is through instruction, because the teacher who has the knowledge as a whole explicitly can lead to knowledge more quickly and easily than anyone can be led by himself, because of this fact that the pupil knows the principles of knowledge only in generality (vaguely).

Reply to Objection 5. Law in practical matters has the same relation as a principle has in speculative matters, but not as a teacher to a pupil. Hence, it does not follow that if one is a law to himself, he can be a teacher to himself.

Reply to Objection 6. The doctor heals not inasmuch as he has health in actuality beforehand, but inasmuch as he has health in the knowledge of his art; but the teacher teaches inasmuch as he has knowledge in actuality. Hence, he who does not have health in actuality can cause health in himself because he has health in the knowledge of the art of healing; but it is not possible that one have knowledge in actuality and yet not have it, so that thus he could be taught by himself.

12

JEAN GERSON
(ca. 1363–ca. 1429)

Jean Charlier de Gerson was born at Gerson, France. His early studies were at the College of Navarre in Paris. He was made chancellor of the University of Paris in 1395, at the same time being appointed a canon of the Cathedral of Notre Dame. A nominalist, he disliked the aridity of much Scholasticism, and argued for a return to the Bible and the fathers in place of theological subtleties. He was devoted to the mystical spirit of the Victorines, such as Hugh. As chancellor of the university he had considerable influence in the councils of the church. He participated actively in the Council of Pisa at which an effort was made to heal the schism between the antipopes of Rome and Avignon; in fact, he was selected to give the address to the new pope, Alexander V.

Pisa having failed to solve the problem adequately, another council was held, this time in 1415 at Constance. It was there that Gerson directed the process against John Hus. After many years of church business, pamphleteering, and the administration of the university, he retired to a monastery of the Celestines in Lyons, where he wrote hymns and mystical pieces.

We are indebted to Prof. Robert Ulich for the present translation of Gerson's work, On Leading Children to

Christ, *evidently the only rendition in English from either the Latin or French texts. This writing demonstrates how even a profound theologian and prominent ecclesiastic could make it a major interest and concern to care for the nurture of the young in Christ, even in the face of bitter criticism from those who thought he was wasting his time and talents in so doing. The writing thus becomes an object lesson in true Christian humility as well as a glimpse into the dynamics of a confessor's relation to young children in the medieval church.*

Gerson's works include The Consolation of Theology *as well as many other treatises on ecclesiastical and theological subjects.*

JEAN GERSON . . .

On Leading Children to Christ

In my defense. Also an admonition to allow me, the unworthy, to lead the children to Christ. ". . . If a man be overtaken in a fault, ye which are spiritual, restore such an one in the spirit of meekness; considering thyself, lest thou also be tempted." (Gal. 6:1.)

A certain man who was a good judge of human customs once said: "The skill of skills is the guiding of souls." Yet there is nothing that the men of our time, even the clergy, approach with less skill than just this. The blind lead the blind. Nobody will be surprised to see this bring forth all kinds of misery! Many persons consider it even below the dignity of a clergyman if, enjoying a good reputation or vested with high ecclesiastical honors, he devotes himself to this task, especially where children are concerned. This attitude has caused me also to become an object of

Gerson, Jean, On Leading Children to Christ, tr. by Robert Ulich, the Fourth Argument of Tractatus de Parvulis trahendis ad Christum, from Joannis Gersonii . . . Opera Omnia, Tomus Tertius, col. 285–291, Antwerp, 1706. Reprinted by permission of the publishers from Ulich, Robert, ed., Three Thousand Years of Educational Wisdom, pp. 181–190. Harvard University Press. Copyright, 1947, 1954, by The President and Fellows of Harvard College.

public controversy and disdain, as in the public's eye I
am of some importance in this question. Indeed, the Lord's
disciples, at the time they had yet little understanding of
things celestial, seem to have harbored the same absurd
notion, in so far as they prevented children's being brought
to the Lord. They thought it unworthy of Christ, their
great master and doctor, to concern himself with such an
insignificant matter. This very opinion shows their mistake, as does also the Lord's example and the above-quoted
word of the apostle, in which he admonishes the clergymen to be the teachers of others, and to be endowed with
the spirit of gentleness, and to look to themselves lest they
be tempted.

It is astonishing to think how rare such men are. Show
me one, and I will tell you that he is spiritually inclined
who judges everything according to spiritual principles,
who has learned to suffer from the sufferings he had to
undergo, who is not interested in himself but in Jesus
Christ, who is filled with love, humility, and piety to such
an extent that vanity and greed find no room within him,
who directs his thoughts toward heaven, who though he
were one of the angels of the Lord and conformed to their
example, could be moved neither by praise nor by remon-
strances, and who, for the sake of baser occupations
neither turns from the high aim nor allows himself to be
drawn into ruinous impurity. For the rest: ". . . What is
a man advantaged, if he gain the whole world, and lose
himself, or be cast away? " (Luke 9:25.) What would be
the benefit if he were not to listen to the command, " Take
pity in thy soul, in order to please God "? (Jesus ben Sirach
30:24.) He, finally, is spiritually inclined who is not attracted or tempted by any physical beauty, but who, entirely removed from all worldliness, dwells on the highest

summit of reason, absorbed in keen conception of the character of the soul.

As long as you lack this, as long as either suspicions bring you suddenly unrest, or threats frighten you, as long as fame makes you proud or slander makes you despair: you are secularly and not spiritually inclined, you are not fitted to teach others in the spirit of gentleness. Thus it happens that I should have been reprimanded for my audacity rather than for my overgreat humility, in so far as I invade the domain of spiritually inclined men with the intention of teaching children who are ensnared in sin, just as though a turtle were to join the company of birds. Yet what shall I do? Some benevolent people think quite differently. They threaten me or the children lest they associate with me, they try this in many different ways; above all they think to demonstrate the justness of their procedure by a fourfold indication. They point out the difference in customs between me and the children; they mention that the dignity of my office reserves me for higher tasks; then they pretend that neither place nor time are suitable; and finally, they fear that the unusualness of the procedure would be condemned by envious people.

We shall discuss in a few words these various charges.

They maintain, and this is correct, that there is a great difference between my customs and those of my pupils. If nevertheless I want to be useful to them, then it is necessary that I adapt my habits to theirs, and that I step down in order to lift them up to my level. "Love and majesty do not go together, nor have they common abode " (Ovid, *Metamorphoses* ii. 846-847). But where there is no love, what good is instruction, as one neither likes to listen to it nor properly believes in the words heard, nor follows the commandments! Therefore it is best to forego all false dignity and to become a child among children. Yet, all sins have to be avoided, and all signs of impure love have to be held at bay. Also, it must be added, that our nature is inclined to resist, as Seneca proves. Our nature prefers guidance to force. Especially gifted people have the further characteristic — as the dumb creatures, the wild animals, and the birds teach us — that they are won and influenced by flattery rather than by words of threat. Why, after all, should extremely shy children hide their sins from one whom they neither hate nor fear? One who, in addition, has convinced them that he is benevolent, loyal, and friendly? But he will not be able to convince them unless he smiles kindly at the laughing ones, encourages those who play, praises their progress in learning, and when remonstrating, avoids all that is bitter or insulting. Then the children will feel he does not hate, but loves them like a brother. . . .

But as regards the opinion held by some that it is my duty to devote my energy to greater things, I do not know if there be anything greater to which to devote my modesty more profitably than, with the help of God, to snatch souls from the very doors of hell and to implant such souls, as it were, once more in the children, or to water a not inconsiderable part of the garden of the church. It is the children of whom I am thinking, bearing in mind that Christ gives them growth. But I am assured that by preaching publicly I should reach this aim in a more splendid manner. It may be that this will cause a greater stir, but in my opinion it will not have more effect and will not bear better fruit. As to the first point, it is Christ who puts us to shame in our pride, if we do not open the lips of wisdom except in the presence of many listeners. He taught by speaking at length to the Samaritan woman,

and to her alone. But I will not deny that I should neglect
the duty imposed by the dignity of the pulpit, if, in order
to serve the profit of others, I should prove unworthy in
the fulfillment of this duty. But in the absence of such
a duty, as is usually the case, who will blame my wholesome activity, since nobody would dare to raise an accusation against me, if I were to enjoy play or rest under these
circumstances?

In a previous argument I have dealt in detail with the
third accusation; namely, that of the unsuitability of time
and place. There can be no place more suitable, and more
nearly above all suspicion, than the church, open to everybody. Thereby, one avoids the proverb, " For everyone
that doeth evil hateth the light " (John 3:20).

Christ's command, too, reads to the effect, " Let your
light so shine before men, that they may see your good
works " (Matt. 5:16), and that one puts his candle in a
candlestick. If others find this annoying by considering
such action ostentatious, vain boasting, passion for glory,
play acting, hypocrisy, or anything similar, let them take
care what they are saying. True, this is an offense which
is being taken, but not offered. It is an offense which Phari-
sees take but not the children. Therefore, it has to be
rejected, because neither the action proper, nor the circumstances under which the action is carried out, harbor anything that could cause spiritual damage. Besides, it must
not surprise us that the beam of light, issuing from a good
work, benefits healthy eyes, but is a nuisance and hateful
to watering, squinting, and inflamed eyes. " We are unto
good a sweet savor of Christ!" exclaims the apostle. And
what does he add? " To the one we are the savor of death
unto death; and to the other the savor of life unto life "
(II Cor. 2:15-16). Whosoever observes how great the

harvest of the Lord is and how few are the laborers — I am speaking of capable laborers, for there are plenty of the other kind, and they are here, as Horace says, " to consume the fruits of the earth " — he will see that at no day, at no hour, at no place, must such work be left undone.

As to the fourth charge, I will not deny that my activity has not been exercised by my predecessors in my office. I console myself with the words of the comedy: " As many people, so many opinions!" (Terence). If one were not free to start something new and excellent, the state would be in a bad way — nay, if the state did not permit that way, it would perish. And yet, this enterprise is neither outstanding nor exceptional, if with the permission or at the order of the bishop of the diocese (who is master of his harvest) one has been commanded to this harvest, which may be reaped now in one, now in another manner. Now, after having obtained this permission, I am protected by the word of Christ: " Pray ye therefore the Lord of the harvest, that he will send forth laborers into his harvest (Matt. 9:38). The same is found in the words of Isaiah (ch. 6:8) when to the question, " Whom shall I send and who will go for us?" he answers, " Here am I; send me."

There is nothing irregular or illegal in my action, because I have obtained permission from my superior, and because I do not undertake or suggest to listen to the confession of boys without informing their teachers of it. Finally, the chancellor of the church of Paris, be it by virtue of his official position, or at the command of the apostolic chair, has a not inconsiderable duty of supervision over the schools of Paris, or many of them, and their pupils. But what could be more suitable for such care than the pious decency of good manners?

However, to repeat what has already been said, friends raise the objection that my enemies will blame the novelty of the matter by pointing out either the curiosity, or the conceit, or the uselessness, or a too-great superficiality, of this or that. This now, dear friends, is nothing new to me. I have reflected a good deal about all this and turned it over in my mind. For what kind of activity would be that of a well-known man who has remained free from blame or from false or absurd criticism? Yet, I swear by the salvation for which all of us hope, and I testify to it before the terrible chair of judgment of the just Lord — since nobody knows what is in man, except the spirit of man, which is in him — that, according to the word of Christ, my work may be known by my fruits. And if perhaps they have found something false, shameless, ignoble, in my teaching or my actions, yet I do not yield, I would rather be considered a wolf in sheep's clothing. But if the fruits of good work are apparent from without, I ask you not to condemn the inside of the tree with malevolence, else one would fall into the sin of thoughtless condemnation of his neighbor and one harms the children thereby, not rarely preventing their being led to Christ. Everyone, whoever he be, has to carry his load; I shall go free. And those who observe me I would beg to consider how much confidence I have in this work, because I have a good conscience. And I have and I invoke the testimony of the children who by their very nature are not apt to conceal anything.

This about my critics. But now I turn to the children, confident in the word of wisdom that " who is simple, let him turn in hither " (Prov. 9:4) without fear and trembling. Let everyone, no matter who he be, at least listen to the good admonitions from my lips. If I claim this virtue for myself, I do so not for myself, but for the Lord. I shall

lead him to the good, if I can; especially if I can make him
examine, with a sorrowful soul, all the years of his life, and
make him sweep out his mind with the broom of his
own tongue. To do this, or anything else, I shall not force
anyone against his will. Furthermore, I shall not try to
ask for things that shall not be revealed; also, I shall
not persuade him to reveal the secrets of his companions —
on the contrary, I shall prevent it! Further, nobody shall
doubt that in every respect I shall preserve unbroken the
seal of confession. I know how much confession is protected. I hope that those who confess will remain silent
about themselves and me, and that they will not let themselves be persuaded by the silly and wrong curiosity of
others to do otherwise.

But perhaps there is one who is afraid of the severity of
the penalty. There is no cause for this fear because I do
not impose a penalty on the unwilling. I prefer the example of William of Paris, and will rather send men to
purgatory with a small penalty, voluntarily fulfilled, than
cast them into hell with an unfulfilled penalty imposed
against their will. Whosoever comes to me conscious of
his sins, no matter how grave they are, he may say
with David in deep contrition: "I have sinned." I will
add immediately, "The Lord hath put away thy sin"
(II Sam. 12:13).

Finally, I am convinced that penitence is perfected if
the sin is wholeheartedly detested and cast off in the act
of confession. Someone else may perhaps think that I hate
and despise those whose confessions I have heard. Nothing
is more erroneous! Rather, I will love him as a faithful
son in Christ, further as a man who, as I know, fears God
and has become good and pure, and further as a man who

has entrusted himself completely to my loyalty, so that he revealed to me the ugly wounds of his soul, which perhaps he would never have shown to his loving parents. And thus I feel in my heart — truth knows it — how I am inclined to be more friendly and loving toward those whom I see liberated from great and serious peril of sin than toward those who suffer from less serious wounds.

There has never, with my will, remained in my heart a trace of revenge or hatred during somebody's confession of sin, were it even the murder of his own parents. I know well that those who confess cannot at once overcome all reluctance and shame; but this is neither necessary nor useful. Reason, at last, will conquer shame, and thereafter this embarrassment will contribute not a little toward diminishing the penalty. Someone will perhaps complain to me, " My mind is cold and unbelieving; what, then, do I profit from confession? " And if this is true, then he should hurry all the more ardently to the warming talk with God. Come to his fire; you will be warmed more than enough.

Sometimes I see many who at the beginning are cold or even avoid or mock such a talk about their sins; but they go away warmed, comforted, and shedding tears. I frequently see such change. Once I felt such a worldly inclination when I wanted to persuade my own sisters to permanent celibacy. Yet, often I felt a deep conflict between my plans and ideas and the power of custom; the goal, which in my piety I had tried to reach, presented itself to me as something contradictory to tradition; I hesitated and changed my opinion and I almost tried to give up my sacred intention by turning my heel backward, till finally, with God's kindly help, my eyes turned from the earth to heaven, from this death to life, from the flesh to eternity, till taught by reason and enlightened by the light of faith, I remembered the proverb: " Vanity of vanities; all is vanity " (Eccl. 1:2). Then I breathed, and was comforted and strengthened. All the more I want to admonish everyone to recognize clearly what is right and pious and to obey pure truth instead of the talks of the crowd and the error of tradition. Let them not aim at what their hearts feel at the moment, but at what they ought to feel.

For the rest, I have the habit, and will not deny it, of advising those who confess to me to observe four things. With regard to their transgressions, I hate it above all if they are given to lies, to perjury, to slander, and further, if their hands are made to apply force and robbery, also lustful and unnatural touch, which is punished by worldly laws. First, they should guard as far as possible against giving others occasions to perdition or to sin; for such actions are of the devil. There is a good command, " Si non caste, tamen caute " (if not chaste, yet discreet), that means secret and alone, without offense or harm to anyone else. The second is that they endeavor to lead to betterment those whom they formerly tempted, or their companions in sin, or, in their stead, others, as far as they can do so unobtrusively, so that they themselves, who formerly did the devil's work, now do the work of the angels. The third is that if they have sinned again — as weak human beings do — they should always, considering time and place, use confession as a remedy; confession is of no use — as I prove again and again — if it has not been a complete one, and if the confessor has not enumerated and explained all the sins he remembers, stressing accompanying details, and, above all, those that change the kind of sin. The fourth point is — although I do not impose this as an obligation, but rather as an admonition — that they take up as their duty a regular but not too strenuous exercise for all the rest of their lives, not only in order to remind them of their sins, but also as a satisfaction for the properly confessed sins, and also as a safeguard against future sins. Hereby, I make it a habit to make them pray daily two " Lord's Prayers " and two " Ave Marias," the one in the morning, the other in the evening, and that, if possible, on their knees.

But I seldom make a change in the arrangement of these exercises, according to the seriousness and the difference of the trespasses, as this is seldom carried out, and as such a change can also be made with other secret exercises of penalty. If, by doing so, I treat those free from sin and those laden with sin in an equal manner, I wish that the innocents would not complain about this. Their obligations are not smaller, since God has taken them under his protection and has prevented them from becoming equal to the sinners.

In order to help children to remember more easily this fourfold observation, I have indulged in the art of poetry:

> Neither by deed nor by word shalt thou ever tempt the others:
> You are guilty enough, if corrupted yourself.
> Have you others corrupted by wicked doings and words,
> Secretly strive to guide them back to the path of right.
> Let not shame prevent your confessing all of your sins,
> Naming distinctly them all; confession, nothing else avails.

If of confession you think, 'gainst relapse it will
    easily guard you;
Therefore a marker think up, which of confession
    reminds.

And finally: " How long, ye simple one, will ye love
simplicity? " (Prov. 1:22.) " How long will you love vanity,
and seek after leasing? " (Ps. 4:2.) Come confidingly!
There is no snare laid on the path; no snake lurks in the
grass. We shall profit from a mutual exchange of spiritual
goods, because I have no desire for your worldly goods.
I offer you instruction, you pay me with prayers; rather,
we will pray mutually for each other's salvation. Thus we
all shall bring joy to our guardian angels, on whose day I
am writing this. In this manner perhaps — but I do not
want to say perhaps, but in certain hope — we will find
mercy by our Heavenly Father, if on the way to him we
obey his voice: I, by admonitions; you, by following them.
There will not be lack of embracing, thanks, and devotion,
giving us comfort in our present misery, and this will be
followed by everlasting unison in complete glory. To this
unity Jesus invites all of us who shall be children in the
spirit; he wants us to answer his call in everlasting enthusiasm: " Suffer the little children to come unto me!"
(Mark 10:14).

PART III

The Reformation and After

13

MARTIN LUTHER
(1483–1546)

_____

The prime mover in the Reformation of the church in Germany was born at Eisleben. After early schooling at Magdeburg and Eisenach, he began the study of jurisprudence at Erfurt, where he himself lectured after 1505 on Aristotle's physics and ethics. He entered an Augustinian monastery at Erfurt, and was ordained priest in 1507. Already marked as a scholarly young man, he was appointed to lecture in philosophy at Wittenberg in 1508, and took his doctorate there in 1512. Incensed over the sale of indulgences, he posted ninety-five theses on October 31, 1517. These were promptly condemned as heretical, but he refused to obey a summons to Rome.

In 1520, Luther published three treatises that were to become influential in the Reformation movement: Address to the Nobles of the German Nation, On the Babylonian Captivity of the Church of God, *and* Christian Liberty. *Thus he began emphasizing the cardinal tenets of the Reformation, such as the Bible as the only rule of faith and practice, the priesthood of believers, and justification by faith alone. His activity led to his excommunication by Pope Leo X, his summons to the imperial Diet of Worms in 1521, his confinement in Wartburg Castle, his marriage to Katharine von Bora, and his unceasing labors on behalf of the new church order in Germany.*

Luther saw that it would be necessary to provide schooling for the children if the full realization of the doctrine of the priesthood of believers was to be achieved. His letter To the Councilmen of All Cities in Germany that They Establish and Maintain Christian Schools *was an appeal and a summons to his countrymen to rise to the challenge of the changed situation, and to do this in terms of quality of instruction and excellence of method. Here we see Luther, the man of the Renaissance, putting his personal learning in the service of the Christian citizenry of his country. Under Melanchthon a virile school system was soon to be established which, along with Luther's translation of the Bible into the vernacular, was to provide a solid groundwork for Reformation education. Here also lay some of the roots of universal education, which much later was to be achieved for the first time in America, discovered only during Luther's boyhood.*

Luther's many writings are currently being published in fresh English translations by Concordia Publishing House under the editorship of Jaroslav Pelikan. Not only did he write sermons, catechisms, hymns, tractates, and innumerable letters, but he also had to address himself to such practical matters as preparing a new liturgy for the separated church in Germany, arranging for the education of the people in the new interpretations of doctrine, and making sure that an adequate theological education should be provided for the clergy who would preach the Word of God. Here I Stand: A Life of Martin Luther, *by Roland H. Bainton (Abingdon Press, 1950), is a fascinating biography. Other writings good to consult are F. V. N. Painter,* Luther on Education *(Lutheran Publication Society, 1890), and James Mackinnon,* Luther and the Reformation, *4 vols. (Longmans, Green & Co., Inc., 1925–1930).*

MARTIN LUTHER . . .

To the Councilmen of All Cities in Germany that They Establish and Maintain Christian Schools

To the Burgomasters and Councilmen of all cities in
Germany.   Martin Luther.

Grace and peace from God our Father and the Lord
Jesus Christ.

Prudent, wise, and dear sirs: Having been put under the
ban some three years ago and declared an outlaw, I should
have remained silent had I feared the command of men
more than God. There are indeed many persons in Germany, both great and small, who on that account, still attack my speaking and writing and shed much blood over
it. But God has opened my mouth and bidden me speak,
and is mightily supporting me and, without my help,
strengthening and spreading my cause the more they rage,
and seems to be laughing and mocking at their rage, as it

Luther, Martin, *To the Councilmen of All Cities in Germany that They
Establish and Maintain Christian Schools* (1524), tr. A. T. W. Stein-
haeuser, in *Works of Martin Luther*, Vol. IV., pp. 103–130, *passim*.
A. J. Holman Company and The Castle Press, 1931. Used by permission of The Muhlenberg Press, present publishers of this work.

is said in the second psalm. . . . And I wish to assure you and declare to you, frankly and confidently, that if you heed me in this matter, you heed not me but Christ, and that if you heed me not, you despise not me but Christ. For I know and am well aware of what I am saying and teaching and for what purpose I say it, and everyone who is willing rightly to consider my teaching will discover it for himself.

First of all, then, we are experiencing today throughout Germany how schools are everywhere allowed to go to wrack and ruin; universities are growing weak, monasteries are declining. . . . For since it is becoming known, through God's Word, how unchristian and devoted only to men's bellies those institutions are; and especially since the carnal multitude see that they are no longer obliged or able to drive their sons and daughters into monasteries and cathedral schools, and to turn them out of their own houses and possessions and plant them in other people's possessions, no one is any longer willing to have children educated. " Tell us," they say, " why should we send them to school, if they are not to become priests, monks, and nuns? They had better learn such things as will help them to make a living!"

From this confession of theirs it is very evident what such people are thinking and on what their minds are set. For if they had not sought only the belly and a temporal living for their children when they sent them into the monasteries and cathedral schools or into their spiritual estates, but had been earnestly concerned for their salvation and blessedness, they would not thus fold their hands, relapse into indifference, and say: " If the spiritual estate is no longer to count for anything, then we will let education be and not bother our heads about it." They would rather say: "If it is true, as the gospel teaches, that this estate is dangerous to our children, why then, dear sirs, show us another way to educate them that will be pleasing to God and profitable to them; we certainly want to provide not only for the bellies of our dear children, but also for their souls." That, at least, is what true Christian and faithful parents would say.

But it is not surprising that the evil one takes this attitude and inspires carnal and worldly hearts to neglect the children and youths. Who can blame him for it? He is a prince and god of this world. How can he possibly be pleased to see his nests, the monasteries and the spiritual gangs, destroyed by the gospel, in which nests he corrupts above all the young folk, who mean so much, yea, everything to him? How can he be expected to permit or promote the proper training of the young? He would indeed be a fool to suffer and help men to establish in his kingdom the very thing by which that kingdom must be most speedily overthrown, as would surely happen if he lost that choice morsel, the dear youth, and had to permit them to be saved for the service of God at his expense and by means of his possessions. . . .

Therefore, I pray you all, my dear sirs and friends, for God's sake and the poor youths', not to treat this subject as lightly as some do, who are not aware of what the prince of this world intends. For it is a serious and important matter that we help and assist our youth, and one in which Christ and all the world are mightily concerned. By helping them we shall be helping ourselves and all men. And reflect that these secret, subtle, and crafty attacks of the devil must needs be met with deep Christian seriousness. If it is necessary, dear sirs, to expend annually such great sums for firearms, roads, bridges, dams, and countless similar items in order that a city may enjoy temporal peace and prosperity, why should not at least as much be devoted to the poor, needy youth so that we might engage one or two competent men to teach school?

Moreover, every citizen should be moved by the following consideration. Formerly he was obliged to give up so much money and property for indulgences, masses, vigils, endowments, testaments, anniversaries, mendicants, brotherhoods, pilgrimages, and other like humbug; but now that he is rid by the grace of God of all that robbing and giving, he ought, out of gratitude to God and for his glory, to give a part of that amount for schools in which to train the poor children, which would indeed be a good and precious investment. . . .

Our second consideration is found in the words of St. Paul in II Corinthians, ch. 6, that we receive not the grace of God in vain nor neglect the day of salvation. For Almighty God has indeed graciously visited us Germans and proclaimed a true year of jubilee. We have at present the most excellent and learned young men, adorned with the languages and all arts, who could be of much service if we made use of them as instructors of the young. Is it not evident that we are now able to prepare a boy in three years, so that at the age of fifteen or eighteen he will know more than all universities and monasteries hitherto? Indeed, what did men learn in those institutions but how to become asses, blockheads, and dunces! For twenty and forty years one sat over one's books without acquiring either Latin or German. I say nothing of the shameful and vicious life, by which the excellent youths were miserably corrupted.

It is true that, rather than have the universities and monasteries continue as before, with no other place for youth to study and live, I should wish no boy ever to study nor to be able to speak; for it is my earnest intention, prayer, and desire that these ass-stables and devil's-schools should either sink into the abyss or be converted into Christian schools. But now that God has so richly blessed us and has given us so many men able to instruct and train our young people aright, surely we ought not to despise the grace of God or suffer him to knock in vain. He is standing at our door; happy are we if we open to him! He is calling to us; blessed is he that answers him. If we let him pass by, who will bring him back? . . .

Our third consideration is by far the most important of all; it is the command of God. Its importance is seen in that he so frequently through Moses urges and enjoins parents to instruct their children that it is said in Psalm 78, " How straitly he commanded our fathers that they should give knowledge unto their children and instruct their children's children." It is seen also in the Fourth Commandment, in which he so urgently enjoins children to obey their parents that he would even have disobedient children sentenced to death. Indeed, for what other purpose do we older folk exist than to care for, instruct, and bring up the young? The foolish youths cannot possibly instruct or protect themselves; God has therefore entrusted them to us who are old and know by experience what is good for them, and he will compel us to render a strict account. . . .

But it is a sin and a disgrace that we must needs urge and be urged to train our children and youths and seek their best interests, when nature itself should drive us to do this and the examples even of the heathen afford us manifold instruction. There is not an irrational animal but looks after its young and teaches them what they need to know, except the ostrich, of which God says that she is hardened against her young ones, as though they were not hers, and leaves her eggs in the earth. And what would it profit us if we possessed and performed all else and became utter saints, and yet neglected the chief purpose of our life, namely, the care of the young? I believe also that among outward sins none so heavily burdens the world in the sight of God nor deserves such severe punishment as the sin we commit against our children by not giving them an education. . . .

"Ah," you say, "but all that is addressed to parents; what business is it of councilmen and magistrates?" Very true: but if the parents neglect it, who is to see to it? Shall it on that account remain undone and the children be neglected? In that case, how will magistrates and councilmen excuse themselves by saying it is no business of theirs? . . .

It therefore becomes the business of councilmen and magistrates to devote the greatest care and attention to the young. For since the property, honor, and life of the whole city are committed to their faithful keeping, they would fail in their duty toward God and man if they did not seek its welfare and improvement with all their powers day and night. Now the welfare of a city consists not alone in gathering great treasures and providing solid walls, beautiful buildings, and a goodly supply of guns and armor. Nay, where these abound and reckless fools get control of them, the city suffers only the greater loss. But a city's best and highest welfare, safety, and strength consist in its having many able, learned, wise, honorable, and well-bred citizens; such men can readily gather treasures and all goods, protect them and put them to a good use. . . .

The civil government must certainly continue. Shall we then permit none but clods and boors to rule, when we

can get better men? That would indeed be a barbarous
and foolish policy. We might as well make rulers of swine
and wolves, and set them over those who will not consider how they may be ruled by men. Moreover, it is in-
human perversity to think no further than this, "We will
rule now; what concern is it of ours how they will fare
who come after us?" Not over human beings, but over
swine and dogs should such persons rule, who seek only
their own profit or honor in governing. Even if we took
the utmost pains to train up none but able, learned, and
skilled rulers, there would still be room enough for toil and
labor in order that the government might prosper. How
shall it prosper if no one takes any pains at all?

"But," you say again, "granted that we must have
schools, what is the use of teaching Latin, Greek, Hebrew,
and the other liberal arts? We can still teach the Bible and
God's Word in German, which is sufficient for our salvation." I reply: Alas! I know well that we Germans must
always remain brutes and stupid beasts, as neighboring
nations call us and as we richly deserve to be called. But
I wonder why we never ask: What is the use of silks, wine,
spices, and strange foreign wares, when we have in Germany not only wine, grain, wool, flax, wood, and stone
enough for our needs, but also the very best and choicest
of them for our honor and ornament? Arts and languages,
which are not only not harmful, but a greater ornament,
profit, honor, and benefit, both for the understanding of
Scripture and for the conduct of government, these we despise; but we cannot do without foreign wares, which we
do not need, which bring us in no profit, and which reduce
us to our last penny. Are we not justly dubbed German
fools and beasts? . . .

Therefore, my beloved Germans, let us open our eyes,

thank God for this precious treasure, and guard it well, lest it be again taken from us and the devil have his will. For though the gospel has come and daily comes through the Holy Spirit alone, we cannot deny that it has come by means of the languages, by which it was also spread abroad, and by which it must be preserved. For when God desired through the apostles to spread abroad the gospel in all the world, he provided tongues for that purpose. And before that he had spread the Greek and Latin languages, by means of the Roman Empire, throughout all lands, in order that his gospel might the more speedily bear fruit far and wide. He has done the same now. No one knew for what purpose God suffered the languages to be revived, until we now begin to see that it was for the sake of the gospel, which he intended afterward to reveal, in order to expose and destroy thereby the kingdom of antichrist. To this end he also gave over Greece to the Turk, in order that the Greeks, driven out and scattered, might spread their language and give an incentive to the study of other languages as well. . . .

Hence the apostles themselves considered it necessary to put the New Testament into Greek and so to bind it fast to that language, doubtless in order to preserve it for us safe and sound as in a sacred ark. For they foresaw all that was to come and now has come to pass, and knew that if it were contained only in men's heads, wild and fearful disorder and confusion, and many various interpretations, fancies, and doctrines would arise in the church, which could be prevented and from which the plain man could be protected only by committing the New Testament to writing and language. Hence it is certain that unless the languages remain, the gospel must finally perish. . . .

Well, this may suffice concerning the necessity and value of languages and Christian schools for the spiritual realm and the salvation of souls. Let us also now consider the body. Let us suppose that there were no soul and no heaven or hell and we had to consider only the temporal government after the manner of the world, and let us see whether it does not need good schools and educated persons more sorely even than the spiritual realm. Hitherto the sophists have shown no concern whatever for the temporal government, and have confined their schools so exclusively to the spiritual estate that it was well nigh a disgrace for an educated man to marry; he had to hear such remarks as, " Behold, he is turning secular and does not care to become a spiritual! " just as if their spiritual estate were alone pleasing to God and the secular estate, as they call it, were altogether of the devil and unchristian. But in the sight of God they themselves become meanwhile the devil's own, and (as happened to Israel in the Babylonian captivity) this poor populace has alone remained in the land and in the right estate, while the better people and the leaders were carried off to the devil with tonsure and cowl to Babylon. . . .

If then there were no soul, as I have said, and if there were no need at all of schools and languages for the sake of the Scriptures and of God, this one consideration should suffice to establish everywhere the very best schools for both boys and girls, namely, that in order outwardly to maintain its temporal estate, the world must have good and skilled men and women, so that the former may rule well over land and people, and the latter may keep house and train children and servants aright. Now such men must come from our boys and such women from our girls. Therefore the thing to do is to teach and train our boys and girls in the proper manner. But I said above that the common man does nothing to bring this about; he cannot, he will not, he does not know how. Princes and lords ought to do it, but they must needs rise in sledges, and drink, and take part in masquerades; they are burdened with high and important business in cellar, kitchen, and bedroom. And though some of them would gladly do it, they must stand in fear of the others, lest they be taken for fools or heretics. It rests, therefore, dear councilmen, altogether with you; you have also more opportunity for doing it than princes and lords. . . .

Now you say: " But who can spare his children for so long a time, and train them all to be young gentlemen? There is work for them to do at home, etc." I reply: It is not in the least of my intention to have such schools established as we had heretofore, in which a boy sat over his Donatus and Alexander for twenty or thirty years and yet learned nothing. We are living in a new world today and things are being done differently. My idea is to let boys go to such a school for one or two hours a day, and spend the remainder of the time working at home, learning a trade or doing whatever their parents desired; so that both study and work might go hand in hand while they were young and able to do both. They spend at least ten times as much time with their peashooters or playing ball or racing and tussling. In like manner, a girl can surely find time enough to go to school one hour a day and still attend to all her duties at home; she sleeps, dances, and plays away more time than that. There is only one thing lacking, and that is the earnest desire to train the young people and to benefit and serve the world with well-bred men and women. The devil very much prefers coarse blockheads and ne'er-do-wells, lest men live too comfortably on earth.

But the exceptional pupils, who give promise of becoming skilled teachers, preachers, and holders of other spiritual positions, should be kept longer at school or altogether dedicated to a life of study, as we read of the holy martyrs who had the training of Sts. Agnes, Agatha, Lucy, and others. That was how the monasteries and cathedral schools originated, which have now, however, been perverted to a very different and damnable use. And there is a great need of such advanced study, for the shaven crowd is fast dwindling; besides, most of them are unfit to teach and rule, for all they know is how to care for the belly, which is indeed all they have been taught. We must certainly have men to administer God's Word and sacraments and to do pastoral work among the people. But where shall we get them if we let our schools decline and do not replace them with others that are Christian? For the schools that have been maintained hitherto, even if they were not to pass away, can produce nothing but lost and pernicious deceivers. . . .

Finally, one thing more should be well considered by all who earnestly desire to have such schools and languages established and maintained in Germany. It is this: no effort or expense should be spared to found good libraries, especially in the larger cities, which can well afford it. For if the Bible and all the arts are to be preserved, they must be contained and held fast in books and writings, as was done by the prophets and the apostles themselves, as I have said above. This is necessary, not only that those who are to be our spiritual and temporal leaders may have books to read and study, but that the good books, the arts and the languages that we now have through the grace of God may be preserved and not lost. . . .

But my advice is not to huddle together indiscriminately all sorts of books and to look only to their number and quantity. I would gather only the best; there is no need of collecting the commentaries of all jurists, the sentences of all theologians, the questions of all philosophers, and the sermons of all monks. Indeed, I would throw out all such dung and furnish my library with the right sort of books, consulting with scholars as to my choice. First of all, there should be in it the Holy Scriptures in Latin, Greek, Hebrew, German, and in whatever other languages they might be had. Then the best commentaries, and if I could find them, the most ancient, in Greek, Hebrew, and Latin. Then books that aid us in acquiring the languages, such as the poets and orators, no matter whether heathen or Christian, Greek or Latin; for it is from such books one must learn grammar. Then should come books of the liberal arts and all the other arts. Lastly, books of law and of medicine, though here too a careful choice among commentaries should be made.

Among the chief books, however, should be chronicles and histories, in whatever language they may be had; for they are of wondrous value for understanding and controlling the course of this world and especially for noting the wonderful works of God. . . .

Therefore I beseech you, my dear sirs, to let this my sincerity and zeal bear fruit among you. Should there be any who count me too insignificant to profit by my advice, or who despise me as one condemned by the tyrants, I pray them to consider that I am not seeking my own advantage, but only the welfare and salvation of all Germany. Even if I were a fool and had hit upon a good idea, certainly no wise man should think it a disgrace to follow me. And if I were a very Turk and a heathen, and my plan were nevertheless seen to benefit not myself but the Christians, they ought not in fairness to spurn my offer. It has happened before that a fool gave better counsel than a whole council of wise men. Moses was obliged to receive instruction from Jethro.

Herewith I commend you all to the grace of God. May he soften and kindle your hearts, that they may be deeply concerned for the poor, miserable and neglected youths and with the help of God assist and help them, to the end that there may be a blessed and Christian government in German lands as to body and soul, with all plenty and abundance, to the praise and glory of God the Father, through Jesus Christ our Savior. Amen.

14

ULRICH ZWINGLI
(1484–1531)

A primary Reformation leader in Switzerland was Ulrich Zwingli, born at Wildhaus, St. Gallen, and educated at Bonn, Vienna, and Basel. In 1506 he became pastor in Glarus, preaching later also at Einsiedeln and Zurich. Actually Zwingli inaugurated the Reformation in Zurich, where it was legalized in 1523. In 1529 he met the German Reformers, notably Luther and Melanchthon, in a colloquy at Marburg, when they reached agreement on many details of the changes that were taking place in church belief and life, but differed in the interpretation of the Lord's Supper. He died in the battle of Kappel while serving as a chaplain.

In the writing reproduced below we see how virtuous living was construed by Zwingli as consisting in what seems to us as a sometimes quaint combination of ascetic behavior with humane learning. The " cue " is to be " the fullest possible absorbing of Christ himself." That is its perennially significant theme.

Zwingli's other writings include Of True and False Religion, A Brief and Clear Exposition of Christian Faith, *and* Treatise on Providence. *For a life and study of Zwingli, see Oskar Farner,* Zwingli the Reformer, *tr. by*

D. G. Sear (Philosophical Library, 1952) and the General Introduction to Zwingli and Bullinger, *Vol. XXIV, pp. 13–40, ed. by G. W. Bromiley, The Library of Christian Classics (The Westminster Press, Philadelphia; S.C.M. Press, London, 1953).*

ULRICH ZWINGLI . . .

Of the Upbringing and Education of Youth in Good Manners and Christian Discipline

PART I

First and chiefly, it is beyond our human capacity to bring the hearts of men to faith in the one God even though we had an eloquence surpassing that of Pericles. For that is something which only our Heavenly Father can do as he draws us to himself. Yet it is still the case, in the words of St. Paul, that "faith cometh by hearing, and hearing by the Word of God," though this does not mean that very much can be accomplished by the preaching of the external word apart from the internal address and compulsion of the Spirit. Therefore it is necessary not merely to instill faith into the young by the pure words, which proceed from the mouth of God, but to pray that

Zwingli, Ulrich, *On the Upbringing and Education of Youth in Good Manners and Christian Discipline, An Admonition by Ulrich Zwingli*, in *Zwingli and Bullinger*, ed. by G. W. Bromiley, Vol. XXIV, pp. 104–105, 108, 113–118. The Library of Christian Classics. The Westminster Press, Philadelphia; S.C.M. Press, London, 1953. (Part II is not used here.) Used by permission.

he who alone can give faith will illuminate by his Spirit
those whom we instruct in his Word.

It seems to me to be quite in keeping with Christ's own
teaching to bring young people to a knowledge of God in
and through external phenomena. For as we bring before
them the fair structure of the universe, pointing them to
each part in particular, we learn that all these things are
changing and destructible, but that he who cojoined them
(and many other things besides) in so lasting and marvelous a whole is necessarily unchanging and immutable.
Again, we learn that he who has so skillfully ordered all
these things need never be suspected of forgetting or dis-
regarding his handiwork, for even with men it is counted
a reproach if the head of the household does not keep a
careful watch over all domestic matters.

Thus the young man is taught that all things are ordained by the providence of God: for of the two sparrows
sold for a farthing not one can fall to the ground except
by decision of the divine providence (which has also numbered the very hairs of our head), nothing being too insignificant for its care.

Hence it is clear that the divine providence appoints
the things necessary for the body as well as the soul. We
see that by it the ravens are liberally fed and the lilies
gloriously arrayed. By such forms of the divine providence
the spirit of man is taught that it ought never to give way
either to anxiety or to ignoble greed. And if the temptation
to greed or anxiety is hewn down and uprooted as soon
as it begins to spring up, we shall keep our soul from a
harmful poison.

For we shall then know in our heart that God is not
only the Lord but also the Father of all those who trust
in him. We shall know that men ought to run to him for

help no less than they do to an earthly father. We shall know that in his words he has promised us that help, indeed he wills that we should make our prayer to him. If, then, we are afflicted by sickness of mind or body, we are taught to look only to him for healing. If we are oppressed by enemies or harassed by envy and hatred, we learn to flee only to him. If we desire wisdom or learning, we are taught to ask it of him alone. Indeed, it is from him that we are to seek even our wife and children, and if riches and honor are showered liberally upon us, we ought to pray to him that our heart may be kept from corruption or from turning aside from him.

I need not say more. Instructed in this way, the soul knows that it ought to ask all things from God. And it knows how shameful it is to ask anything which God cannot fittingly give. In fact, it will be ashamed either to ask or to have anything that it cannot fittingly receive from God. It will keep before it and lay up for itself only the things which are a true source of blessing. . . .

Therefore those who have rightly understood the mystery of the gospel will exert themselves to live rightly. As far as possible, then, we should learn the gospel with all exactness and diligence. And as occasion offers we should study what services will be most pleasing to God: and undoubtedly these are the very ones which he himself renders to us, righteousness, fidelity, and mercy. For God is a spirit, and he can be truly worshiped only with the sacrifice of a consecrated spirit. The young man should see to it, then, that he studies to grow up a man of God, righteous in life and as nearly like God as possible. For God does good to all and is profitable to all. He does hurt only to those who first do hurt to him. So, too, the man who is most like God is the one who studies to be profitable to all, to

be all things to all men, and to keep himself from all forms
of evil. When we consider our own powers, these things
are very difficult, but " to him that believeth all things are
possible." . . .

<h2 style="text-align:center">PART III</h2>

The noble spirit must first consider the fact that Christ
gave himself up to death on our behalf and became ours:
therefore we ought to give up ourselves for the good of all
men, not thinking that we are our own, but that we belong
to others. For we are not born to live to ourselves, but to
become all things to all men.

From early boyhood, then, the young man ought to
exercise himself only in righteousness, fidelity, and constancy: for with virtues such as these he may serve the
Christian community, the common good, the state, and
individuals. Only the weak are concerned to find a quiet
life: the most like to God are those who study to be of
profit to all even to their own hurt.

In this connection, however, we must be careful to see
that the things undertaken for God's honor or the state or
the common good are not corrupted by the devil or by
self-pleasing, so that in the long run we turn to our own
interest that which we want to be regarded as undertaken
in the interests of others. For many begin well at the
first, but they are quickly perverted and turned aside from
all that is good by that vainglory which is the bane of all
good counsels.

As regards the good or evil fortunes of others, a Christian spirit will conduct itself as if they were his own. When
fortune comes to another he will think of it as coming
to himself, and similarly with adversity. For he will look
upon the whole fellowship only as one household or fam-

ily, indeed as one body, in which all the members rejoice and suffer together and help one another, so that what-. ever happens to one happens to all.

So then he will " rejoice with them that do rejoice and weep with them that weep," looking upon the fortunes of others as his own; for as Seneca says, What happens to one can happen to everyone.

Yet the Christian ought not to show joy or grief after the common manner, being carried away by good fortune and plunged into despair by evil. On the contrary, seeing we must always be affected either by the one emotion or the other, we ought so to moderate them (if we are wise) that we never trespass the bounds of due decorum. And that is how we are to rejoice at the prosperity of others as at our own, and that is how we are also to weep, bearing all things with moderation and self-control.

I do not believe that a young man should be debarred from seemly pleasures, for instance at those times when the sexes are accustomed to come together publicly, the marriage of relatives, annual games, carnivals, and festivals: for I note that Christ himself did not despise the wedding feast. Seeing such things are necessary, I am better pleased if they are done publicly and not in corners or secretly, for the multitude of witnesses is more frightening to some than their own conscience, and if there are any who are shameless enough to conduct themselves indecorously in public, no good can be expected of them.

When communal gatherings of this kind do take place, the young man ought always to study to profit by them, so that he will not return home any the worse (which was the complaint of Socrates). To that end he should mark those who are behaving honorably and decorously, that

he may be able to follow them, and also those who are behaving scandalously and dishonorably, that he may avoid
them.

But these things are not suitable for adults. For that
reason it is my advice that the young ought to be allowed
to attend such gatherings as infrequently as possible. In-
evitably there is an almost frantic enthusiasm for associating with others in this way, but recovery from this enthusiasm should be swift. To help toward recovery, reasons can
be offered which will satisfy those who realize that we are
intent always upon better things.

When a neighbor is in trouble, we ought not to allow
anything to hinder us from going. We should be the first
there and the last away, and we must exert ourselves to
weigh the hurt, treating it and removing it and proffering
counsel.

Next to immortal God our parents ought to be held in
highest esteem, as is customary even amongst pagans and
unbelievers. To our parents we ought always to yield. And
though at times they may not act accordingly to the mind
of Christ (which is our mind), we must not oppose them
violently, but tell them as gently as possible what they
ought to say and do. And if they will not listen, it is better to leave them than to insult or reproach them.

Anger (as the natural scientists tell us) is a product of
heat; and as youth is the time of heat, the young man
ought to keep a careful watch against anger, that his words
and actions may not be impelled by it. Since anger con-
tinues with us, we ought to mistrust anything that might
give rise to it.

If an insult is offered which we cannot swallow because
it is too bitter, it is better to bring the matter before a

magistrate or to take it to court. For if we give back word for word or reproach those who reproach us, we only make ourselves like those whom we reproach.

At the proper time there is no reason why you should not play games with your equals, but they ought to be useful either educationally or as bodily exercise. Games with educational value are those which involve numbers (from which we learn arithmetic), or strategy, as for example chess, which teaches how to advance and retreat, and how to keep careful watch behind and before; for the main lesson we learn from this game is not to assume anything rashly. But even in this, moderation is to be observed, for there are some who push aside the serious affairs of life and give themselves to this one thing alone. For my part, I would allow such recreations only occasionally and as a pastime. Dicing and card games I condemn absolutely.

The games which exercise the body are running, jumping, throwing, fighting and wrestling, but the latter only in moderation, for it often takes on a serious character. Such sports are common to almost all peoples, but especially amongst the Swiss, who find them useful in many different circumstances. I do not find the same value in swimming, though at the proper time it is pleasurable to stretch one's limbs in water and imitate the fish. And on occasion swimming has also proved useful, as with the man who swam from the capitol and told Camillus of the pitiable state to which the city had been reduced by covetousness. Chloelia too escaped to her own people by swimming.

Our conversation and speech should all be of a kind to profit those with whom we live. If we have to reprove or

punish, we ought to do it wisely and wittily, and so good
humoredly and considerately that we not only drive away
the offence but win over the offender, binding him more
closely to us.

We ought to follow after truth with such consistency
and singleheartedness that we weigh not only our own
speech but that of others, lest it contain any deceit or
falsehood. A man of noble spirit is never more perturbed
than when he involuntarily lets slip an untruth — not to
mention his shame and horror when he lets out a flood
of idle and empty gossip invented by himself or repeated
from others. The Christian is commanded to speak truth
with his neighbor. Christ himself is the truth. Therefore
the Christian must cleave steadfastly to the truth. " A
double-minded man is unstable in all his ways." A man who
is inconsistent in his speech cannot be trusted. The heart
declares itself in speech. If the speech be empty and un-
truthful and inconsistent, it is a sure sign that things are
far worse inwardly. At the same time, lies cannot be con-
cealed indefinitely, although they may be for a long time.
For that reason it is foolish to cherish or mitigate a secret
evil by hoping that it will remain secret.

But we must study to be truthful not only in our words
but in all our actions. We must never do anything which
is manifestly false. The face and hands and all the external
features must not pretend to be other than the heart,
which is the source of all our actions. If someone enters
in a way quite different from that which his nature demands, his affected walk is quite enough to show us what
manner of man he is, frivolous, and of a dissolute spirit.

But what need I say more? The young man ought to fix
his whole attention upon the fullest possible absorbing of

Christ himself. Where that is done, he will be a rule to himself. And acting rightly, he will never be lifted up or cast down. He will increase daily, but he will see to it that he himself decreases. He will progress, but he will always reckon himself the least of all. He will do good to others, but he will never hold it against them, for that was the way of Christ. And to be perfect, we must set ourselves to follow Christ alone.

These then, my dear Gerold, are what appear to me to be the essentials in the instruction of a young nobleman. I need not draw attention to the disjointedness of their presentation, for that is easily perceived. It is for you to ponder them in your mind and then to express in your conduct that which I have roughly sketched out on paper. In so doing, you will give order to that which is scattered and disorderly, and you will be a living example of the rules which I have written out for you. Indeed, if you apply yourself to them, may it not be that you will attain a greater completeness and perfection than I have been able to show in words. But you will have to stretch every nerve, which will have the useful result of banishing indolence, the mother of all mischief, to which so many are of evil custom shamefully addicted, as though their only ambition were to live upon others and to fulfill all manner of wickedness. But turn your own youth to good account, as the poet said, for the time passes quickly and the latter days are seldom better than the former.

The true Christian is not the one who merely speaks about the laws of God, but the one who with God's help attempts great things. And for that reason, noble youth, see to it that you adorn more illustriously and with true adornment the fair gifts of race, physique, and patrimony with which you have been endowed. I say less than I ought? Rank, beauty, and wealth are not genuine riches, for they are subject to chance. The only true adornments are virtue and honor. May God so lead you through the things of this world that you may never be separated from him. Amen.

15

JOHN CALVIN
(1509–1564)

Another of the principal Reformers was John Calvin, whose French name is Jean Cauvin. He was born at Noyon, Picardy. After studying at Paris, Orleans, and Bourges, he became a Protestant in 1528. In 1536, when he was less than thirty years old, he published his monumental Institutes of the Christian Religion. In that same year he went to Geneva, where he was persuaded to become the spiritual leader of the city. In addition to his heavy responsibilities as a pastor he forged interpretations that were destined to become characteristic of the Reformed-Presbyterian tradition throughout the world as well as in Geneva. His grave was unmarked, at his request, in order that people might not revere his memory but only give glory to God. That was characteristically in keeping with Calvin's emphasis on the sovereignty of God and the servanthood of the creature.

In 1599 he had founded the academy at Geneva. That was one evidence of his interest in formal education. He also fashioned a teaching instrument, a catechism, the introduction to which is offered below. We include it here as an example of the device which played so large a part in Reformation approaches to the teaching of doctrine.

Calvin's Institutes of the Christian Religion appears in

Vols. XX and XXI of The Library of Christian Classics, ed. by John T. McNeill (The Westminster Press); and various Theological Treatises in Vol. XXII of that same series, ed. by J. K. S. Reid (1954). For biographical and interpretative material, consult R. N. Carew Hunt, Calvin (The Centenary Press, London, 1933); James Mackinnon, Calvin and the Reformation (Longmans, Green & Co., Inc., London, 1936); Thomas Henry Lewis Parker, Portrait of Calvin (S.C.M. Press, London, 1954); John Thomas McNeill, The History and Character of Calvinism (Oxford University Press, 1954). Various catechisms are discussed, and their texts set forth in The School of Faith: The Catechism of the Reformed Church, ed. by Thomas F. Torrance (James Clarke & Company, Ltd., London, 1959).

JOHN CALVIN . . .

The Catechism of the Church of Geneva

LETTER TO THE READER

It has always been a practice and diligent care of the
church that children be rightly brought up in Christian
doctrine. To do this more conveniently, not only were
schools formerly opened and individuals enjoined to teach
their families properly, but also it was accepted public
custom and practice to examine children in the churches
concerning the specific points which should be common
and familiar to all Christians. That this be done in order, a
formula was written out, called catechism, or institute.
After this, the devil, miserably rending the church of God
and bringing upon it his fearful destruction (of which the
marks are all too evident in most parts of the world), sub-
verted this sacred policy; nor did he leave surviving anything more than certain trivialities, which give rise only
to superstitions, without any edifying fruit. Of this kind

Calvin, John, *The Catechism of the Church of Geneva, that is, a Plan
for Instructing Children in the Doctrine of Christ,* in *Calvin: Theological
Treatises,* ed. by J. K. S. Reid, Vol. XXII, pp. 88–91. The Library of
Christian Classics. The Westminster Press, Philadelphia; S.C.M. Press,
London, 1954. Used by permission.

is that confirmation, as they call it, made up of gesticulations which are more than ridiculous and suited rather to monkeys, and rest on no foundation. What we now bring forward, therefore, is nothing else than the use of a practice formerly observed by Christians and the true worshipers of God, and never neglected until the church was wholly corrupted.

John Calvin to the Faithful Ministers of Christ Who Preach the Pure Doctrine of the Gospel in East Friesland

Since it is proper for us by every means to endeavor to make that unity of faith shine forth among us which is so highly commended by Paul, the solemn profession of faith which is joined to our common Baptism ought to be directed chiefly to this end. It might therefore be wished, not only that there exist a perpetual consent by all in pious doctrine, but that there be also a single form of catechism for all churches. But since for many reasons it will hardly ever be otherwise than that each church have its own catechism, we should not too strenuously resist it; provided, however, that the variety in the kind of teaching be such that we are all directed to the one Christ, by whose truth, if we be united in it, we may grow together into one body and one spirit, and with one mouth also proclaim whatever belongs to the sum of the faith. Catechists who do not pursue this end, besides seriously injuring the church by the dissemination of material of dissension in religion, introduce also an impious profanation of Baptism. For what further use is Baptism, unless this remains its foundation, that we all agree in one faith? Those who publicly bring out catechisms ought therefore to be all the more diligently careful, lest by producing something rashly they do grave harm to piety and inflict a deadly wound upon the church, not only for the present but also in posterity.

I wanted to say this by way of preface to testify to my readers that I also, as is right, have made it a first charge on my attention, not to transmit anything in this catechism of mine that is not agreeable to the doctrine held by all the pious. This declaration of mine will not be found vain by those that bring candor and sound judgment to their reading. I trust I have succeded so far that, even if it be not entirely satisfying, my work may be acceptable to all good men, so that it be considered useful by them.

I have written it in Latin, and, even if this decision perhaps does not commend itself to some, I had many reasons for it, though it would be unprofitable to refer to them all here. I shall select such as seem to be enough to obviate censure. First, in this confused and divided state of Christendom, I judge it useful to have public testimonies by which churches that agree in Christian doctrine though widely separated in space may mutually recognize each other. For besides the fact that this contributes not a little to mutual confirmation, what is more desirable than that mutual congratulations should pass between them, and that they should devoutly commend each other to the Lord? To this end, while a consensus of faith still existed and flourished among us, bishops used once to send synodal letters across the sea, with which, as by tokens, they might establish sacred communion between the churches.

How much more necessary is it now, in the dreadful devastation of the Christian world, that those churches, which worship God rightly, few and dispersed and hedged about by the profane synagogues of antichrist as they are, should give and receive mutually this sign of holy fellowship, and thereby be incited to that fraternal embrace of which I have spoken? And if this be necessary for today, what are we to think of posterity? About it I am more anxious than I almost dare to think. For unless God give miraculous assistance from heaven, I cannot avoid thinking that the world is threatened with extreme barbarism. I could wish that our children do not shortly find this to be a true prophecy and no mere conjecture. All the more, then, must we labor to gather by our writings such remains of the church as may persist or even emerge after our death. There are other kinds of writing to show what are our views in all matters of religion; but what agreement in doctrine our churches had among themselves cannot be observed with clearer evidence than from the catechisms. For in them there appears not only what someone or another once taught, but what were the rudiments with which both the learned and the unlearned among us were from youth constantly instructed, all the faithful holding them as the solemn symbol of Christian communion. This indeed was my chief reason for publishing this catechism.

A second reason, however, carried not a little weight with me: that I heard that it was desired by a great many, who hoped it might not be unworthy of reading. Whether they were right or wrong is not for me to say; but it was a right thing to do as they wished. It was almost necessity that was laid upon me, and I could not rightly decline. For since, seven years earlier, there was edited by me a brief summary of religion under the name of catechism, I feared, unless I anticipated by bringing this one forward, the other would be driven into the background; and this I did not wish.

Hence consideration of the public good required me to take care that this one which I preferred should occupy the position. Besides I think it belongs to good example to testify to the world that we, who undertake the restitution of the church, faithfully exert ourselves everywhere for the rightful return of the use of catechism abolished some centuries ago under the papacy. For this holy custom cannot be sufficiently commended for its usefulness: nor can the papists be sufficiently condemned for the flagrant corruption, because by turning it into puerile trifles they not only set it aside, but also basely misused it as the occasion of impure and impious superstition. For they deck out that spurious confirmation, which they have substituted in its place, like a harlot, with great splendor of ceremonies and splendid pomps without measure. They even, in wanting to adorn it, ornament it with execrable blasphemies, giving out that it is a sacrament of greater dignity than Baptism and calling only half-Christians those that have not been besmeared with their rank oil. In fact the whole business consists in nothing but theatrical gesticulations, or rather, the wanton sporting of monkeys, without even imitative skill.

To you, my very dear brothers in the Lord, I have chosen to dedicate this work, because some of your number besides showing me that they loved me and that the most part of them take pleasure in my writings, also expressly demanded in letters that I undertake it for their sake. For the rest, there was one just and sufficient reason: that I learned long since from the statement of serious and pious men things concerning you that bound me to you with my whole soul. Now I ask of you what I trust you will do of your own accord, that you take in good part this testimony of my good will toward you. Farewell. The

Lord daily increase you more and more in the spirit of wisdom, prudence, zeal, and fortitude, to the edification of his church.

Geneva, November 27, 1545.

16

ROGER ASCHAM

(1515–1568)

Roger Ascham was born at Kirby Wiske, Yorkshire, England, and died at London. He was a student at St. John's College, Cambridge, at that time a center of broad studies in the humanities, where he specialized in Greek. It is assumed that Queen Elizabeth I became a devotee of the classics during his tutelage of her when she was a young princess. Later he served his queen in the capacity of Latin secretary, a sort of ambassadorial role. He wrote a treatise on archery called Toxophilus *(1545).*

The title page of The Scholemaster *(to use its original spelling) contains this long subtitle: " or plain and perfect way of teaching children to understand, write, and speak, in Latin tongue, but specially purposed for the private bringing up of youth in gentlemen and noble men's houses, and commodious also for all such, as have forgot the Latin tongue, and would by themselves, without a scholemaster, in short time, and with small pains, recover a sufficient ability to understand, write, and speak Latin." The book was published posthumously in London in 1570, and dedicated by his wife, Margaret, to " The Honorable Sir William Cecill, Knight, principal Secretarie to the Quene's most excellent Maiestie." Part I is concerned with " teaching the bringing up of youth "; Part II with " teaching the ready way to the Latin tongue."*

In a time when learning was made difficult for children, Ascham can be credited with humane concern for the pupils, and a recognition of their youthful need to be motivated. His emphasis on readiness and on the plasticity of the youthful mind and spirit was avant garde *for his century!*

ROGER ASCHAM . . .

The Schoolmaster

By Socrates' judgment, a good father and a wise schoolmaster should choose a child to make a scholar of, that hath, by nature, the aforesaid perfect qualities and comely furniture, both of mind and body; hath memory, quick to receive, sure to keep, and ready to deliver; hath love to learning, hath list to labor, hath desire to learn of others, hath boldness to ask any question, hath mind wholly bent to win praise by well doing.

The two first points be special benefits of nature: which nevertheless be well preserved and much increased by good order. But as for the five last: love, labor, gladness to learn of others, boldness to ask doubts, and will to win praise, be won and maintained by the only wisdom and discretion of the schoolmaster. Which fine points, whether a schoolmaster shall work sooner in a child, by fearful beating or courteous handling, you that be wise, judge.

Yet some men, wise in deed, but in this matter, more

Ascham, Roger, *The Scholemaster*, "The First Book Teachyng The Brynging Up of Youth." London, Printed by John Daye, 1570. The first edition of 1570 was collated with the second edition of 1571 by Edward Arber and published in London in 1870 in a series entitled " English Reprints." The editor has modernized the spelling from the original work.

by severity of nature than any wisdom at all, do laugh
at us, when we thus wish and reason that young children
should rather be allured to learning by gentleness and
love than compelled to learning by beating and fear. They
say our reasons serve only to breed forth talk and pass
away time, but we never saw a good schoolmaster do so,
nor never read of a wise man that thought so.

Yes, forsooth, as wise as they be, either in other men's
opinion or in their own conceit, I will bring the contrary
judgment of him, who, they themselves shall confess, was
as wise as they are, or else they may be justly thought to
have small wit at all: and that is Socrates; in English thus:
No learning ought to be learned with bondage; for bodily
labors, wrought by compulsion, hurt not the body; but
any learning wrought by compulsion, tarrieth not long in
the mind. And why? For whatsoever the mind doth learn
unwillingly with fear, the same it doth quickly forget without care. And lest proud wits, that love not to be contraried
but have lust to wrangle or trifle away truth, will say that
Socrates meaneth not this of children's teaching, but of
some other higher learning, hear what Socrates in the same
place doth more plainly say: My dear friend, bring not up
your children in learning by compulsion and fear, but
by playing and pleasure. . . . And in this counsel, judgment, and authority of Socrates I will repose myself, until I meet with a man of the contrary mind, whom I may
justly take to be wiser than I think Socrates was. Fond
schoolmasters neither can understand, nor will follow, this
good counsel of Socrates; but wise riders in their office can
and will do both: which is the only cause that commonly,
the young gentlemen of England go so unwillingly to
school, and run so fast to the stable. For in very deed fond
schoolmasters, by fear, do beat into them the hatred of

learning, and wise riders, by gentle allurements, do breed up in them the love of riding. They find fear and bondage in schools; they feel liberty and freedom in stables, which causeth them utterly to abhor the one, and most gladly to haunt the other. And I do not write this, that in exhorting to the one, I would dissuade young gentlemen from the other; yea, I am sure, with all my heart, that they be given no more to riding than they be. For, of all outward qualities, to ride fair is more comely for himself, more necessary for his country; and the greater he is in blood, the greater is his praise, the more he doth exceed all others therein.

But, to our purpose, by any means. . . . When by the time they come to their own rule, they carry commonly from the school with them a perpetual hatred of their master, and a continual contempt of learning. If ten gentlemen be asked, why they forget so soon in Court that which they were learning so long in school, eight of them, or let me be blamed, will lay the fault on their ill handling by their schoolmasters.

Yet some will say that children of nature love pastime and mislike learning because, in their kind, the one is easy and pleasant, the other hard and wearisome; which is an opinion not so true as some men ween. For the matter lieth not so much in the disposition of them that be young, as in the order and manner of bringing up by them that be old, nor yet in the difference of learning and pastime. For, beat a child, if he dance not well, and cherish him, though he learn not well, ye shall have him unwilling to go to dance, and glad to go to his book. Knock him always, when he draweth his shaft ill, and favor him again, though he fault at his book, ye shall have him very loathe to be in the field, and very willing to be in the school. Yea, I say more, and not of myself, but the judgment of those, from whom few wise men will gladly dissent, that if ever the nature of man be given at any time, more than other, to receive goodness, it is in innocency of young years, before that experience of evil have taken root in him. For the pure, clean wit of a sweet young babe is like the newest wax, most able to receive the best and fairest printing; and like a new, bright silver dish never occupied, to receive and keep clean, any good thing that is put into it.

And thus, will in children, wisely wrought withal, may easily be won to be very well willing to learn. And wit in children, by nature, namely memory, the only key and keeper of all learning, is readied to receive, and surest to keep any manner of thing that is learned in youth. This, lewd and learned, by common experience, know to be most true. For we remember nothing so well when we be old as those things which we learned when we were young. And this is not strange, but common in all nature's works. Every man sees (as I said before) new wax is best for printing; new clay fittest for working; new-shorn wool aptest for soon and surest dyeing; new, fresh flesh for good and durable salting. And this similitude is not rude, not borrowed of the larder house, but out of his school-house, of whom the wisest of England need not be ashamed to learn. Young grafts grow not only soonest but fairest, and bring always forth the best and sweetest fruit; young whelps learn easily to carry; young popingays learn quickly to speak. And so, to be short, if in all other things, though they lack reason, sense, and life, the similitude of youth is fittest to all goodness, surely nature, in mankind, is most beneficial and effectual in this behalf.

Therefore, if to the goodness of nature be joined the wisdom of the teacher in leading young wits into a right and plain way of learning, surely children, kept up in God's fear and governed by his grace, may most easily be brought well to serve God and country both by virtue and wisdom. . . .

And thus the children, kept up in God's fear and preserved by his grace, finding pain in ill-doing and pleasure in well-studying, should easily be brought to honesty of life and perfectness of learning, the only mark that good and wise fathers do wish and labor that their children should most busily and carefully shoot at. . . .

And God is a good God, and wisest in all his doings, that will place virtue and displace vice, in those kingdoms where he doth govern. For he knoweth that nobility, without virtue and wisdom, is blood indeed, but blood truly without bones and sinews. . . .

17

JOHN AMOS COMENIUS
(1592–1670)

Comenius was born in Moravia, his family name being Komensky, later Latinized. Born a Czech, he was destined to live richly and deeply in an international circle. His education took place at Herborn Gymnasium in Nassau and at the University of Heidelberg. In 1618 he became pastor of the congregation of the Unitas Fratrum (Unity of Brethren) at Fulnek. When that town was destroyed in the Thirty Years' War, he sought refuge in Bohemia. There he wrote Labyrinth of the World. Again, he had to move elsewhere, for all Protestant pastors were exiled by the emperor. He went next to Leszno, Poland, where he served as co-rector of the local gymnasium. Now his fame was rising as an educational authority. In 1641 he was invited for educational consultations to Sweden and England. Later he directed the reform of the Hungarian school system. During the Polish-Swedish War most of his manuscripts were destroyed. In 1632 he had been elected bishop of the Unitas Fratrum; in 1648 he was their only remaining bishop.

The Great Didactic, from which we publish only a brief selection, is one of the foundational educational treatises of all time. It is especially noteworthy in that it is informed by a deeply spiritual concept of man as the creature of

God. *It is at once a philosophy of Christian education and a compendium of teaching method that takes the whole range of human learning into account,* sub specie aeternitatis.

Comenius' writings include A Pattern of Universal Knowledge, Janua linguarum reserata, Via lucis, Orbis pictus (*one of the earliest textbooks with pictures*), *and* The Analytical Didactic (*available in a translation by Vladimir Jelinek* [*The University of Chicago Press, 1953*]). *The introduction to another work,* The School of Infancy, *ed. by Ernest M. Eller* (*The University of North Carolina Press, 1956*), *pp. 3–53, contains an excellent short life.*

JOHN AMOS COMENIUS . . .

The Great Didactic

Man Is the Highest, the Most Absolute, and the Most Excellent of Things Created

When Pittacus of old gave to the world his saying " Know thyself," the sentiment was received by the wise with so much approval, that, in order to impress it on the people, they declared that it had fallen from heaven, and caused it to be written in golden letters on the temple of the Delphic Apollo, where great assemblies of men used to collect. Their action was prudent and wise; but their statement was false. It was, however, in the interests of truth, and is of great importance to us.

For what is the voice from heaven that resounds in the Scriptures but " Know thyself, O man, and know me ": me the source of eternity, of wisdom and of grace; thyself, my creation, my likeness, my delight.

For I have destined thee to be the companion of my eternity; for thy use I designed the heaven, the earth, and all that in them is; to thee alone I gave all those things in

Comenius, John Amos, *The Great Didactic*, tr. by M. W. Keatinge. Adam and Charles Black, London, 1896. Chapter I, pp. 177 f., and Chapter VII, pp. 209–212, are used here by permission.

conjunction, which to the rest of creation I gave but singly, namely, Existence, Vitality, Sense, and Reason. I have made thee to have dominion over the works of my hands. I have placed all things under thy feet, sheep and oxen and the beasts of the field, the fowl of the air and the fish of the sea, and I have crowned thee with glory and with honor (Ps. 8). To thee, finally, lest anything should be lacking, I have given myself in personal communion, joining my nature to thine for eternity, and in this distinguishing thee from all created things, visible and invisible. For what creature in heaven or in earth can boast that God was manifest in his flesh and was seen of angels (I Tim. 3:16), not, forsooth, that they might only see and marvel at him whom they desired to see (I Peter 1:12), but that they might adore God made manifest in the flesh, the Son of God and of man (Heb. 1:6; John 1:51; Matt. 4:11). Know therefore that thou art the cornerstone and epitome of my works, the representative of God among them, the crown of my glory.

Would that this were inscribed, not on the doors of temples, not on the title pages of books, not on the tongues, ears, and eyes of all men, but on their hearts! Would that this could be done to all who undertake the task of educating men, that they might learn to appreciate the dignity of the task and of their own excellence, and might bring all means to bear on the perfect realization of their divinity!

A Man Can Most Easily Be Formed in Early Youth, and Cannot Be Formed Properly Except at This Age

From what has been said it is evident that the circumstances of men and of trees are similar. For, as a fruit tree (an apple, a pear, a fig, or a vine) is able to grow from its own stock and of its own accord, while a wild tree will not bring forth sweet fruits until it be planted, watered, and pruned by a skilled gardener, so does a man grow of his own accord into a human semblance (just as any brute resembles others of his own class), but is unable to develop into a rational, wise, virtuous, and pious creature, unless virtue and piety are first engrafted in him. We will now show that this must take place while the plants are young.

From the human point of view there are six reasons for this. First, the uncertainty of our present life. For that we must leave it is certain, but when and how is uncertain. And that any should be snatched away unprepared is a danger greatly to be dreaded since a man is thus doomed eternally. For, just as a man must go through life without a limb if he leave his mother's womb bereft of it, so, if, when we leave this world, our minds have not been molded to the knowledge of and participation in God, there will be no further opportunity given us. And therefore, as the matter is of such importance, the greatest haste is necessary, lest any man be lost.

And although death be far off and a long life be assured, the formation of character should nonetheless begin early, because life must be spent not in learning but in acting. We should therefore be prepared for the actions of life as soon as possible, since we may be compelled to desist from action before we have learned our lesson properly. Indeed, if any wish to devote his life to learning, the multitude of objects which the Creator has placed before his happy gaze is infinite, and, if he chance to have a life like Nestor's, he will find his most useful occupation in discerning the treasures of divine wisdom that the Creator has provided, and in thus preparing for himself the bulwarks of a happy life. Man's senses, therefore, must be early brought to bear on the world that surrounds him, since throughout his whole life he has much to learn, to experience, and to accomplish.

It is the nature of everything that comes into being, that while tender it is easily bent and formed, but that, when it has grown hard, it is not easy to alter. Wax, when soft, can be easily fashioned and shaped; when hard it cracks readily. A young plant can be planted, transplanted, pruned, and bent this way or that. When it has become a tree these processes are impossible. New-laid eggs, when placed under a hen, grow warm quickly and produce chickens; when they are old they will not do so. If a rider wishes to train a horse, a ploughman an ox, a huntsman a dog or a hawk, a bear-leader a bear for dancing, or an old woman a magpie, a raven or a crow to imitate the human voice, they must choose them for the purpose when quite young; otherwise their labor is wasted.

It is evident that this holds good with man himself. His brain, which we have already compared to wax, because it receives the images of external objects that present themselves to its organs of sense, is, in the years of childhood, quite wet and soft, and fit for receiving all images that come to it. Later on, as we find by experience, it grows hard and dry by degrees, so that things are less readily impressed or engraved upon it. Hence Cicero's remark, " Boys pick up countless things with rapidity." In the same way it is only in the years of boyhood, when the muscles are still capable of being trained, that the hands and the other members can be trained to produce skilled work. If a man is to become a good writer, painter, tailor, smith, cabinet-maker, or musician, he must apply himself to the art from his early youth, when the imagination is active and the fingers flexible: otherwise he will never produce anything.

If piety is to take root in any man's heart, it must be engrafted while he is still young; if we wish anyone to be virtuous, we must train him in early youth; if we wish him to make great progress in the pursuit of wisdom, we must direct his faculties toward it in infancy, when desire burns, when thought is swift, and when memory is tenacious. "An old man who has still to learn his lessons is a shameful and ridiculous object; training and preparation are for the young, action for the old " (Seneca, Epistle 36).

In order that man may be fashioned to humanity, God has granted him the years of youth, which are unsuitable for everything but education. While the horse, the ox, the elephant, and other beasts, mere animated masses, come to maturity in a few years, man alone scarcely does so in twenty or thirty. Now, if any imagine that this arises from chance or from some accidental cause or other, he surely betrays his folly. To all other things, forsooth, God has meted out their periods, while in the case of man alone, the lord of all, he allows them to be fixed by chance! Or are we to suppose that nature finds it easier to complete the formation of man by slow processes?: nature, who with no trouble can produce vaster bodies in a few months. We can only suppose, therefore, that the Creator, of deliberate intent, interposed the delay of youth, in order that our period of training might be longer; and ordained that for some time we should take no part in the action of life, that, for the rest of our lives, and for eternity, we might be the more fitted to do so.

In man, that alone is lasting which has been imbibed in early youth, as is clear from the same examples. A jar, even though broken, preserves the odor with which it was imbued when new. When a tree is young its branches spread out all round it, and remain in this position for hundreds of years, until it is cut down. Wool is so tenacious of the color with which it is first dyed, that it cannot be bleached. The wooden hoop of a wheel, which has been bent into a curve, will break into a thousand pieces rather than return to straightness. And similarly, in a man, first impressions cling so fast that nothing but a miracle can remove them. It is therefore most prudent that men be shaped to the standard of wisdom in early youth.

Finally, it is most dangerous if a man be not imbued with the cleanly precepts of life from his early cradle. For, when the external senses begin to fulfill their functions, the mind of man cannot remain at rest, and, if not engaged with what is useful, it occupies itself with the vainest and even with harmful things (a process which is assisted by the evil examples of a corrupt age), while later on, if it wish to unlearn what it has acquired, it finds this impossible or very difficult; as we have already shown. Hence the world is full of enormities which neither the civil magistrates nor the ministers of the church are able to quell, since no serious attention is given to the source from which the evil flows.

If, then, each man have the welfare of his own children at heart, and if that of the human race be dear to the civil and ecclesiastical guardians of human affairs, let them hasten to make provision for the timely planting, pruning, and watering of the plants of heaven, that these may be prudently formed to make prosperous advances in letters, virtue, and piety.

18

THOMAS FULLER
(1608–1661)

The English clergyman Thomas Fuller was born and died in London. He was appointed curate of the Savoy, London, after completing studies at Cambridge about the time of the beginning of the English Civil War. He was stoutly loyal to the crown during that conflict, attaching himself to the king at London in 1643 and serving after the Restoration as chaplain to King Charles II.

His analysis of the types of schoolmasters has a relevance for today as well as his own time. Some may quarrel with his prescription about the teacher's functioning as " an absolute monarch in his school," yet few will fail to applaud his recommendation that moderation should be employed in inflicting deserved punishment! Withal, he is sensitive to the schoolteacher's role as one that will either impede or encourage his pupils toward enlightenment and true spiritual wisdom.

" The Good Schoolmaster " is a chapter in The Holy State and the Profane State *(1642). He wrote also* The History of the Holy War, A Pisgah-sight of Palestine, History of the University of Cambridge, *and* History of the Worthies of England.

THOMAS FULLER . . .

The Good Schoolmaster

There is scarce any profession in the commonwealth more necessary, which is so slightly performed. The reasons whereof I conceive to be these: First, young scholars make this calling their refuge; yea, perchance, before they have taken any degree in the university, commence schoolmasters in the country; as if nothing else were required to set up their profession, but only a rod and a ferula. Secondly, others, who are able, use it only as a passage to better preferment; to patch the rents in their present fortune, till they can provide a new one, and betake themselves to some more gainful calling. Thirdly, they are disheartened from doing their best, with the miserable reward which in some places they receive — being masters to their own children, and slaves to their parents. Fourthly, being grown rich, they grow negligent; and scorn to touch the school, but by the proxy of an usher. But see how well our schoolmaster behaves himself.

I. *His genius inclines him with delight to his profession.*

Fuller, Thomas, " The Good Schoolmaster," Chapter XVI in Book II, *The Holy State and the Profane State*, ed. by James Nichols, pp. 99–102. London, printed for Thomas Tegg, 1841.

Some men had as lief be schoolboys as schoolmasters — to be tied to the school, as Cooper's *Dictionary* and Scapula's *Lexicon* are chained to the desk therein; and, though great scholars, and skillful in other arts, are bunglers in this. But God of his goodness hath fitted several men for several callings, that the necessity of church and state, in all conditions, may be provided for. So that he who beholds the fabric thereof may say: " God hewed out this stone, and appointed it to lie in this very place; for it would fit none other so well, and here it doth most excellent." And thus God moldeth some for a schoolmaster's life; undertaking it with desire and delight, and discharging it with dexterity and happy success.

II. *He studieth his scholars' natures as carefully as they their books.* And ranks their dispositions into several forms. And though it may seem difficult for him in a great school to descend to all particulars, yet experienced schoolmasters may quickly make a grammar of boys' natures, and reduce them all (saving some few exceptions) to these general rules:

1. *Those that are ingenious and industrious.* The conjunction of two such planets in a youth presage much good unto him. To such a lad a frown may be a whipping, and a whipping a death; yea, where their master whips them once, shame whips them all the week after. Such natures he useth with all gentleness.

2. *Those that are ingenious and idle.* These think, with the hare in the fable, that, running with snails (so they count the rest of their schoolfellows), they shall come soon enough to the post, though sleeping a good while before their starting. O! a good rod would finely take them napping!

3. *Those that are dull and diligent.* Wines, the stronger

they be, the more lees they have when they are new. Many
boys are muddyheaded till they be clarified with age; and
such afterward prove the best. Bristol diamonds are both
bright, and squared, and pointed by nature, and yet are
soft and worthless; whereas Orient ones, in India, are
rough and rugged naturally. Hard, rugged, and dull natures of youth acquit themselves afterward the jewels
of the country; and, therefore, their dullness at first is to
be borne with, if they be diligent. That schoolmaster deserves to be beaten himself, who beats nature in a boy
for a fault. And I question whether all the whipping in the
world can make their parts which are naturally sluggish,
rise one minute before the hour which nature hath appointed.

4. *Those that are invincibly dull and negligent also.*
Correction may reform the latter, not amend the former.
All the whetting in the world can never set a razor's edge
on that which hath no steel in it. Such boys he consigneth
over to other professions. Shipwrights and boat makers
will choose those crooked pieces of timber which other
carpenters refuse. Those may make excellent merchants
and mechanics who will not serve for scholars.

III. *He is able, diligent, and methodical in his teaching.*
Not leading them rather in a circle than forward. He
minces his precepts for children to swallow; hanging clogs
on the nimbleness of his own soul, that his scholars may go
along with him.

IV. *He is, and will be known to be, an absolute monarch
in his school.* If cockering mothers proffer him money, to
purchase their sons an exemption from his rod (to live, as
it were, in a peculiar, out of their master's jurisdiction),
with disdain he refuseth it, and scorns the late custom in
some places of commuting whipping into money, and ran-

soming boys from the rod at a set price. If he hath a stubborn youth, correction-proof, he debaseth not his authority
by contesting with him, but fairly (if he can) puts him
away, before his obstinacy hath infected others.

V. *He is moderate in inflicting deserved correction.*
Many a schoolmaster better answereth the name *paido-
tribes* than *paidogogos,* rather " tearing his scholars' flesh
with whipping, than giving them good education." No
wonder if his scholars hate the Muses, being presented
unto them in the shapes of fiends and furies. Junius com-
plains of the excessive torture inflicted on him by his
schoolmaster, who lacerated him with thongs seven or
eight times every day. Yea, hear the lamentable verse of
poor Tusser, in his own *Life:*

> " From Paul's I went,
>   To Eaton sent,
>   To learn straughtways
>   The Latin phrase;
>   Where fifty-three
>   Stripes given to me
>   At once I had.

> " For fault but small,
>   Or none at all,
>   It came to pass
>   Thus beat I was;
>   See, Udal,* see
>   The mercy of thee
>   To me, poor lad! "

Such an Orbilius mars more scholars than he makes. Their
tyranny hath caused many tongues to stammer, which
spake plain by nature, and whose stuttering at first was

---

* Nicholas Udal was schoolmaster of Eaton during the reign of
Henry VIII.

nothing else but fears quavering on their speech at their master's presence; and whose mauling them about their heads hath dulled those who in quickness exceeded their master.

VI. *He makes his school free to him who sues to him* in forma pauperis. And, surely, learning is the greatest alms that can be given. But he is a beast, who, because the poor scholar cannot pay him his wages, pays the scholar in his whipping. Rather are diligent lads to be encouraged with all excitements to learning. This minds me of what I have heard concerning Mr. Bust, that worthy late schoolmaster of Eaton, who would never suffer any wandering, begging scholar (such as justly the statute hath ranked in the forefront of rogues) to come into his school, but would thrust him out with earnestness (however privately charitable unto him) lest his schoolboys should be disheartened from their books, by seeing some scholars, after their studying in the university, preferred to beggary.

VII. *He spoils not a good school, to make thereof a bad college.* Therein to teach his scholars logic. For, besides that logic may have an action of trespass against grammar for encroaching on her liberties, syllogisms are solecisms taught in the school; and oftentimes they are forced afterward, in the university, to unlearn the fumbling skill they had before.

VIII. *Out of his school, he is no whit pedantical in carriage or discourse.* Contenting himself to be rich in Latin, though he doth not jingle with it in every company wherein he comes.

To conclude: let this, amongst other motives, make schoolmasters careful in their place, that the eminencies of their scholars have commended the memories of their schoolmasters to posterity, who, otherwise in obscurity, had altogether been forgotten. Who had ever heard of R. Bond, in Lancashire, but for the breeding of learned Ascham his scholar? Or of Hartgrave, in Burnley school, in the same county, but because he was the first who did teach worthy Dr. Whitaker? Nor do I honor the memory of Mulcaster for anything so much as for his scholar, that gulf of learning, Bishop Andrews. This made the Athenians, the day before the great feast of Theseus their founder, to sacrifice a ram to the memory of Conidas, his schoolmaster, that first instructed him.

19

JOHN MILTON
(1608–1674)

The poet-essayist Milton lived in London most of his lifetime. Educated at St. Paul's School and Cambridge University (Christ's College), he had originally planned on entering the ministry. However, during a period of leisurely study at his father's estate at Horton from 1632 to 1638, he changed his mind. He determined to make poetry the chief interest of his life. That he had genuine talent and made a wise decision soon became evident in his early compositions, such as On the Morning of Christ's Nativity, L'Allegro, Il Penseroso, Comus, Lycidas. *During a grand tour of Europe in 1638 he met many Italian literary leaders and other outstanding persons such as Galileo. When Civil War threatened Europe, he temporarily deserted the muse for politics, writing numerous tracts. One of these,* Areopagitica *(1644), was a strident plea for freedom from censorship that has continued to be a principal argument. He even entered Cromwell's government as secretary for foreign tongues. By 1652 he had become totally blind. In his later years he wrote the massive* Paradise Lost, Paradise Regained, *and* Samson Agonistes.

Though theoretical and never put into practice, his scheme of education is interesting for its blend of culture and religion.

JOHN MILTON . . .

On Education

To Master Samuel Hartlib

I am long since persuaded, Master Hartlib, that to say or do aught worth memory and imitation no purpose or respect should sooner move us than simply the love of God, and of mankind. Nevertheless to write now the reforming of education, though it be one of the greatest and noblest designs that can be thought on, and for the want thereof this nation perishes; I had not yet at this time been induced, but by your earnest entreaties and serious conjurements; as having my mind for the present half diverted in the pursuance of some other assertions, the knowledge and use of which cannot but be a furtherance both to the enlargement of truth and honest living with much more peace. Nor should the laws of any private friendship have prevailed with me to divide thus, or transpose my former thoughts, but that I see those aims, those actions, which have won you with me the esteem of a person sent hither by some good providence from a far country to be the occasion and incitement of great good to this island.

From *The Prose Works of John Milton,* Vol. III, ed. by J. A. St. John, pp. 462–478. Henry G. Bohn, London, undated.

And, as I hear, you have obtained the same repute with men of most approved wisdom, and some of the highest authorities among us; not to mention the learned correspondence which you hold in foreign parts, and the extraordinary pains and diligence which you have used in this matter, both here and beyond the seas; either by the definite will of God so ruling, or the peculiar sway of nature, which also is God's working. Neither can I think that so reputed and so valued as you are, you would, to the forfeit of your own discerning ability, impose upon me an unfit and overponderous argument; but that the satisfaction which you profess to have received, from those incidental discourses which we have wandered into, hath pressed and almost constrained you into a persuasion, that what you require from me in this point, I neither ought nor can in conscience defer beyond this time both of so much need at once, and so much opportunity to try what God hath determined.

I will not resist, therefore, whatever it is, either of divine or human obligement, that you lay upon me; but will forthwith set down in writing, as you request me, that voluntary idea, which hath long, in silence, presented itself to me, of a better education, in extent and comprehension far more large, and yet of time far shorter, and of attainment far more certain than hath been yet in practice. Brief I shall endeavor to be; for that which I have to say, assuredly this nation hath extreme need should be done sooner than spoken. To tell you, therefore, what I have benefited herein among old renowned authors, I shall spare; to search what many modern Januas and Didactics, more than ever I shall read, have projected, my inclination leads me not. But if you can accept of these few observations which have flowered off, and are as it were the

burnishing of many studious and contemplative years, altogether spent in the search of religious and civil knowledge, and such as pleased you so well in the relating, I
here give you them to dispose of.

The end then of learning is to repair the ruins of our
first parents by regaining to know God aright, and out of
that knowledge to love him, to imitate him, to be like him,
as we may the nearest by possessing our souls of true virtue, which being united to the heavenly grace of faith,
makes up the highest perfection. But because our understanding cannot in this body found itself but on sensible
things, nor arrive so clearly to the knowledge of God and
things invisible, as by orderly conning over the visible and
inferior creature, the same method is necessarily to be
followed in all discreet teaching. And seeing every nation
affords not experience and tradition enough for all kinds
of learning, therefore we are chiefly taught the languages
of those people who have at any time been most industrious after wisdom; so that language is but the instrument
conveying to us things useful to be known. And though
a linguist should pride himself to have all the tongues that
Babel cleft the world into, yet if he have not studied the
solid things in them, as well as the worlds and lexicons,
he were nothing so much to be esteemed a learned man, as
any yeoman or tradesman competently wise in his mother
dialect only.

Hence appear so many mistakes which have made learning generally so unpleasing and so unsuccessful; first, we
do amiss to spend seven or eight years merely in scraping
together so much miserable Latin and Greek as might be
learned otherwise easily and delightfully in one year. And
that which casts our proficiency therein so much behind,
is our time lost partly in too oft idle vacancies given both

to schools and universities; partly in a preposterous exaction, forcing the empty wits of children to compose themes, verses, and orations, which are the acts of ripest judgment, and the final work of a head filled with long reading and observing, with elegant maxims and copious invention. These are not matters to be wrung from poor striplings, like blood out of the nose, or the plucking of untimely fruit. Besides the ill habit which they get of wretched barbarizing against the Latin and Greek idiom, with their untutored Anglicisms, odious to be read, yet not to be avoided without a well-continued and judicious conversing among pure authors digested, which they scarce taste. Whereas, if after some preparatory grounds of speech by their certain forms got into memory, they were led to the praxis thereof in some chosen short book lessoned thoroughly to them, they might then forthwith proceed to learn the substance of good things, and arts in due order, which would bring the whole language quickly into their power. This I take to be the most rational and most profitable way of learning languages, and whereby we may best hope to give account to God of our youth spent herein.

And for the usual method of teaching arts, I deem it to be an old error of universities, not yet well recovered from the scholastic grossness of barbarous ages, that instead of beginning with arts most easy (and those be such as are most obvious to the sense), they present their young unmatriculated novices, at first coming, with the most intellective abstractions of logic and metaphysics; so that they having but newly left those grammatic flats and shallows, where they stuck unreasonably to learn a few words with lamentable construction, and now on the sudden transported under another climate, to be tossed and turmoiled with their unballasted wits in fathomless and unquiet deeps of controversy, do for the most part grow into hatred and contempt of learning, mocked and deluded all this while with ragged notions and babblements, while they expected worthy and delightful knowledge; till poverty or youthful years call them importunately to their several ways, and hasten them, with the sway of friends, either to an ambitious and mercenary, or ignorantly zealous divinity: some allured to the trade of law, grounding their purposes not on the prudent and heavenly contemplation of justice and equity, which was never taught them, but on the promising and pleasing thoughts of litigious terms, fat contentions, and flowing fees; others betake them to state affairs, with souls so unprincipled in virtue and true generous breeding, that flattery and court-shifts and tyrannous aphorisms appear to them the highest points of wisdom; instilling their barren hearts with a conscientious slavery; if, as I rather think, it be not feigned. Others, lastly, of a more delicious and airy spirit, retire themselves (knowing no better) to the enjoyments of ease and luxury, living out their days in feast and jollity; which indeed is the wisest and safest course of all these, unless they were with more integrity undertaken. And these are the errors, and these are the fruits of misspending our prime youth at the schools and universities as we do, either in learning mere words, or such things chiefly as were better unlearned.

I shall detain you now no longer in the demonstration of what we should not do, but straight conduct you to a hillside, where I will point you out the right path of a virtuous and noble education; laborious indeed at the first ascent, but else so smooth, so green, so full of goodly prospect, and melodious sounds on every side, that the harp of Orpheus was not more charming. I doubt not but ye shall have more ado to drive our dullest and laziest youth, our stocks and stubs, from the infinite desire of such a happy nurture, than we have now to hale and drag our choicest and hopefullest wits to that asinine feast of sow-thistles and brambles, which is commonly set before them as all the food and entertainment of their tenderest and most docible age. I call therefore a complete and generous education, that which fits a man to perform justly, skillfully, and magnanimously all the offices, both private and public, of peace and war. And how all this may be done between twelve and one and twenty, less time than is now bestowed in pure trifling at grammar and sophistry, is to be thus ordered.

First, to find out a spacious house and ground about it fit for an academy, and big enough to lodge a hundred and fifty persons, whereof twenty or thereabout may be attendants, all under the government of one, who shall be thought of desert sufficient, and ability either to do all, or wisely to direct and oversee it done. This place should be at once both school and university, not needing a remove to any other house of scholarship, except it be some peculiar college of law, or physic, where they mean to be practitioners; but as for those general studies which take up all our time from Lily to commencing, as they term it, master of art, it should be absolute. After this pattern, as many edifices may be converted to this use as shall be needful in every city throughout this land, which would tend much to the increase of learning and civility everywhere. This number, less or more thus collected, to the convenience of a foot company, or interchangeably two troops of cavalry, should divide their day's work into three parts as it lies orderly: their studies, their exercise, and their diet.

For their studies: first, they should begin with the chief

and necessary rules of some good grammar, either that now used, or any better; and while this is doing, their speech is to be fashioned to a distinct and clear pronunciation, as near as may be to the Italian, especially in the vowels. For we Englishmen being far northerly, do not open our mouths in the cold air wide enough to grace a southern tongue; but are observed by all other nations to speak exceeding close and inward, so that to smatter Latin with an English mouth, is as ill a hearing as law French. Next to make them expert in the usefullest points of grammar, and withal to season them and win them early to the love of virtue and true labor, ere any flattering seducement or vain principle seize them wandering, some easy and delightful book of education would be read to them, whereof the Greeks have store, as Cebes, Plutarch, and other Socratic discourses. But in Latin we have none of classic authority extant, except the two or three first books of Quintilian, and some select pieces elsewhere.

But here the main skill and groundwork will be, to temper them to such lectures and explanations, upon every opportunity as may lead and draw them in willing obedience, inflamed with the study of learning and the admiration of virtue; stirred up with high hopes of living to be brave men, and worthy patriots, dear to God, and famous to all ages. That they may despise and scorn all their childish and ill-taught qualities, to delight in manly liberal exercises, which he who hath the art and proper eloquence to catch them with, what with mild and effectual persuasions, and what with the intimation of some fear, if need be, but chiefly by his own example, might in a short space gain them to an incredible deligence and courage, infusing into their young breasts such an ingenuous and noble ardor, as would not fail to make many of them renowned and matchless men. At the same time, some other hour of the day, might be taught them the rules of arithmetic; and soon after the elements of geometry, even playing, as the old manner was. After evening repast, till bedtime, their thoughts would be taken up in the easy grounds of religion, and the story of Scripture.

The next step would be to the authors of agriculture, Cato, Varro, and Columella, for the matter is most easy; and, if the language be difficult, so much the better, it is not a difficulty above their years. And here will be an occasion of inciting, and enabling them hereafter to improve the tillage of their country, to recover the bad soil, and to remedy the waste that is made of good; for this was one of Hercules' praises. Ere half these authors be read (which will soon be with plying hard and daily) they cannot choose but be masters of any ordinary prose. So that it will be then seasonable for them to learn in any modern author the use of the globes, and all the maps, first, with the old names, and then with the new; or they might be then capable to read any compendious method of natural philosophy.

And at the same time might be entering into the Greek tongue, after the same manner as was before prescribed in the Latin; whereby the difficulties of grammar being soon overcome, all the historical physiology of Aristotle and Theophrastus are open before them, and, as I may say, under contribution. The like access will be to Vitruvius, to Seneca's natural questions, to Mela, Celsus, Pliny, or Solinus. And having thus passed the principles of arithmetic, geometry, astronomy, and geography, with a general compact of physics, they may descend in mathematics to the instrumental science of trigonometry, and from thence to fortification, architecture, enginery, or navigation. And in natural philosophy they may proceed leisurely from the history of meteors, minerals, plants, and living creatures, as far as anatomy.

Then also in course might be read to them, out of some not tedious writer, the institution of physic, that they may know the tempers, the humors, the seasons, and how to manage a crudity; which he who can wisely and timely do is not only a great physician to himself and to his friends, but also may, at some time or other, save an army by this frugal and expenseless means only; and not let the healthy and stout bodies of young men rot away under him for want of this discipline; which is a great pity, and no less a shame to the commander. To set forward all these proceedings in nature and mathematics, what hinders but that they may procure, as oft as shall be needful, the helpful experience of hunters, fowlers, fishermen, shepherds, gardeners, apothecaries; and in the other sciences, architects, engineers, mariners, anatomists; who doubtless would be ready, some for reward, and some to favor such a hopeful seminary. And this will give them such a real tincture of natural knowledge, as they shall never forget, but daily augment with delight. Then also those poets which are now counted most hard, will be both facile and pleasant, Orpheus, Hesiod, Theocritus, Aratus, Nicander, Oppian, Dionysius; and in Latin, Lucretius, Manilius, and the rural part of Virgil.

By this time, years and good general precepts, will have furnished them more distinctly with that act of reason which in ethics is called Proairesis; that they may with some judgment contemplate upon moral good and evil. Then will be required a special reinforcement of constant and sound indoctrinating, to set them right and firm, instructing them more amply in the knowledge of virtue and the hatred of vice; while their young and pliant affections are led through all the moral works of Plato, Xenophon, Cicero, Plutarch, Laertius, and those Locrian remnants; but still to be reduced in their nightward studies wherewith they close the day's work, under the determinate sentence of David or Solomon, or the evangelists and apostolic Scriptures. Being perfect in the knowledge of personal duty, they may then begin the study of economics. And either now or before this, they may have easily learned, at any odd hour, the Italian tongue. And soon after, but with wariness and good antidote, it would be wholesome enough to let them taste some choice comedies, Greek, Latin, or Italian; those tragedies also, that treat of household matters, as Trachiniae, Alcestis, and the like.

The next removal must be to the study of politics; to know the beginning, end, and reasons of political societies; that they may not, in a dangerous fit of the commonwealth, be such poor, shaken, uncertain reeds, of such a tottering conscience, as many of our great counselors have lately shewn themselves, but steadfast pillars of the state. After this, they are to dive into the grounds of law, and legal justice; delivered first and with best warrant by Moses; and as far as human prudence can be trusted, in those extolled remains of Grecian lawgivers, Lycurgus, Solon, Zaleucus, Charondas, and thence to all the Roman edicts and tables with their Justinian: and so down to the Saxon and common laws of England, and the statutes.

Sundays also and every evening may be now understandingly spent in the highest matters of theology, and church history, ancient and modern; and ere this time the Hebrew tongue at a set hour might have been gained, that the Scriptures may be now read in their own original; whereto it could be no impossibility to add the Chaldee and the Syrian dialect. When all these employments are well conquered, then will the choice histories, heroic poems, and Attic tragedies of stateliest and most regal argument, with all the famous political orations, offer themselves; which if they were not only read, but some of them got by memory, and solemnly pronounced with right accent and grace, as might be taught, could endue them even with the spirit and vigor of Demosthenes or Cicero, Euripides or Sophocles.

And now, lastly, will be the time to read with them those organic arts, which enable men to discourse and write perspicuously, elegantly, and according to the fittest style, of lofty, mean, or lowly. Logic, therefore, so much as is useful, is to be referred to this due place with all her well-couched heads and topics, until it be time to open her contracted palm into a graceful and ornate rhetoric, taught out of the rule of Plato, Aristotle, Phalereus, Cicero, Hermogenes, Longinus. To which poetry would be made subsequent, or indeed rather precedent, as being less subtile and fine, but more simple, sensuous, and passionate. I mean not here the prosody of a verse, which they could not but have hit on before among the rudiments of grammar; but that sublime art which in Aristotle's poetics, in Horace, and the Italian commentaries of Castelvetro, Tasso, Mazzonei, and others, teaches what the laws are of a true epic poem, what of a dramatic, what of a lyric, what decorum is, which is the grand masterpiece to observe. This would make them soon perceive what despicable creatures our common rhymers and playwriters be; and show them what religious, what glorious and magnificent use might be made of poetry, both in divine and human things.

From hence, and not till now, will be the right season

of forming them to be able writers and composers in every excellent matter, when they shall be thus fraught with an universal insight into things. Or whether they be to speak in parliament or council, honor and attention would be waiting on their lips. There would then also appear in pulpits other visage, other gestures, and stuff otherwise wrought than what we now sit under, ofttimes to as great a trial of our patience as any other that they preach to us. These are the studies wherein our noble and our gentle youth ought to bestow their time, in a disciplinary way, from twelve to one and twenty: unless they rely more upon their ancestors dead, than upon themselves living. In which methodical course it is so supposed they must proceed by the steady pace of learning onward, as at convenient times, for memory's sake, to retire back into the middle ward, and sometimes into the rear of what they have been taught, until they have confirmed and solidly united the whole body of their perfected knowledge, like the embattling of a Roman legion. Now will be worth the seeing, what exercises and recreations may best agree, and become these studies. . . .

20

JOHN LOCKE

(1632–1704)

John Locke was born at Wrington, near Bristol, England. He studied at Westminster and Oxford. His own feeble health led to an interest in medicine, which he studied without any intention to practice it professionally. He served for a year as secretary to the English ambassador to Berlin, after which he returned to Oxford, where he served as educational mentor for the son of the Earl of Shaftesbury. When Shaftesbury was banished from England, Locke followed him to Holland, not returning until 1688. Eventually, in 1695, he was appointed by King William as commissioner of trade and plantations. Failing health necessitated his leaving public life after a few years, and he retired to Oates, Sussex, where he lived until his death.

Locke is important to the whole modern science of education for his emphasis, in An Essay Concerning Human Understanding *(1689), on man's being born not with innate general principles or primary notions, but with a mind akin to a* tabula rasa, *on which experience writes the individual's history. From the standpoint of religious or moral education, this view long held sway and paved the way for the later emergence of some of the distinctively liberal emphases.*

Some Thoughts Concerning Education *was published in*

1693, and was elaborated in The Conduct of the Understanding, *published posthumously in 1706. The writing
from which we have excerpts below was composed during
his stay in Holland, and is in the form of notes to a friend,
Edward Clarke. Other friends requested that these notes be
enlarged into a book. Locke's ideas influenced Rousseau,
La Chatolais (in that writer's* Eassai d'Education Nation-
ale) *and Pestalozzi. Locke wrote also an* Essay on the Reasonableness of Christianity as Delivered in the Scriptures
(1695). On Locke's life, see Richard Ithamer Aaron, John
Locke *(Oxford University Press, 1937). The* Correspondence of John Locke and Edward Clarke *is edited by
B. Rand (Oxford University Press, 1927). A convenient
assortment of Locke's writings is contained in* Selections,
*ed. by Sterling P. Lamprecht (Charles Scribner's Sons,
1928).*

JOHN LOCKE . . .

Some Thoughts Concerning Education

A sound mind in a sound body, is a short but full description of a happy state in this world: he that has these two, has little more to wish for; and he that wants either of them, will be but little the better for anything else. Men's happiness or misery is most part of their own making. He whose mind directs not wisely, will never take the right way; and he whose body is crazy and feeble, will never be able to advance in it. I confess there are some men's constitutions of body and mind so vigorous and well framed by nature, that they need not much assistance from others, but by the strength of their natural genius, they are from their cradles carried toward what is excellent; and, by the privilege of their happy constitutions are able to do wonders. But examples of these are but few; and I think I may say that, of all the men we meet with, nine parts of ten are what they are, good or evil, useful or not, by their education. 'Tis that which makes the great difference in mankind. The little, and almost insensible im-

Locke, John, *Some Thoughts Concerning Education,* in Adamson, John William, *The Educational Writings of John Locke,* pp. 25–218, *passim.* Cambridge University Press, London, 1922. Used by permission.

pressions on our tender infancies, have very important and lasting consequences; and there 'tis, as in the fountains of some rivers, where a gentle application of the hand turns the flexible waters into channels, that make them take quite contrary courses; and by this little direction, given them at first in the source, they receive different tendencies, and arrive at last at very remote and distant places.

REVERENCE

When, by making your son sensible that he depends on you, and is in your power, you have established your authority; and by being inflexibly severe in your carriage to him, when obstinately persisting in any ill-natured trick which you have forbidden, especially lying, you have imprinted on his mind that awe which is necessary; and on the other wise, when (by permitting him the full liberty due to his age, and laying no restraint in your presence to those childish actions, and gaiety of carriage, which, whilst he is very young, is as necessary to him as meat or sleep) you have reconciled him to your company, and made him sensible of your care and love of him by indulgence and tenderness, especially caressing him on all occasions wherein he does anything well, and being kind to him after a thousand fashions, suitable to his age, which nature teaches parents better than I can: when, I say, by these ways of tenderness and affection, which parents never want for their children, you have also planted in him a particular affection for you, he is then in the state you could desire, and you have formed in his mind that true reverence, which is always afterward carefully to be increased and maintained in both parts of it, love and fear, as the great principles whereby you will always have hold upon him to turn his mind to the ways of virtue and honor.

Virtue

I place virtue as the first and most necessary of those endowments that belong to a man or a gentleman, as absolutely requisite to make him valued and beloved by others, acceptable or tolerable to himself; without that, I think, he will be happy neither in this nor the other world.

God

As the foundation of this, there ought very early to be imprinted on his mind a true notion of God, as of the independent Supreme Being, Author and Maker of all things, from whom we receive all our good, who loves us, and gives us all things; and, consequent to it, a love and reverence of this Supreme Being. This is enough to begin with, without going to explain this matter any farther, for fear, lest by talking too early to him of spirits, and being unseasonably forward to make him understand the incomprehensible nature of that infinite being, his head be either filled with false, or perplexed with unintelligible notions of him. Let him only be told upon occasion, of God, that made and governs all things, hears and sees everything, and does all manner of good to those that love and obey him. You will find, that being told of such a God, other thoughts will be apt to rise up fast enough in his mind about him; which, as you observe them to have any mistakes, you must set right. And I think it would be better, if men generally rested in such an idea of God, without being too curious in their notions about a being, which all must acknowledge incomprehensible; whereby many, who have not strength and clearness of thought to distinguish between what they can, and what they cannot know, run themselves into superstition or atheism, making God like themselves, or (because they cannot comprehend anything else) none at all. (And I am apt to think the keeping children constantly morning and evening to acts of devotion to God, as to their Maker, Preserver, and Benefactor, in some plain and short form of prayer, suitable to their age and capacity, will be of much more use to them in religion, knowledge, and virtue, than to distract their thoughts with curious inquiries into his inscrutable essence and being.)

SPIRITS

Having by gentle degrees, as you find him capable of it, settled such an idea of God in his mind, and taught him to pray to him, forbear any discourse of other spirits, till the mention of them coming in his way, upon occasion hereafter to be set down, and his reading the Scripture history, put him upon that inquiry.

TRUTH

Having laid the foundations of virtue in a true notion of a God, such as the Creed wisely teaches, as far as his age is capable, and by accustoming him to pray to him, the next thing to be taken care of, is to keep him exactly to speaking of truth, and by all the ways imaginable inclining him to be good-natured. Let him know, that twenty faults are sooner to be forgiven, than the straining of truth to cover any one by an excuse. And to teach him betimes to love and be good-natured to others, is to lay early the true foundation of an honest man; all injustice generally springing from too great love of ourselves and too little of others.

This is all I shall say of this matter in general, and is enough for laying the first foundations of virtue in a child.

As he grows up, the tendency of his natural inclination must be observed; which, as it inclines him, more than is convenient, on one or t'other side, from the right path of virtue, ought to have proper remedies applied. For few of Adam's children are so happy as not to be born with some bias in their natural temper, which it is the business of education either to take off, or counterbalance: but to enter into particulars of this would be beyond the design of this short treatise of education. . . .

WISDOM

Wisdom I take, in the popular acceptation, for a man's managing his business ably and with foresight in this world. This is the product of a good natural temper, application of mind and experience together, and not to be taught children. The greatest thing that in them can be done toward it, is to hinder them, as much as may be, from being cunning; which, being the ape of wisdom, is the most distant from it that can be: and as an ape, for the likeness it has to a man, wanting what really should make him so, is by so much the uglier. Cunning is only the want of understanding; which, because it cannot compass its ends by direct ways, would do it by a trick and circumvention; and the mischief of it is, a cunning trick helps but once, but hinders ever after. No cover was ever made either so big or so fine as to hide itself. Nobody was ever so cunning as to conceal their being so: and when they are once discovered, everybody is shy, everybody distrustful of crafty men; and all the world forwardly join to oppose and defeat them: whilst the open, fair, wise man has everybody to make way for him, and goes directly to his business. To accustom a child to have true notions of things, and not to be satisfied till he has them; to raise his mind to great and worthy thoughts; and to keep him at a distance from falsehood and cunning, which has always a broad mixture of falsehood in it, is the fittest preparation of a child for wisdom, which being learned from time, experience, and observation, and an acquaintance with men, their tempers and designs (is) not to be expected in the ignorance and inadvertency of childhood, or the inconsiderate heat and unwariness of youth: all that can be done toward it, during this unripe age, is, as I have said, to accustom them to truth and submission to reason; and, as much as may be, to reflection on their own actions.

READING

. . . The Lord's Prayer, the Creeds, and Ten Commandments, 'tis necessary he should learn perfectly by heart; but, I think, not by reading them himself in his primer, but by somebody's repeating them to him, even before he can read. But learning by heart, and learning to read, should not, I think, be mixed, and so one made to clog the other. But the learning to read should be made as little trouble or business to him as might be.

What other books there are in English of the kind of those above-mentioned (e.g., Aesop's *Fables* and *Reynard the Fox*), fit to engage the liking of children, and tempt them to read, I do not know; but am apt to think that children, being generally delivered over to the method of schools, where the fear of the rod is to enforce, and not any pleasure of the employment to invite, them to learn; this sort of useful books, amongst the number of silly ones that are of all sorts, have yet had the fate to be neglected; and nothing that I know has been considered of this kind out of the ordinary road of the hornbook, primer, Psalter, Testament, and Bible.

As for the Bible, which children are usually employed in to exercise and improve their talent in reading, I think, the promiscuous reading of it through by chapters as they lie in order, is so far from being of any advantage to children, either for the perfecting their reading or principling their religion, that perhaps a worse could not be found. For what pleasure or encouragement can it be to a child, to exercise himself in reading those parts of a book where he understands nothing? And how little are the Law of Moses, the Song of Solomon, the prophecies in the Old, and the Epistles and Apocalypse in the New Testament, suited to a child's capacity? And though the history of the evangelists and the Acts have something easier; yet, taken all together, it is very disproportionate to the understanding of childhood. I grant, that the principles of religion are to be drawn from thence, and in the words of the Scripture; yet none should be proposed to a child but such as are suited to a child's capacity and notions. But it is far from this to read through the whole Bible, and that for reading's sake. And what an odd jumble of thoughts must a child have in his head, if he have any at all, such as he should have concerning religion, who in his tender age reads all the parts of the Bible indifferently, as the word of God, without any other distinction. I am apt to think that this, in some men, has been the very reason why they never had clear and distinct thoughts of it all their life-time.

And now I am by chance fallen on this subject, give me leave to say, that there are some parts of the Scripture which may be proper to put into the hands of a child to engage him to read; such as are the story of Joseph and his brethren, of David and Goliath, of David and Jonathan, etc., and others, that he should be made to read for his instruction; as that, " What you would have others do unto you, do you the same unto them"; and such other easy and plain moral rules, which, being fitly chosen, might often be made use of, both for reading and instruction together. But this reading of the whole Scripture indifferently is what I think very inconvenient for children, till, after having been made acquainted with the plainest fundamental parts of it, they have got some kind of general view of what they ought principally to believe and practice, which yet, I think, they ought to receive in the very words of the Scripture, and not in such, as men prepossessed by systems and analogies, are apt in this case to make use of, and force upon them. Dr. Worthington (John, Master of Jesus College, Cambridge), to avoid this, has made a Catechism which has all its answers in the precise words of the Scripture, a thing of good example and such a sound form of words, as no Christian can except against as not fit for his child to learn. Of this, as soon as he can say the Lord's Prayer, Creed, and Ten Commandments by heart, it may be fit for him to learn a question every day, or every week, as his understanding is able to receive and his memory to retain them. And when he has this catechism perfectly by heart, so as readily and roundly to answer to any question in the whole book, it may be convenient to lodge in his mind the moral rules, scattered up and down in the Bible, as the best exercise of his memory, and that which may be always a rule to him, ready at hand, in the whole conduct of his life.

Conclusion

Though I am now come to a conclusion of what obvious remarks have suggested to me concerning education, I would not have it thought that I look on it as a just treatise on this subject. There are a thousand other things that may need consideration; especially if one should take in the various tempers, different inclinations, and particular defaults, that are to be found in children; and prescribe proper remedies. The variety is so great, that it would require a volume; nor would that reach it. Each man's mind has some peculiarity, as well as his face, that distinguishes him from all others; and there are possibly scarce two children who can be conducted by exactly the same method. Besides that, I think a prince, a nobleman, and an ordinary gentleman's son, should have different ways of breeding. But having had here only some general views, in reference to the main end and aims in education, and those designed for a gentleman's son, who being then very little, I considered only as white paper, or wax, to be molded and fashioned as one pleases, I have touched little more than those heads, which I judged necessary for the breeding of a young gentleman of his condition in general; and have now published these my occasional thoughts, with this hope, that, though this be far from being a complete treatise on this subject, or such as that everyone may find what will just fit his child in it; yet it may give some small light to those, whose concern for their dear little ones makes them so irregularly bold, that they dare venture to consult their own reason, in the education of their children, rather than wholly to rely upon old custom.

21

JEAN BAPTISTE DE LA SALLE
(1651–1719)

Jean Baptiste de la Salle was born in Reims into a devout Roman Catholic family, two of his brothers becoming priests in addition to himself, and a sister becoming a nun. He was enrolled in the Collège des Bon Enfants in his home city, and had determined by the age of eleven to become a priest. He took his baccalaureate and advanced degrees at the University of Reims, also studying theology at the Sorbonne in Paris. He spent some years establishing the Congregation of the Sisters of the Holy Child Jesus, the foundations for which had been laid by his spiritual director, Nicolas Roland. Troubled over the fact that most of the children in the large cities were not receiving an adequate elementary education, de la Salle and colleagues (clerical and lay) sought to provide free schools for the children. The result was the Institute of the Brothers of the Christian Schools. De la Salle later went to Paris, where schools were established even in face of great opposition from the operators of tuition schools, who feared that the coming of free schools would deprive them of pupils. He also directed the development of a school for the training of teachers and a " Christian Academy," in which ambitious boys were given instruction on Sundays in geometry, architecture, drawing, and similar fields.

In The Conduct of the Schools *de la Salle drew up a uniform plan for the use of all the schools of the Brothers. When published in 1720 its provisions were immediately adopted. In the preceding year its author had died at St. Yon, near Rouen, where he had opened a home for the Brothers and a boarding school for practical vocational training.*

These detailed instructions for the teacher's procedures in the classroom as recommended by de la Salle were rather characteristic of pedagogical method in his century and for a long time afterward until the advent of the more informal educational procedures advocated by men like Pestalozzi and Froebel. Readers will notice the teacher-centered situation, aimed at imparting perfect knowledge of the matter of the Catechism being presented in the class.

At his death de la Salle left a work entitled Explication de la méthode d'oraison. *For a fascinating story of his career and pedagogical theories, see F. de la Fontainerie's introduction to* The Conduct of the Schools of Jean-Baptiste de la Salle (*McGraw-Hill Book Co., Inc., 1935*), *pp. 1–41.*

JEAN BAPTISTE DE LA SALLE . . .

The Conduct of the Schools

Manner of Asking Questions on the Catechism

The teacher will not speak to the pupils during Catechism as though he were preaching, but he will ask them almost continuously questions and subquestions. In order to make them understand what he is teaching them, he will ask several pupils, one after another, the same question. Sometimes he will ask it of seven or eight (or even of ten or twelve, and sometimes even of a greater number). He will question the pupils according to the order of the benches. If, however, he remarks that several, one after another, cannot answer the question or do not do so well, he may call upon one or several out of the regular order and in different parts of the class. Then, after having struck the signal once, he will make a sign to one to answer; and after one or several have answered, he will make the one answer upon whom he had called before in the regular order. He will question all his pupils each day — several times, even if he is able to do so. However, from time to

De la Salle, Jean Baptiste, *The Conduct of the Schools*, tr. by F. de la Fontainerie, pp. 129–135, from Chapter IX, "The Catechism." McGraw-Hill Book Co., Inc., 1935. Used by permission.

time he will interrupt the regular order and the sequence to question those whom he has observed to be inattentive, or even the more ignorant. He will be especially careful to question, and much more often than the others, those whose minds are slow and dull and who have difficulty in remembering, particularly on the abridgment of Christian doctrine, and even more so on those questions in it which every Christian is obliged to know.

. . . In his questions, he will make use of only the simplest expressions and words which are very easily understood and which need no explanation, if this is possible, and he will make his questions as short as he can.

He will never permit an answer to be given word by word, but will require that the entire answers be given in sequence. If it should happen that some little child or some ignorant one is unable to give an entire answer, he will divide the question in such a way that the pupil may give in three answers what he had not been able to give in one.

If it ever happens that some pupil has so slow a mind that he cannot repeat properly an answer that several others have given one after another, in order to make him retain it, the teacher will have it repeated four or five times alternately by a pupil who knows it well and by the one who does not know it, so as to afford him a greater facility for learning it.

Duties of the Teacher During Catechism

One of the principal tasks of the teacher during Catechism is to conduct the lessons in such a manner that all the pupils will be very attentive and may easily retain all he says to them. To this effect, he will always keep all his pupils in sight and will observe everything they do. He will take care to talk very little and to ask a great many questions.

He will speak only on the subject assigned for the day, and he will guard himself against departing from his subject. He will always speak in a serious manner, such as will inspire the pupils with respect and restraint, and he will never say anything that might cause laughter. He will be careful not to speak in an indolent manner which could produce weariness. He will not fail to indicate in every lesson some practices to the pupils, and to instruct them as thoroughly as it is possible for him to do concerning those things which pertain to morals and to conduct which should be observed in order to live as a true Christian. But he will reduce these practices and these matters of morals to questions and answers, which will make the pupils very much more attentive and make them retain them more easily. He will take care not to disturb the Catechism lesson by untimely reprimands and corrections; and if it happens that some pupils deserve punishment, he will postpone it ordinarily until the next day, just before the Catechism, without letting them know it. He may, however, sometimes, but rarely, when he considers it unavoidable, give a few blows of the ferule during this time.

On Sundays and holy days, when the Catechism lasts three times as long as on the other days, he will always choose some story that the pupils will enjoy and tell it to them in a way that will please them and renew their attention. He will tell it with details that will prevent them from being bored. He will say nothing during the Catechism lessons that he has not read in some well-approved book and of which he is not very certain; he will never decide whether a sin is venial or mortal.

He may only say, when he judges such to be the case:

" That will offend God very much." " It is a sin very much
to be feared." " It is a sin that has evil consequences." " It
is a grievous sin." Although sins should not be considered
more grievous than they are, it is, however, more dangerous to make them appear slight and trifling. A great horror of sins, however slight they may appear, must always
be inspired; an offense against God cannot be slight, and
nothing that concerns him can be trifling.

He will take care that the questions, the subquestions,
and the answers to the subquestions fulfill the following
four conditions: 1. They must be short. 2. They must
make complete sense. 3. They must be accurate. 4. The
answers must not be suited to the capacity of the most
able and most intelligent pupils, but to that of the average
ones, so that the majority may be able to answer the questions that are asked them.

The teachers will be so careful of the instruction of all
their pupils that they will not leave a single one in ignorance, at least of those things which a Christian is obliged
to know, in reference both to doctrine and to practice.
In order not to neglect a matter of such great importance,
they should often consider attentively that they will render account to God and that they will be guilty in his sight
of the ignorance of the children who have been under
their care and of the sins into which this ignorance has led
them, if they who have been in charge of them have not
applied themselves with sufficient care to deliver them
from their ignorance, and that there will be nothing on
which God will examine them, and by which he will
judge them, more severely than on this point.

The teachers will help the pupils to acquire a perfect
application to the Catechism. This is not naturally easy
for them and is ordinarily of very short duration. For this

purpose, they will employ the following means: 1. They will take care not to rebuff or to confuse them, either by words or in any other manner, when they are unable to answer properly the question which has been asked of them. 2. They will encourage and even help them to say what they have difficulty in recalling. 3. They will offer rewards, which they will give from time to time to those who have been the best behaved and the most attentive — sometimes even to the more ignorant who have made the greatest effort to learn well. They will employ various other similar means, which prudence and charity will enable them to find, to encourage the pupils to learn the Catechism more readily and to retain it more easily.

DUTIES OF THE PUPILS DURING CATECHISM

During the time when the Catechism is being taught, the pupils will be seated, their bodies erect, their faces and eyes turned toward the teacher, their arms crossed, and their feet in order. The teacher will make a sign with his signal to the first whom he wishes to question. The latter, before answering, will rise and uncover, then make the sign of the cross, removing his gloves if he is wearing them, and, having crossed his arms, will answer the questions which have been asked him in such a manner that, by including the question, the answer will make complete sense.

When the first pupil has almost finished his answer, the one who comes next will rise, make the sign of the cross, saying the words in a tone low enough not to interrupt the one who is reciting, taking care to have made the sign of the cross by the time the other one is finished, and repeat the same answer, unless the teacher should ask him another question. All the others who follow on the same bench or on the next bench will do the same.

If the teacher should happen to call upon one or several pupils in succession out of the regular order, he whose turn it is to answer will remain standing during this time, until he is notified to speak. He will also remain standing if the other says something by way of explanation, and will answer as soon as the latter has finished speaking. A pupil, when answering during Catechism, will keep his eyes modestly lowered and will not stare fixedly at the teacher nor yet turn his head slightly to one side. He will keep his body erect and both feet properly placed on the floor. He will speak in a moderate tone but rather low than loud, so that, if possible, he will not be heard by the other classes and the other pupils will be more attentive. He will, above all, speak very slowly and distinctly, so that not only the words but also all the syllables may be heard. The teacher will see that he pronounces them all, particularly the last ones.

All the pupils will be very attentive during the entire Catechism lesson. The teacher will take care that they do not cross their legs and that they do not put their hands under their garments, in order that they may not do the least thing contrary to good behavior. He will not permit any pupil to laugh when another has not answered properly or any one of them to prompt another who is unable to answer a question. He will take care that the pupils go out of the room the least possible number of times during Catechism and only in case of great necessity.

22

AUGUST HERMANN FRANCKE
(1663–1727)

Francke was born at Lübeck, Germany, and died at Halle, a city with which his name is indissolubly linked. He belonged to the pietistic sect of Lutherans who put a strong emphasis on personal religious living and ascetic discipline. He served as pastor in Glaucha, suburban to Halle (Prussia) and as professor of divinity in the new University of Halle. In 1695 he received a donation of a small amount of money which inspired him to establish a charity school. Friends and admirers contributed to his cause, with the result that by 1714 a whole series of elementary, secondary, and normal training schools had been founded. Religion was the core of the curriculum in these schools. Vocational courses were combined with catechetical and Biblical instruction. He also stressed scientific study. Only a minimal emphasis was retained from the earlier classical instruction. At Halle there were established also an orphans' home and a printing plant. These were known collectively as the Francke Institutions. The basic work on Francke's life is A. Otto, August Hermann Francke, 2 vols. (Verlag des Waisenhauses, Halle, 1902– 1904). *Francke's work was entitled* Pietas Hallensis.

The beginning of a humane concern for the teaching process and for the pupil as a person is reflected in these selections.

AUGUST HERMANN FRANCKE . . .

Thoughts on Teaching

Thoughts on Teaching

Especially must a teacher be careful that his pupils should not notice anything wicked in him. For children notice everything, whether good or bad. . . . Children who see their teachers or fathers drunk, angry, or unchaste and hear them swear and slander and observe through their example the vanity of the world and the pleasures of the flesh and luxurious life will thereafter not easily be brought to a fundamental hatred for these vices.

You should not be sullen, angry, boring, or impatient but must show yourself always full of love and friendliness toward the children, so that you will win their love, upon which so much depends. However, an understanding teacher will see to it that no unrestrained familiarity develops.

It generally happens that most teachers out of lack of adequate experience and love try to compel goodness

Otto, A., *August Hermann Francke*, Verlag des Waisenhauses, 2 vols., 1902, 1904. Tr. in Cole, Luella, *A History of Education:* Socrates to Montessori, pp. 389–394, *passim*. Rinehart & Company, Inc., 1950. Used by permission.

through sharp external punishment rather than to enfold those entrusted to their care in a spirit of love and to bring their hearts to goodness with fatherly loyalty, patience, and foresight.

Whoever has such paternal affection . . . will not neglect admonition and punishment; however, in so far as is possible he will not disrupt education by use of physical force and harshness, nor give in in the least to the feeling of anger, but with all kindness and sweetness he will plant in their hearts a childish fear of God and a love toward God and Christ. With friendliness a teacher makes more progress than with everlasting scolding and beating. . . .

No child should be scolded or punished because he is slow to learn. . . . The teacher should not become impatient and angry if a child, because of limited ability, cannot immediately grasp something, but he should in gentleness and patience that much the more diligently teach. . . . Profane words and ridicule are absolutely not to be used to the children, since they are more hurt than helped thereby. A teacher may not call them, out of impatience, oxen, asses, pigs, dogs, beasts, fools, scoundrels, swineherds, and so on, and still less children of the devil. One shall not swear at them or wish them evil. . . .

No child is to be struck on the head with the hand, with a stick, a ruler, or a book. Still less may one box a child's ears . . . because the children do not profit thereby and much harm may be done to both their spirit and their health. No child should be pulled hither by the arms, yanked by the hair, nor flicked with the stick on the hands or fingers. . . .

In all punishment one must consider the individuality of the child. A teacher should take care to learn the disposition of his children, so that he will not discipline the shy and sensitive spirits as he does the hardened and impudent children; for more children can be won with words than with blows.

You should not give children books that are too long, but those that are as short as possible; for in this way they do not lose their interest so easily, if they soon come to the end and can begin something new. Education must be carried on in the mother tongue; otherwise unrest easily arises and the children pay more attention to the words than to the meaning.

Love of truth can be instilled if (1) you will teach children that all lies are frightful sins and the main characteristic of Satan, who was a liar from the beginning . . . ; (2) if you take care that children do not listen to fairy stories or other tales from old women or from the domestic help, through which the children become accustomed to lie busily; (3) if the children do not observe that their parents consider the so-called "white" lies only minor offenses; (4) if you do not awaken in a child a love for comedies, jokes, novels, or love stories, political nonsense, or other foolishness; (5) if you watch carefully over children's talk and do not let the tiniest lie go unpunished; (6) if you do not repeat children's lies and laugh over them, since the children are likely to hear and to be strengthened in their wickedness.

PLAN OF TEACHING

(For the teacher's time. While certain children are being taught, the others are presumably studying, writing, or reading.)

Hours	*Weekdays*	*Sunday*
7–8	Song, prayer, and reading from the Bible; repetition of the Catechism	Attendance at the morning service in church
8–9	½ hour reading of Biblical selections; ½ hour catechism with the older pupils	
9–10	½ hour explaining quotations and proverbs to the younger children; ½ hour study of psalms and the New Testament by the older children	
10–11	Writing hour	
2–3	Prayer and Bible-reading. Reading, music, and reading for the smaller children, on different days	Attendance at the afternoon service in church
3–4	½ hour reading by the younger and study of quotations and sayings by the older pupils; ½ hour recitation of the sayings, while the little children listen	
4–5	Catechism	
5–6	Evening prayers in the church.	

23

COTTON MATHER

(1663–1728)

The first American to appear in our collection was born in Boston, where he lived all his life. After taking A.B. and A.M. degrees at Harvard College, he became minister of the Second Church in Boston in 1685, serving there for the entire span of his ministry, and becoming one of the acknowledged great leaders of Congregationalism. He was sympathetic to the local political aspirations of the colony and took part in opposition to the British governor, Sir Edmund Andros, in 1688–1689. His father, Increase Mather, had been president of Harvard, and it is said that Cotton Mather also aspired to that office, though it was never offered him. Instead, he turned his interests to Yale, which he hoped would be a more diligent defender of orthodoxy than Harvard had become.

Internationally recognized for scholarly attainments, Mather was elected to membership in the Royal Society of London in 1713, and was granted an honorary degree by Aberdeen University in 1710. He was in many ways very conservative, as in his belief in diabolic possession (witchcraft). At the same time he was generous in his views, as when in 1718 he helped ordain a Baptist minister. Married three times, he was survived by only two of his fifteen children.

The name of Mather has not usually been associated with Christian education so much as with history and theology. It is therefore all the more refreshing to go through his pamphlets and to discover that he was deeply concerned also with questions of Christian nurture. A Brief Essay to Direct and Excite Family Religion *shows a profound concern for what in recent decades has been re-emphasized as " family life education." One notes how Mather anticipated some of the now " advanced " methods of adult and family education, such as meetings in homes for discussion.*

Mather's Magnalia Christi Americana, *a collection of historical materials on the church history of New England, is an important document. The Congregational Library in Boston has many tracts and pamphlets by Mather, many of which, in addition to the one used here, deserve more thorough attention than they have yet received from students of the history of Christian education.*

COTTON MATHER . . .

A Brief Essay to Direct and Excite Family Religion

That a family should have a sacrifice: We will, by a few proper steps, advance to those proposals, which we have now to make, for the welfare of the families in our neighborhood.

I. Every society, and therefore every family, does owe religious acknowledgments unto that God, whom all men are to acknowledge in all their ways. No man questions, whether it be the duty of every man to glorify his Maker with religious acknowledgments of his glories. . . .

II. A family cannot, nor can any other society, duly acknowledge the blessed God without a sacrifice. The religion of the world, from the very beginning of the world, that is to say, ever since there was any sin in the world, hath had a sacrifice attending of it. Sacrifices were undoubtedly at first an institution of God. We cannot imagine that they should have been accepted by God, if they had

---

Mather, Cotton, *A Brief Essay to Direct and Excite Family Religion; and Produce the Sacrifices of Righteousness in Our Families.* Boston, printed by B. Green and J. Allen; sold by B. Eliot, 1703. The editor has modernized the spelling from the original work.

not been appointed by him; and it was immediately after the Fall of man, that God gave order for them. . . .

Accordingly, there is but one propitiatory sacrifice, with which a family can acknowledge the blessed God; and that is, the sacrifice of our Lord Jesus Christ. There was an eternal covenant of redemption made between God and our Lord-Messiah. . . . A faith in a sacrificed Messiah is to be one ingredient in all our acknowledgments of God. A family which does not appear before God, with that sacrifice, and acknowledge the power, and wisdom, and justice, and goodness of God, with faith in the sacrifice of the Lord Jesus Christ, is a very miserable family.

But then there is an eucharistical sacrifice in every religious exercise performed by a family. After having first considered the Lord Jesus Christ as the sacrifice, by which the favor of God and the pardon of sin is procured, a family must proceed then unto a sacrifice of thanksgiving to the Lord. When we present ourselves unto God, with our obedient respects, unto his holy and just and good commandments, we do ourselves become unto him a sacrifice of thanksgiving. . . .

I have now laid in sufficient preliminaries, whereupon we may pass to discourse on our important and intended case. What is to be done by a Christian householder, that so his family may have a sacrifice?

I. A Christian householder must ascribe unto the sacrifice of the Lord Jesus Christ, all the blessings of his family; all the comforts which his family should be or hath been blessed withal. . . .

II. You doubtless foresaw, that I could not long forbear the point, which now even ere we are aware, we are fallen into; a point, which indeed were a boundless ocean, if it were to be fully prosecuted. Prayer, prayer, even family

prayer, is the family sacrifice, which every Christian householder should and will offer with his family, and this no
less than twice every day. A family that has no prayer is
most certainly a family that has no sacrifice. . . .

III. The Scriptures of God are to be read, with our prayers to God, in our families; and so read, as to make an
edifying part of our family sacrifice. . . . When we are
going to prayer with our families, there is ordinarily a call
from heaven unto us, like what was given unto Augustine:
" Take up and read! Take up and read! " Don't I want wisdom? Here is the word that will make me wise unto salvation. Would not I be directed in the path of light? Here
is the light. Would not I have myself discovered unto myself? Here is the glass. Would not I have my mind nour-
ished with everlasting truth? Here is my food. Would I
not have my soul healed of all its distempers? Here is my
medicine. Would not I be assisted against the enemies of
my salvation? Here is my armory. Don't I want spiritual
blessings for my family? Here is the blessed storehouse
of them. Think thus, and read unto thy family, the letter
which comes from the glorious king of heaven unto them.
Read, with all the reverence imaginable; such a letter
should not be rudely handled.

IV. But there is another pleasant and charming stroke
sometimes to belong unto our family sacrifice: Awake,
awake, O Christian householder, awake, awake, and utter
a song. The singing of psalms is intended. . . .

V. Family instruction is a notable family sacrifice; a
Christian householder must carefully instruct his family
in the things of God. Yea, the great God says of such a man,
Gen. 18:19, " I know him, that he will command his children and his household after him, and they shall keep
the way of the Lord." In a family sacrifice under the Law,

there was part of it burnt unto the Lord, but part of it
eaten by the folks in the family. Truly, in feeding a family
with the truths of God, while we at the same time adore
the great God in our hearty owning of those truths, we
have a family sacrifice. We have a family sacrifice, yea,
we make our family itself become a most happy sacrifice
when by our good instruction, our houses become like that
of the martyr Hooper, of whom 'tis recorded that in every
corner of his house there was a savor of godliness; and like
that of the martyr Cranmer, of whom 'tis recorded, that his
house was a very school of godliness. It is recorded of
Constantine the Great, one of the greatest men that ever
lived on the face of the earth, in every room of his house
the name of Jesus Christ was written in observable capitals.
Oh! happy sacrifice in a family, if the people in every room
of the house might come to know, and love, and seek the
Lord Jesus Christ, our great Sacrifice. As a family sacrifice,
then, O Christian householder, endeavor to catechize thy
children and servants. But then let it not suffice to have
them recite the words of the Catechism like parrots without some clear apprehension and understanding of them.
Endeavor to make them apprehend the meaning of what
they say; and therefore distinctly divide and apply their
answers, and, if you can, win their young hearts to comply
with the duty to be inferred from the answer. As now,
when they say, " God made me, he keeps me, and he can
save me," do you whet it over again upon them. Ask,
" Who is it that made you and all the world? " And, " Why
did he make you? Was it that you might serve him? " And,
" Is it your desire that he would make you willing and able
to do so? " . . .

Christian, while thou art thus endeavoring to shape thy

little folks, that even they themselves may be a sacrifice of praise unto God, who can tell but the spirit of God may fall down with an holy fire from heaven upon the sacrifice, and cause the hearts of the little folks to burn within them? Yea, we are to take frequent opportunities for conferring with our families about the things of their everlasting peace. We should frequently be instilling into them the knowledge of those things, which to know is life eternal. We should frequently lay our charge upon them, to pray by themselves, and shun evil company, and give themselves up to God in the Lord Jesus Christ, and wisely to consider their latter end. It may be, you will find this the best way to repeating the public sermons to your little folks; put every stroke of the public sermons, as far as you judge proper, into a conference with them; and expect at least an intelligent Yes or No, an acknowledgment of the truth which will sanctify them, upon every stroke. Every such conference will be a lovely sacrifice.

VI. A Christian householder should banish every profane and unclean thing out of his family; and allow nothing there that may pollute the family sacrifice. The profane and unclean were of old chased from the sacrifices. We should be desirous that our families may not be filled with profane and unclean persons, of whom it may be said, their sacrifices are an abomination to God; and, our sacrifices will be abominable to them. That our family sacrifice to heaven may not be prejudiced, let our families be as like heaven as they can; heaven, I say, whereunto there enters nothing that may defile it. . . .

VII. A Christian householder should with a suitable behavior answer the various dealings of God with his family, as he finds his family either favored or afflicted of the Lord. A family sacrifice of old was to acknowledge God, in his various dispensations toward the family; so it should still be so.

VIII. I would make a proposal, for family meetings, to be so managed and ordered among us, that they may prove serviceable sacrifices in our families. It hath been a laudable custom, in many places, for a dozen families in a vicinity to combine into a design of meeting at each other's houses, at fit seasons, to spend an hour together, in prayers and psalms, and repetition of sermons, and religious conferences about the things of God. It would be a real service to religion, yea, and unto themselves also, if the pastors of our churches would animate and encourage such family meetings among their well-disposed people. We may see religion prosper or wither in our churches very much according to the encouragement given unto these exercises of piety among the neighbors; and unto their frequent coming together for the sacrifices of the gospel. Give me leave to commend unto the Christians which may compose these family meetings, that good management which may still make their coming together to be for the better and not for the worse. Wherefore, sirs, as you will uphold the exercises of piety at your meetings, I hope you will study very particularly to be blessings to one another in courtesy and condescension upon all occasions, and everyone of you will please his neighbor to his good for edification; but also make it a one special intention of your supplications to obtain the blessings of God upon the families where you are entertained. This will render you great blessings to one another; and lay it as a law upon yourselves, both to cover one another's infirmities, and to give lovingly and to take lovingly, all the admonitions for which you may see occasions in one another's infirmities. And so it will for you to agree upon giving to each other all the charitable succors, reliefs, and assistances you can, and bear one another's burdens, in whatever distresses the providence of God may bring upon any of your families. . . . Christians, there would be fat sacrifices to heaven in and from your families if such exercises of piety were carried on among them! Consider what I say, and the Lord give you understanding for all such things as these.

24

ISAAC WATTS

(1674–1748)

The Congregational hymn writer, Isaac Watts, known to most churchgoers chiefly for his well-known hymns such as " O God, Our Help in Ages Past," *was born at Southampton, England, into a family of religious Independents. He attended the Nonconformist Academy at Stoke Newington, London. Later, he became a tutor in the family of Sir John Hartopp. At the age of twenty-four he became assistant pastor of the Independent congregation of Mark Lane, London, assuming the full pastorate two years later.*

Watts's writings are of three types. His theological interests were expressed in such writings as Doctrine of the Trinity (1722) *and* Essay on the Freedom of the Will (1732). *His educational concerns were shown in* Logick; or the Right Use of Reason in the Enquiry After Truth (1725) *and* The Knowledge of the Heavens and the Earth Made Easy; or the First Principles of Geography and Astronomy Explained (1726). *His hymnody produced* Horae Lyricae (1706), Hymns (1709), The Psalms of David (1719), *and* Divine and Moral Songs for Children (1720). *His* Posthumous Works *were published in two collections, 1773 and 1779.*

Watts's tract on Christian Discipline; or the Character of a Polite Young Gentleman *is reminiscent of Ulrich*

Zwingli's piece in Chapter 14. It is, however, definitely characteristic of a type of writing that was very popular in the eighteenth and nineteenth centuries, both in Great Britain and the United States: heavily moralistic, didactic, and with a strong emphasis on personal piety and religious experience.

ISAAC WATTS . . .

Christian Discipline: or the Character of a Polite Young Gentleman

Eugenio is just out of his minority, and in the twenty-second year of his age he practices the man with all that virtue and decency that makes his father's acquaintance covet his company; and indeed they may learn by his discourse the art of good reasoning, as well as the precepts of piety from his example. He is an entertaining companion to the gay young gentlemen his equals; and yet divines and philosophers take a pleasure to have Eugenio amongst them. He is caressed by his superiors in honor and years; and though he is released from the discipline of parental education, yet he treats the lady, his mother, with all that affectionate duty that could be desired or demanded of him ten years ago. His father is content to see his own youth outshined by his son, and confesses that Eugenio already promises greater things than Agathus did at thirty.

If you ask whence these happy qualities arise, I grant

Watts, Isaac, *Christian Discipline: or the Character of a Polite Young Gentleman;* by which the proper degrees of liberty and restraint, in the education of a son, are beautifully illustrated in the examples of Agathus and Eugenio. Boston, Reprinted by Benjamin Mecom, n.d.

there was some foundation for them in the very make of his nature; there was something of a complexional virtue mingled with his frame; but it is much more owing to the wise conduct of his parents from his very infancy, and the blessing of divine grace attending their labors, their prayers, and their hopes.

He was trained up from the very cradle to all the duties of infant virtue, by the allurements of love and reward, suited to his age; and never was driven to practice anything by a frown or a hasty word, where it was possible for kinder affections to work the same effect by indulgence and delay.

As fast as his reasoning powers began to appear and exert themselves, they were conducted in an easy track of thought, to find out and observe the reasonableness of every part of his duty, and the lovely character of a child obedient to reason and to his parents' will; while every departure from duty was shown to be so contrary to reason, as laid an early foundation for conscience to work upon. Conscience began here to assume its office, and to manifest its authority in dictates, and reproofs, and reflections of mind, peaceful or painful, according to his behavior. When his parents observed this inward monitor to awake in his soul, they could better trust him out of their sight.

When he became capable of conceiving of an almighty and invisible Being who made this world and every creature in it, he was taught to pay all due regards to this God his maker; and from the authority and love of his father on earth, he was led to form right ideas (as far as childhood permitted) of the power, government, and goodness of all in heaven.

He was informed why punishment was due to an offense against God or his parents, that his fear might become a useful passion to awaken and guard his virtue; but he was instructed, at the same time, that where he heartily repented of a fault, and returned to his duty with new diligence, there was forgiveness to be obtained both of God and man.

When at any time a friend interceded for him to his father, after he had been guilty of a fault, he was hereby directed into the doctrine of Jesus, the mediator between God and man; and thus he knew him as an intercessor, before he could well understand the notion of his sacrifice and atonement.

In his younger years he passed but twice under the correction of the rod: once for a fit of obstinacy and persisting in a falsehood. Then he was given up to severe chastisement, and it dispelled and cured the sullen humor forever; and once for the contempt of his mother's authority he endured the scourge again, and he wanted it no more.

He was enticed sometimes to the love of letters, by making his lesson a reward of some domestic duty; and a permission to pursue some parts of learning was the appointed recompense of his diligence and improvement in others.

There was nothing required of his memory but what was first (as far as possible) let into his understanding. And by proper images and representations, suited to his years, he was taught to form some conception of the things described, before he was bid to learn the words by heart. Thus he was freed from the danger of treasuring up the cant and jargon of mere names, instead of the riches of solid knowledge.

Where any abstruse and difficult notions occurred in his course of learning, his preceptor postponed them till he had gone through that subject in a more superficial way. For this purpose he passed twice through all the sciences; and to make the doctrines of Christianity easy to him in his childhood, he had two or three Catechisms composed by his tutor, each of them suited to his more early or more improved capacity, till at twelve years old he was thought fit to learn that public form, which is more universally taught and approved.

As he was inured to reasoning from his childhood, so he was instructed to prove everything, according to the nature of the subject, as far as his years would admit. And thus he drew much of his early knowledge from reason or from revelation by the force of his judgment, and not merely from his teachers by the strength of his memory.

His parents were persuaded indeed that they ought to teach him the principles of virtue while he was a child, and the most important truths of religion both natural and revealed, before he was capable of deriving them from the fund of his own reason, or of framing a religion for himself out of so large a book as the Bible. They thought themselves under the obligation of that divine command, " Train up a child in the way he should go, and when he is old he will not depart from it " (Prov. 22:6). And therefore from a child they made him acquainted with the Holy Scriptures, and persuaded him to believe that they were given by the inspiration of God, before it was possible for him to take in the arguments from reason, history, tradition, etc., which must be joined together to confirm the sacred canon, and prove the several books of the Bible to be divine. Thus like Timothy he " continued in the things which he had learned and had been assured of, knowing of whom he had learned them " (II Tim. 3:14-16). Yet as his years advanced, they thought it requisite to show him the solid and rational foundations of his faith, that his hope might be built upon the authority of God and not of men.

Thus the apostles and prophets were made his early companions; and being instructed in the proofs of the Christian religion, and the divine Original of his Bible, he pays a more constant and sacred regard to it, since his judgment and reason assure him that it is the word of God, than when he was a child, and believed it because his mother told him so. He reads the Scriptures daily now, not like the lessons of his infancy, but as the infallible rule of his faith and practice; he searches them every day in his closet, not to confirm any articles and doctrines that he is resolved to believe, but (as the noble Bereans did) to examine and try whether those doctrines and articles ought to be believed or no, which he was taught in the nursery.

After he arrived at fifteen he was suffered to admit nothing into his full assent till his mind saw the rational evidence of the proposition itself; or at least till he felt the power of those reasons which obliged him to assent upon moral evidence and testimony where the evidences of sense or of reason were not to be expected. He knew that he was not to hope for mathematical proofs that there is a pope at Rome, that the Turks have dominion over Judea, that St. Paul wrote an epistle to the Romans, that Christ was crucified without the gates of Jerusalem, and that in three days time he rose from the dead; and yet that there is just and reasonable evidence to enforce and support the belief of all these. Where truths were too sublime for present comprehension, he would never admit them as a part of his faith till he saw full evidence of a speaking God and a divine revelation.

His tutor never imposed anything upon him with a

magisterial air, but by way of advice recommended to him such studies and such methods of improvement, as his experience had long approved; he gave frequent hints of the danger of some opinions, and the fatal consequences of some modish and mistaken principles. He let him know generally what sentiments he himself embraced among the divided opinions of the age, and what clear and comprehensive knowledge, what satisfaction of judgment, serenity of mind, and peace of conscience were to be found in the principles which he had chosen; but he exhorted his pupil still to choose wisely for himself, and led him onward in the sciences, and in common and sacred affairs, to frame his own sentiments by just rules of reasoning. Though Eugenio did not superstitiously confine his belief to the opinions of his instructor, yet he could not but love the man that indulged him such a liberty of thought, and gave him such an admirable clue by which he let himself into the secrets of knowledge, human and divine. Thus under the happy and insensible influences of so prudent a supervisor, he traced the paths of learning, and enjoyed the unspeakable pleasure of being his own teacher, and of framing his opinions himself. By this means he began early to use his reason with freedom, and to judge for himself without a servile submission to the authority of others; and yet to pay a just and solemn deference to persons of age and experience, and particularly to those who were the proper and appointed guides of his youth, and who led him on so gently in the paths of knowledge.

He loves to call himself by the honorable name of Christian, and though his particular sentiments approach much nearer to the opinions of some parties than to others, yet he likes not to be called by the name of any party; for he is wise and bold enough to be a bigot to none. He practices a noble and extensive charity to those that, in lesser matters, differ widely from him, if they do but maintain the most essential and necessary parts of Christianity; nor does he seclude them from his communion, nor withhold himself from theirs; but as the providence of God gives him just occasions, he eats and drinks with them at the table of their common Lord, provided always that they impose nothing upon his practice contrary to his conscience.

Yet his charity has its limits, too: for he hardly knows how to worship the Son of God in the most solemn ordinance of Communion with those that esteem him but a mere man; nor can he join with an assembly of professed Socinians to commemorate the death of Christ who deny it to be a proper atonement for the sins of men.

He dares to believe the doctrines of original sin, the satisfaction of Christ, the influence of the blessed Spirit, and other despised truths of the gospel; and this not because his ancestors believed them, but because he cannot avoid the evidence of them in Scripture. And if in some few points of less importance he takes leave to differ from the sentiments of his elders, it is with such a becoming modesty that convinces his father how unwilling he is to dissent from him; and yet he maintains his opinion with such an appearance of argument, and such an honest concern for truth and piety that makes it plain to his friends that he is under the strong constraint of an inward conviction. Thus, though he has perhaps some new apprehensions of things, yet he is by no means led into them by licentious humor of opposing his teachers, nor a wanton pride of freethinking.

He was not kept a stranger to the errors and follies of mankind, nor was he let loose amongst them, either in books or in company, without a guard and a guide. His preceptor let him know the gross mistakes and iniquities of men, ancient and modern, but inlaid him with proper principles of truth and virtue, and furnished him with such rules of judgment as led him more easily to distinguish between good and bad. And thus he was secured against the infection and the poison, both of the living and the dead.

He had early caution given him to avoid the bantering tribe of mortals, and was instructed to distinguish a jest from an argument, so that a loud laugh at his religion never puts him nor his faith out of countenance. He is ever ready to tender a reason of his Christian hope, and to defend his creed; but he scorns to enter the lists with such a disputant that has no artillery but squib and flash, no arguments besides grimace and ridicule. Thus he supports the character of a Christian with honor. He confines his faith to his Bible, and his practice to all the rules of piety; and yet thinks as freely as that vain herd of atheists and deists that arrogate the name of " Freethinkers " to themselves.

You will inquire, perhaps, how he came to attain so manly a conduct in life at so early an age, and how every thing of the boy was worn off so soon. Truly, besides other influences, it is much owing to the happy management of Eraste (that was the name of the lady, his mother). She was frequent in the nursery, and inspired sentiments in his childhood becoming riper years. When there was company in the parlor, with whom he could use such a freedom, she brought her son in among them, not to entertain them with his own noise and tattle from impertinence, but to hear their discourse, and sometimes to answer a little question or two they might ask him. When he was grown up to a youth, he was often admitted to a room with his father's acquaintance, and was indulged the liberty to ask and enquire on subjects that seemed to be able his years. He was encouraged to speak a sentence or two of his own thoughts, and thus to learn and practice a modest assurance. But when the company was gone, he was approved and praised, if he behaved well, or received kind hints of admonition that he might know when he had been too silent, and when too forward to speak. Thus by enjoying the advantage of society above the level of his own age and understanding, he was always aspiring to imitation; and the excesses and defects of his conduct were daily noticed and cured.

His curiosity was gratified abroad with new sights and scenes as often as his parents could do it with convenience, that he might not stare and wonder at every strange object or occurrence; but he was made patient of restraint and disappointment when he seemed to indulge in excessive desire of any needless diversion. If he saw any criminal pleasures or diversions attended with great danger and inconvenience, the pursuit of them was absolutely forbidden; but it was done in so kind a manner as made the guilt or peril of them appear in the strongest light, and thereby they were rendered hateful or formidable, rather than the objects of wish or desire.

Some of the wild young gentlemen of the age may happen to laugh at him for being so much a boy still, and for showing such subjection to the old folks (as they call them). With a scornful smile they bid him, " break off his leading strings, and cast away his yokes of bondage." But for the most part he observes, that the same persons shake off all yokes at once, and at once break the bonds of nature, duty, and religion. They pay but little regard to their superior in heaven, any more than to those on earth, and have forgot God and their parents together. " Nor will I ever be moved," says he, " with the reproaches of those who make a jest of things sacred as well as civil, and treat their mother and their Maker with the same contempt."

PART IV

The Eighteenth Century and Beyond

25

JOHANN HEINRICH PESTALOZZI
(1746–1827)

Pestalozzi was born at Zurich and died at Brig. This Swiss educational reformer began his personal educational career by studying theology and jurisprudence at Zurich. Influenced by Rousseau's Émile, he turned for a while to agriculture. In 1775 he started a school for poor children at Neuhof which he hoped would be supported by popular subscriptions, but these failed to materialize. The school was closed in 1780. Next he started a school at Stans; this one, though assisted by government support, also proved to be a failure, lasting only a year. Finally he took charge of a school at Burgdorf, successively removed to Münchenbuchsee and to Yverdon, where it continued until 1825.

Pestalozzi must be included in any anthology of educational writings, and his place in general education history is not to be stressed at the expense of his distinctively Christian orientation. Emil Brunner has designated Pestalozzi as perhaps the Christian educator par excellence (see Brunner's appreciative estimate of Pestalozzi in Christianity and Civilization, *Vol. II, pp. 43–56, passim,* The Gifford Lectures, Nisbet and Co., Ltd., London, 1948). *One need only mention his stress on "loving discipline" and the insistence that the child learns through experiences of observation as well as by rote.*

Pestalozzi's most important writings are these: Evening Hours of a Hermit, Leonard and Gertrude, How Gertrude Teaches Her Children, Memoirs of Burgdorf and Yverdon, Views and Experiences on Ideas of Elementary Training (Ansichten und Erfahrungen). *See J. A. Green,* Life and Work of Pestalozzi (*University Tutorial Press, Ltd., London, 1913*); *Hermann Krüsi,* Pestalozzi: His Life and Work (*Wilson and Meyer, 1927*); *Kate Silber,* Pestalozzi: The Man and His Work (*Routledge and Kegan Paul, London, 1960*).

JOHANN HEINRICH PESTALOZZI . . .

Leonard and Gertrude

Gertrude's Method of Instruction

It was quite early in the morning when Arner, Glülphi,
and the pastor went to the mason's cottage. The room was
not in order when they entered, for the family had just
finished breakfast, and the dirty plates and spoons still
lay upon the table. Gertrude was at first somewhat dis-
concerted, but the visitors reassured her, saying kindly,
" This is as it should be; it is impossible to clear the table
before breakfast is eaten! "

The children all helped with the dishes, and then seated
themselves in their customary places before their work.
The gentlemen begged Gertrude to let everything go on
as usual, and after the first half hour, during which she
was a little embarrassed, all proceeded as if no stranger
were present. First the children sang their morning hymns,
and then Gertrude read a chapter of the Bible aloud, which
they repeated after her while they were spinning, rehears-
ing the most instructive passages until they knew them by

Leonard and Gertrude. Translated and abridged by Eva Channing.
D. C. Heath & Company, 1885. Copyright, 1885, by Eva Channing. Used
by permission. The material used here comprises Chapters XXV, pp. 129–
131; XXXI, pp. 152–155; and a portion of XXXII, pp. 156–158.

heart. In the meantime, the oldest girl had been making the children's beds in the adjoining room, and the visitors noticed through the open door that she silently repeated what the others were reciting. When this task was completed, she went into the garden and returned with vegetables for dinner, which she cleaned while repeating Bible verses with the rest.

It was something new for the children to see three gentlemen in the room, and they often looked up from their spinning toward the corner where the strangers sat. Gertrude noticed this, and said to them: " Seems to me you look more at these gentlemen than at your yarn." But Harry answered: " No, indeed! We are working hard, and you'll have finer yarn today than usual."

Whenever Gertrude saw that anything was amiss with the wheels or cotton, she rose from her work, and put it in order. The smallest children, who were not old enough to spin, picked over the cotton for carding with a skill which excited the admiration of the visitors.

Although Gertrude thus exerted herself to develop very early the manual dexterity of her children, she was in no haste for them to learn to read and write. But she took pains to teach them early how to speak; for, as she said, " Of what use is it for a person to be able to read and write, if he cannot speak? — since reading and writing are only an artificial sort of speech." To this end she used to make the children pronounce syllables after her in regular succession, taking them from an old A–B–C book she had. This exercise in correct and distinct articulation was, however, only a subordinate object in her whole scheme of education, which embraced a true comprehension of life itself. Yet she never adopted the tone of instructor toward her children; she did not say to them: " Child, this is your head, your nose, your hand, your finger," or "Where is your eye, your ear?"—but instead, she would say: "Come here, child, I will wash your little hands," "I will comb your hair," or "I will cut your finger nails." Her verbal instruction seemed to vanish in the spirit of her real activity, in which it always had its source. The result of her system was that each child was skillful, intelligent, and active to the full extent that its age and development allowed.

The instruction she gave them in the rudiments of arithmetic was intimately connected with the realities of life. She taught them to count the number of steps from one end of the room to the other, and two of the rows of five panes each, in one of the windows, gave her an opportunity to unfold the decimal relations of numbers. She also made them count their threads while spinning, and the number of turns on the reel, when they wound the yarn into skeins. Above all, in every occupation of life she taught them an accurate and intelligent observation of common objects and the forces of nature.

All that Gertrude's children knew, they knew so thoroughly that they were able to teach it to the younger ones; and this they often begged permission to do. On this day, while the visitors were present, Jonas sat with each arm around the neck of a smaller child, and made the little ones pronounce the syllables of the A–B–C book after him; while Lizzie placed herself with her wheel between two of the others, and while all three spun, taught them the words of a hymn with the utmost patience.

When the guests took their departure, they told Gertrude they would come again on the morrow. "Why?" she returned. "You will only see the same thing over again." But Glülphi said: "That is the best praise you

could possibly give yourself." Gertrude blushed at this
compliment, and stood confused when the gentlemen
kindly pressed her hand in taking leave.

The three could not sufficiently admire what they had
seen at the mason's house, and Glülphi was so overcome
by the powerful impression made upon him, that he
longed to be alone and seek counsel of his own thoughts.
He hastened to his room, and as he crossed the threshold,
the words broke from his lips, " *I* must be schoolmaster in
Bonnal! " All night visions of Gertrude's schoolroom floated
through his mind, and he only fell asleep toward morning.
Before his eyes were fairly open, he murmured, " I will
be schoolmaster! " — and hastened to Arner to acquaint
him with his resolution.

The Organization of a New School

Glülphi was full of the idea of his school, and could
speak of nothing else with Arner and the pastor. He used
all his spare time in visiting Gertrude in order to talk it
over with her; but she seemed quite unable to explain her
method in words, and usually deprecated the idea of her
advice being necessary. Occasionally, however, she would
let drop some significant remark which the lieutenant
felt went to the root of the whole matter of education. For
example, she said to him one day: " You should do for your
children what their parents fail to do for them. The reading, writing, and arithmetic are not, after all, what they
most need; it is all well and good for them to learn something, but the really important thing is for them to *be*
something — for them to become what they are meant to
be, and in becoming which they so often have no guidance
or help at home."

Finally, the day arrived on which the new schoolmaster

was to be formally presented to the village. Arner and the pastor led him solemnly between them to the church, which was crowded with the inhabitants of Bonnal. The good clergyman preached a sermon on the ideal function of the school in its relation to the home, and to the moral development of the community; after which Arner led Glülphi forward to the railing of the choir, and introducing him to the people, made a short but earnest plea in his behalf. The lieutenant was much affected, but mastered his emotion sufficiently to express in a few words his sense of the responsibility conferred upon him, and his hope that the parents would co-operate with him in his undertaking.

Arner was anxious to make the occasion of Glülphi's installation a festival for the school children, so after the services at the church, he invited all the little folks to the parsonage, where, with the help of the pastor's wife, preparations had been made to receive them. It was a time-honored custom that every year, at Christmas and Easter, eggs and rolls should be distributed among the children of Bonnal. On this day, on entering the parsonage, the young people beheld even more beautifully painted eggs than they had seen at Easter; and beside each child's portion lay a bright nosegay.

The lieutenant, who knew nothing of the whole matter, was in an adjoining room, when suddenly the door was thrown open, and the children, at a sign from Theresa, struck up with one accord their prettiest song, and Glülphi found himself surrounded by the lively throng of his future charges. He was much moved, and when the song was concluded, he greeted them kindly, shaking many of them by the hand, and chatting pleasantly with them. Arner ordered some of his own wine to be brought, and the children drank to the health of their new schoolmaster.

On the following morning the lieutenant began his school, and Gertrude helped him in the arrangement of it. They examined the children with regard to their previous studies, and seated those together who were equally advanced. First there were those who had not learned their letters, then those who could read separate words, and finally, those who already knew how to read. Besides reading, all were to learn writing and arithmetic, which previously had only been taught to the more wealthy, in private lessons.

At first Glülphi found it harder than he had expected; but every day, as he gained in experience, his task became easier and more delightful. A good and capable woman named Margaret, who came to take charge of the sewing, spinning, etc., proved a most valuable and conscientious helper in the work. Whenever a child's hand or wheel stopped, she would step up and restore things to their former condition. If the children's hair was in disorder, she would braid it up while they studied and worked; if there was a hole in their clothes, she would take a needle and thread, and mend it; and she showed them how to fasten their shoes and stockings properly, besides many other things they did not understand.

The new master was anxious, above all, to accustom his charges to strict order, and thus lead them to the true wisdom of life. He began school punctually on the stroke of the clock, and did not allow anyone to come in late. He also laid great stress on good habits and behavior. The children were obliged to come to school clean in person and apparel, and with their hair combed. While standing, sitting, writing, and working, they always were taught to keep the body erect as a candle. Glülphi's schoolroom must be clean as a church, and he would not suffer a pane of glass to be missing from the window, or a nail to be driven crooked in the floor. Still less did he allow the children to throw the smallest thing upon the floor, or to eat while they were studying; and it was even arranged that in getting up and sitting down they should not hit against each other.

Before school began, the children came up to their teacher one by one, and said, " God be with you." He looked them over from head to foot, so that they knew by his eye if anything was wrong. If this glance was not sufficient, he spoke to them, or sent a message to their parents. A child would not infrequently come home with the word: " The schoolmaster sends greetings, and wants to know whether you have no needles and thread," or " whether water is dear," etc. At the close of school, those who had done well went up to him first, and said, " God be with you." He held out his hand to each one, replying, " God be with you, my dear child! " Then came those who had only done partly well, and to these he merely said, " God be with you! " without giving them his hand. Finally, those who had not done well at all had to leave the room without even going to him.

The lieutenant's punishments were designed to remedy the faults for which they were inflicted. An idle scholar was made to cut firewood, or to carry stones for the wall which some of the older boys were constructing under the master's charge; a forgetful child was made school messenger, and for several days was obliged to take charge of all the teacher's business in the village. Disobedience and impertinence he punished by not speaking publicly to the child in question for a number of days, talking with him only in private, after school. Wickedness and lying were punished with the rod, and any child thus chastised was not allowed to play with the others for a whole week; his name was registered in a special notebook of offenses, from which it was not erased until plain evidence of improvement was given. The schoolmaster was kind to the children while punishing them, talking with them more then than at any other time, and trying to help them correct their faults.

A Good Pastor and Schoolmaster;
The Opening of a New Era

In his instruction, Glülphi constantly sought to lay the foundation of that equanimity and repose which man can possess in all circumstances of life, provided the hardships of his lot have early become a second nature to him. The success of this attempt soon convinced the pastor that all verbal instruction, in so far as it aims at true human wisdom, and at the highest goal of this wisdom, true religion, ought to be subordinated to a constant training in practical domestic labor. The good man, at the same time, became aware that a single word of the lieutenant's could accomplish more than hours of his preaching. With true humility, he profited by the superior wisdom of the schoolmaster, and remodeled his method of religious instruction. He united his efforts to those of Glülphi and Margaret, striving to lead the children, without many words, to a quiet, industrious life, and thus to lay the foundations of a silent worship of God and love of humanity. To this end, he connected every word of his brief religious teachings with their actual, everyday experience, so that when he spoke of God and eternity, it seemed to them as if he were speaking of father and mother, house and home, in short, of the things with which they were most familiar. He pointed out to them in their books the few wise and pious passages which he still desired them to learn by heart, and completely ignored all questions involving doctrinal differences. He no longer allowed the children to learn any long prayers by rote, saying that this was contrary to the spirit of Christianity, and the express injunctions of their Savior.

The lieutenant often declared that the pastor was quite unable to make a lasting impression on men, because he spoiled them by his kindness. Glülphi's own principles in regard to education were very strict, and were founded on an accurate knowledge of the world. He maintained that love was only useful in the education of men when in conjunction with fear; for they must learn to root out thorns and thistles, which they never do of their own accord, but only under compulsion, and in consequence of training.

He knew his children better in eight days than their parents did in eight years, and employed this knowledge to render deception difficult, and to keep their hearts open before his eyes. He cared for their heads as he did for their hearts, demanding that whatever entered them should be plain and clear as the silent moon in the sky. To insure this, he taught them to see and hear with accuracy, and cultivated their powers of attention. Above all, he sought to give them a thorough training in arithmetic; for he was convinced that arithmetic is the natural safeguard against error in the pursuit of truth.

Despite the children's rapid progress in their school, the lieutenant did not please everybody in the village, and a rumor soon spread abroad that he was too proud for a schoolmaster. It was in vain that the children contradicted this report; their parents only answered, "Even if he is good to you, he may be proud all the same." It was not until three weeks after the beginning of the school, that an event occurred which accomplished for him what the children's defense had been unable to do.

For the last twenty years the old rotten footbridge opposite the schoolhouse had been out of repair, so that in a rainy season the children must get wet above their ankles in crossing the lane to school. The first time the road was in this condition, Glülphi planted himself in the middle of the street in all the rain, and as the children came, lifted them, one after the other, across the brook. Now it happened that some of the very persons who had complained most of the lieutenant's pride, lived just across the way. It amused them greatly to see him get wet through and through in his red coat, and they fancied it would not be many minutes before he would call to them for help. When, however, he kept on patiently lifting the children over, until his hair and clothes were dripping wet, they began to say behind the windowpanes: " He must be a good-natured fool, and we were certainly mistaken; if he were proud, he would have given it up long ago." Finally, they came out, and offered to relieve him from his task, while he went home and dried himself. But this was not all; when school was out that day, the children found a footbridge built, over which they could go home dry-shod. And from that day forth, not a word more was heard of the schoolmaster's pride. . . .

26

JOHANN FRIEDRICH HERBART
(1776–1841)

Herbart was born at Oldenburg. After studying under the philosopher Fichte at Jena, he repudiated the idealistic philosophy in his early twenties. When he visited Pestalozzi's school at Burgdorf, he became enamored of education. He was appointed to a teaching position at Göttingen, but in 1809 went to Königsberg as professor of philosophy in a chair once held by Immanuel Kant. At Königsberg he established a demonstration school and teachers' training college, which developed into the first pedagogical seminary. Definitely intellectualistic and systematic in his inclinations, he developed a method of instruction that came to be known as the "Herbartian method." This method stressed presenting knowledge to the child in a clear manner, relating this new knowledge to material already learned, associating the new knowledge with the pupil's total experience, and applying the knowledge to new facts. He was one of the first psychologists in the modern sense, differentiating even between the consciousness and unconsciousness, a matter that later psychologists explored in great detail. He believed that education should serve a moral and religious purpose.

Since the "Herbartian method" had great vogue in the United States, it was inevitable that his influence came to *be felt strongly not only in the secular schools but also, eventually, in Sunday school curriculum writing. His concern with moral education has its late echo in character education emphases through the " moral and spiritual values" approach. But Herbart did not think of moral education as separate from the life of the Christian church: " Religious instruction culminates . . . in the rite of confirmation, and the subsequent admission to the Holy Communion." At the same time, he made a definite correlation between the ethical and the church dimensions of religious instruction, urging that denominational goals be accompanied by a concern for the whole Christian community.*

Herbart's works include: ABC of Sense Perception, Outlines of Educational Doctrine, Manual of Psychology, The Science of Education, Brief Encyclopaedia of Practical Philosophy.

JOHANN FRIEDRICH HERBART . . .

Outlines of Educational Doctrine

INTRODUCTION

1. The plasticity, or educability, of the pupil is the fundamental postulate of pedagogics.

The concept plasticity, or capacity for being molded, extends far beyond the confines of pedagogics. It takes in even the primary components of matter. It has been traced as far as the elementary substances entering into the chemical changes of organic bodies. Signs of plasticity of will are found in the souls of the higher animals. Only man, however, exhibits plasticity of will in the direction of moral conduct.

2. Pedagogics as a science is based on ethics and psychology. The former points out the goal of education; the latter the way, the means, and the obstacles.

This relationship involves the dependence of pedagogics on experience, inasmuch as ethics includes application

Herbart, John Frederick, *Outlines of Educational Doctrine,* tr. by Alexis F. Lange, annotated by Charles de Garmo. Pp. 1–14 — Introduction and Chapter I, "The Ethical Basis" in Part I, "The Double Basis of Pedagogics"; pp. 219–222 — Chapter I, "Religion" in Part III, "Special Applications of Pedagogics." The Macmillan Company, 1913. Used by permission.

to experience, while psychology has its starting point, not in metaphysics alone, but in experience correctly interpreted by metaphysics. But an exclusively empirical knowledge of man will not suffice for pedagogics. It is the less adequate in any age the greater the instability of morals, customs, and opinions; for, as the new gains on the old, generalizations from former observations cease to hold true.

3. Philosophical systems, involving either fatalism or its opposite, pure caprice of will, are logically shut out from pedagogics, because the notion of plasticity, implying as it does a transition from the indeterminate to the determinate, cannot by such systems be brought in without inconsistency.

4. On the other hand, the assumption of unlimited plasticity is equally inadmissible; it is for psychology to guard against this error. The educability of the child is, to begin with, limited by his individuality. Then, too, the possibility of determining and molding him at will through education is lessened by time and circumstances. Lastly, the established character of the adult develops by an inner process which in time passes beyond the reach of the educator.

5. Education seems thus to find a barrier, first, in the order of nature, and later in the pupil's own will. The difficulty is indeed a real one, if the limitations of education are overlooked: hence an apparent confirmation of fatalism as well as of the doctrine of absolute free will.

6. The power of education must be neither over- nor under-estimated. The educator should, indeed, try to see how much may be done; but he must always expect that the outcome will warn him to confine his attempts within reasonable bounds. In order not to neglect anything essential, he needs to keep in view the practical bearings of the

whole theory of ideas; in order to understand and interpret correctly the data furnished by observation of the child, the teacher must make constant use of psychology.

7. In scientific study, concepts are separated which in practice must always be kept united. The work of education is continuous. With an eye to every consideration at once, the educator must always endeavor to connect what is to come with what has gone before. Hence a mode of treatment which, following the several periods of school life, simply enumerates the things to be done in sequence, is inadequate in a work on pedagogics. In an appendix this method will serve to facilitate a bird's-eye view; the discussion of general principles, according to fundamental ideas, must needs precede. But our very first task will necessarily consist in dealing, at least briefly, with the ethical and the psychological basis of pedagogics.

The Ethical Basis

The term *virtue* expresses the whole purpose of education. Virtue is the idea of inner freedom which has developed into an abiding actuality in an individual. Whence, as inner freedom is a relation between insight and volition, a double task is at once set before the teacher. It becomes his business to make actual each of these factors separately, in order that later a permanent relationship may result.

But even here at the outset we need to bear in mind the identity of morality with the effort put forth to realize the permanent actuality of the harmony between insight and volition. To induce the pupil to make this effort is a difficult achievement; at all events, it becomes possible only when the twofold training mentioned above is well under way. It is easy enough, by a study of the example of others, to cultivate theoretical acumen; the moral application to the pupil himself, however, can be made, with hope of success, only in so far as his inclinations and habits have taken a direction in keeping with his insight. If such is not the case, there is danger lest the pupil, after all, knowingly subordinates his correct theoretical judgment to mere prudence. It is thus that evil in the strict sense originates.

Of the remaining practical or ethical concepts, the idea of perfection points to health of body and mind; it implies a high regard for both, and their systematic cultivation.

The idea of good will counsels the educator to ward off temptation to ill will as long as such temptation might prove dangerous. It is essential, on the other hand, to imbue the pupil with a feeling of respect for good will.

The idea of justice demands that the pupil abstain from contention. It demands, furthermore, reflection on strife, so that respect for justice may strike deep root.

The idea of equity is especially involved in cases where the pupil has merited punishment as requital for the intentional infliction of pain. Here the degree of punishment must be carefully ascertained and acknowledged as just.

Where a number of pupils are assembled there arises, naturally, on a small scale, a system of laws and rewards. This system, and the demands which in the world at large spring from the same ideas, must be brought into accord.

The concept of an administrative system has great significance for pedagogics, since every pupil, whatever his rank or social status, must be trained for co-operation in the social whole to fit him for usefulness. This requirement may assume very many different forms.

Of the system of civilization only the aspect of general culture, not that of special training, must be emphasized at this point.

For the business of education, the idea of perfection, while it does not rise into excessive prominence, stands out above all others on account of its uninterrupted application. The teacher discovers in the as yet undeveloped human being a force which requires his incessant attention to intensify, to direct, and to concentrate.

The constant presence of the idea of perfection easily introduces a false feature into moral education in the strict sense. The pupil may get an erroneous impression as to the relative importance of the lessons, practice, and performance demanded of him, and so be betrayed into the belief that he is essentially perfect when these demands are satisfied.

For this reason alone, if others were wanting, it is necessary to combine moral education proper, which in everyday life lays stress continually on correct self-determination, with religious training. The notion that something really worthy has been achieved needs to be tempered by humility. Conversely, religious education has need of the moral also to forestall cant and hypocrisy, which are only too apt to appear where morality has not already secured a firm foothold through earnest self-questioning and self-criticism with a view to improvement. Finally, inasmuch as moral training must be put off until after insight and right habits have been acquired, religious education, too, should not be begun too early; nor should it be needlessly delayed.

RELIGION

The content of religious instruction is for theologians to determine, while philosophy bears witness that no knowledge is able to surpass the trust of religious faith. But both the beginning and the end of religious instruction call for remarks from the point of view of pedagogy.

Religious instruction culminates, if it does not end, in the rite of confirmation, and the subsequent admission to the Holy Communion. The former is characteristic of a particular Christian denomination; the latter, on the contrary, of the whole brotherhood of Christians. Now the profound emotion which marks the first Communion service should imply a conquest over the feeling of separation from other denominations, especially since the mere admission to Communion is conditioned on the general requirement of earnest ethical aspiration. It is thus assumed that members of other confessions, provided they are communicants at all, have fulfilled the same condition. Preparatory instruction must work toward this end all the more, since with many persons Christian love for those who differ from them in important articles of faith belongs to the more difficult duties. Moreover, the fact that this same instruction necessarily had to set forth clearly fundamental denominational differences, lends additional weight to the necessity of inculcating the virtue of Christian charity.

In academic schools, if Greek is begun early enough, it is possible to deepen the impressions of Christian teaching by the dialogues of Plato that bear on the death of Socrates, particularly the *Crito* and the *Apology*. Being the weaker, however, impressions of this sort should precede the time when the solemn initiation into Christian fellowship produces its whole powerful effect.

Going back in thought, we find that the portion of religious instruction which deals with characteristic denominational distinctions, presupposes that which deals with tenets common to all Christians, and we find that this in turn has been preceded by Bible stories, including those of the Old Testament. But the question arises, " Must we not go back to something more fundamental still? "

Religion cannot possibly be adequately presented by treating of it merely as a perpetuation of something historical and past. The teacher must needs make use also of the present testimony furnished by the adjustment of means to end, in nature. But even this, for which some knowledge of nature is prerequisite, and which leads up to the ideas of wisdom and power, is not the first step.

True family feeling is elevated easily and directly to the idea of the Father, of the father and mother. Only where such feeling is wanting does it become necessary to make churches and Sunday observance the starting point as indications of humility and gratitude. An all-pervading love, providence, and watchful care constitute the first concept of the Highest Being — a concept limited by the mental horizon of the child, and expanding and becoming more elevated only by degrees.

The process of elevating religious concepts and purifying them of unworthy admixtures must, however, have taken place, and the true concepts must have been deeply impressed, before the mythological conceptions of antiquity become known; in which case the latter will produce the right effect by the contrast between the manifestly fabulous and crude, and the worthy and sublime. If managed properly, this subject presents no difficulties.

But there are other difficulties — difficulties growing out of individual peculiarities. While some would be harmed by much talk about sin, because they would thus either become acquainted with it, or else be filled with fantastic terror, there are others whom only the strongest language can move, and still others who themselves preach against the sins of the world, and, at the same time, front the world in proud security. Then there are those who brood over ethical problems, and who, without having heard of Spinoza, argue that what the Highest Judge has permitted to happen he has approved of, whence might is the practical proof of right. There are condemners of mere morality, who think that prayers will consecrate their evil actions. Isolated traces of such perversions may indeed be met with even in children, especially if their glib reproduction of the sermon, or worse yet, their praying aloud, has happened to receive praise.

Hence it is necessary to observe the effect of religious instruction on each individual: another task for home training.

27

FRIEDRICH FROEBEL
(1782–1852)

When Friedrich Wilhelm August Froebel was a boy, he displayed no special interest in studying, but in his later years his studious interests developed into a rich flowering. Early apprenticed to a woodcutter, he became interested in nature and decided to go to the University of Jena to study science for a brief period. Eventually his interests turned to teaching. He helped in a model school at Frankfurt and worked for a while under Pestalozzi at Yverdon. Going back to the university, he enrolled at Berlin and Göttingen. While fighting in the war against Napoleon, he met two men who became his disciples, Heinrich Langethal and Wilhelm Middendorf. With them he founded a school in 1816 at Griesheim, later moved to Keilhau. They thought of this school in terms of its being a community, and the curriculum was worked out on the basis of the needs and nature of individual pupils. While conducting a school at Lucerne, Switzerland, Froebel decided that instruction should start even before children were of formal school age. The result was the first kindergarten (literally, " children's garden "), opened at Blankenburg, Thüringia, in 1837. It failed. During the crisis situation of 1848 the government feared that Froebel's ideas were akin to those of one of his relatives who had shown *definite socialist affinities. Thus in 1851 it was decreed that schools of the type he had advocated should be banned in the country. He died a year later, at Marienthal.*

Froebel's works include the following titles: Autobiography, Letters on the Kindergarten, The Pedagogics of the Kindergarten, *and his major work,* The Education of Man. *In the excerpt from* The Education of Man *published here we can see the spiritual basis of Froebel's educational theory. He interprets the aims of education in terms of what he defines as the " Divine Unity," the groundwork of all pedagogy. By education " the divine essence of man should be unfolded, brought out, lifted into consciousness, and man himself raised into free, conscious obedience to the divine principle that lives in him." His philosophical groundwork sounds in retrospect to be strongly akin to the emphasis on " natural religion " which was the antecedent of much " liberal " religious education of the first part of the 1900's.*

On Froebel's life, see Baroness B. von Marenholz-Bülow, Reminiscences of Friedrich Froebel, *tr. by Mrs. Horace Mann (Lee and Shepherd, 1895);* Friedrich Froebel and English Education, *ed. by Evelyn Lawrence (University of London Press, London, 1952);* P. P. Claxton, Sketches of Froebel's Life and Times (*Milton Bradley Co., 1914*).

FRIEDRICH FROEBEL . . .

The Education of Man

GROUNDWORK OF THE WHOLE

In all things there lives and reigns an eternal law. To him whose mind, through disposition and faith, is filled, penetrated, and quickened with the necessity that this cannot possibly be otherwise, as well as to him whose clear, calm mental vision beholds the inner in the outer and through the outer, and sees the outer proceeding with logical necessity from the essence of the inner, this law has been and is enounced with equal clearness and distinctness in nature (the external), in the spirit (the internal), and in life which unites the two. This all-controlling law is necessarily based on an all-pervading, energetic, living, self-conscious, and hence eternal Unity. This fact, as well as the Unity itself, is again vividly recognized, either through faith or through insight, with equal clearness and comprehensiveness; therefore, a quietly observant human mind, a thoughtful, clear human intellect, has never failed, and will never fail, to recognize this Unity.

This Unity is God. All things have come from the Divine

Froebel, Friedrich, *The Education of Man*, tr. by W. N. Hailmann, pp. 1–18, *passim.* D. Appleton and Co., 1907. Used by permission.

Unity, from God, and have their origin in the Divine Unity, in God alone. God is the sole source of all things. In all things there lives and reigns the Divine Unity, God. All things live and have their being in and through the Divine Unity, in and through God. All things are only through the divine effluence that lives in them. The divine effluence that lives in each thing is the essence of each thing.

It is the destiny and lifework of all things to unfold their essence, hence their divine being, and, therefore, the Divine Unity itself — to reveal God in their external and transient being. It is the special destiny and lifework of man, as an intelligent and rational being, to become fully, vividly, and clearly conscious of his essence, of the divine effluence in him, and, therefore, of God; to become fully, vividly, and clearly conscious of his destiny and lifework; and to accomplish this, to render it (his essence) active, to reveal it in his own life with self-determination and freedom.

Education consists in leading man, as a thinking, intelligent being, growing into self-consciousness, to a pure and unsullied, conscious and free representation of the inner law of Divine Unity, and in teaching him ways and means thereto.

The knowledge of that eternal law, the insight into its origin, into its essence, into the totality, the connection, and intensity of its effects, the knowledge of life in its totality, constitute *science, the science of life;* and, referred by the self-conscious, thinking, intelligent being to representation and practice through and in himself, this becomes *science of education.*

The system of directions, derived from the knowledge and study of that law, to guide thinking, intelligent beings in the apprehension of their lifework and in the accomplishment of their destiny, is *the theory of education.*

The self-active application of this knowledge in the direct development and cultivation of rational beings toward the attainment of their destiny, is *the practice of education.*

The object of education is the realization of a faithful, pure, inviolate, and hence holy life.

To be wise is the highest aim of man, is the most exalted achievement of human self-determination.

To educate one's self and others, with consciousness, freedom, and self-determination, is a twofold achievement of wisdom: it *began* with the first appearance of man upon the earth; it *was manifest* with the first appearance of full self-consciousness in man; it *begins now* to proclaim itself as a necessary, universal requirement of humanity, and to be heard and heeded as such. With this achievement man enters upon the path which alone leads to life; which surely tends to the fulfillment of the inner, and thereby also to the fulfillment of the outer, requirement of humanity; which, through a faithful, pure, holy life, attains beatitude.

By education, then, the divine essence of man should be unfolded, brought out, lifted into consciousness, and man himself raised into free, conscious obedience to the divine principle that lives in him, and to a free representation of this principle in his life.

Education, in instruction, should lead man to see and know the divine, spiritual, and eternal principle which animates surrounding nature, constitutes the essence of nature, and is permanently manifested in nature; and, in living reciprocity and united with training, it should express and demonstrate the fact that the same law rules both (the divine principle and nature), as it does nature and man.

Education, as a whole, by means of instruction and training, should bring to man's consciousness, and render efficient in his life, the fact that man and nature proceed from God and are conditioned by him — that both have their being in God.

Education should lead and guide man to clearness concerning himself and in himself, to peace with nature, and to unity with God; hence it should lift him to a knowledge of himself and of mankind, to a knowledge of God and of nature, and to the pure and holy life to which such knowledge leads.

In all these requirements, however, education is based on considerations of the innermost.

The inner essence of things is recognized by the innermost spirit (of man) in the outer and through outward manifestations. The inner being, the spirit, the divine essence of things and of man, is known by its outward manifestations. In accordance with this, all education, all instruction and training, all life as a free growth, start from the outer manifestations of man and things, and, proceeding from the outer, act upon the inner, and form its judgments concerning the inner. Nevertheless, education should not draw its inferences concerning the inner from the outer directly, for it lies in the nature of things that always in some relation inferences should be drawn inversely. Thus, the diversity and multiplicity in nature do not warrant the inference of multiplicity in the ultimate cause — a multiplicity of gods — nor does the unity of God warrant the inference of finality in nature; but, in both cases, the inference lies conversely from the diversity in nature to the oneness of its ultimate cause, and from the unity of God to an eternally progressing diversity in natural developments.

The failure to apply this truth, or rather the continual sinning against it, the drawing of direct inferences concerning the inner life of childhood and youth from certain external manifestations of life, is the chief cause of antagonism and contention, of the frequent mistakes in life and education. This furnishes constant occasion for innumerable false judgments concerning the motives of the young, for numberless failures in the education of children, for endless misunderstanding between parent and child, for so much needless complaint and unseemly arraignment of children, for so many unreasonable demands made upon them. Therefore, this truth, in its application to parents, educators, and teachers, is of such great importance that they should strive to render themselves familiar with its application in its smallest details. This would bring into the relations between parents and children, pupils and educators, teacher and taught, a clearness, a constancy, a serenity which are now sought in vain; for the child that seems good outwardly often is not good inwardly; i.e., does not desire the good spontaneously, or from love, respect, and appreciation; similarly, the outwardly rough, stubborn, self-willed child that seems outwardly not good, frequently is filled with the liveliest, most eager, strongest desire for spontaneous goodness in his actions; and the apparently inattentive boy frequently follows a certain fixed line of thought, that withholds his attention from all external things.

Therefore, education in instruction and training, originally and in its first principles, should necessarily be *passive, following* (only guarding and protecting), not *prescriptive, categorical, interfering.*

Indeed, in its very essence, education should have these

characteristics; for the undisturbed operation of the Divine Unity is necessarily good — cannot be otherwise than good. This necessity implies that the young human being — as it were, still in process of creation — would seek, although still unconsciously, as a product of nature, yet decidedly and surely, that which is itself best; and, moreover, in a form wholly adapted to his condition, as well as to his disposition, his powers, and means. Thus the duckling hastens to the pond and into the water, while the young chicken scratches the ground, and the young swallow catches its food upon the wing and scarcely ever touches the ground. Now, whatever may be said against the previously enounced law of converse inference, and against this other law of close sequence, as well as against their application to and in education, they will be fully vindicated in their simplicity and truth among the generations that trust in them fully and obey them.

We grant space and time to young plants and animals because we know that, in accordance with the laws that live in them, they will develop properly and grow well; young animals and plants are given rest, and arbitrary interference with their growth is avoided, because it is known that the opposite practice would disturb their pure unfolding and sound development; but the young human being is looked upon as a piece of wax, a lump of clay, which man can mold into what he pleases. O man, who roamest through garden and field, through meadow and grove, why dost thou close thy mind to the silent teaching of nature? Behold even the weed, which, grown up amid hindrances and constraint, scarcely yields an indication of inner law; behold it in nature, in field or garden, and see how perfectly it conforms to law — what a pure inner life it shows, harmonious in all parts and features: a beauti-

ful sun, a radiant star, it has burst from the earth! Thus,
O parents, could your children, on whom you force in
tender years forms and aims against their nature, and who,
therefore, walk with you in morbid and unnatural deform-
ity — thus could your children, too, unfold in beauty and
develop in all-sided harmony! . . .

The prescriptive, interfering education, indeed, can be
justified only on two grounds: either because it teaches
the clear, living thought, self-evident truth, or because
it holds up a life whose ideal value has been established in
experience. But, where self-evident, living, absolute truth
rules, the eternal principle itself reigns, as it were, and
will on this account maintain a passive, following character. For the living thought, the eternal divine principle as
such demands and requires free self-activity and self-determination on the part of man, the being created for
freedom in the image of God.

Again, a life whose ideal value has been perfectly established in experience never aims to serve as model in its
form, but only in its essence, in its spirit. It is the greatest
mistake to suppose that spiritual, human perfection can
serve as a model in its form. This accounts for the common
experience that the taking of such external manifestations
as examples, instead of elevating mankind, checks, nay,
represses, its development.

Jesus himself, therefore, in his life and in his teachings,
constantly opposed the imitation of external perfection.
Only spiritual, striving, living perfection is to be held fast
as an ideal; its external manifestation — on the other hand
— its form should not be limited. The highest and most
perfect life which we, as Christians, behold in Jesus — the
highest known to mankind — is a life which found the pri-
mordial and ultimate reason of its existence clearly and

distinctly in its own being; a life which, in accordance with the eternal law, came from the eternally creating All-Life, self-acting and self-poised. This highest eternally perfect life itself would have each human being again become a similar image of the eternal ideal, so that each again might become a similar ideal for himself and others; it would have each human being develop from within, self-active and free, in accordance with the eternal law. This is, indeed, the problem and the aim of all education in instruction and training; there can and should be no other. We see, then, that even the eternal ideal is following, passive, in its requirements concerning the form of being.

Nevertheless, in its inner essence (and we see this in experience), the living thought, the eternal spiritual ideal, ought to be and is categorical and mandatory in its manifestations; and we see it, indeed, sternly mandatory, inexorable, and inflexible, but only when the requirement appears as a pronounced necessity in the essence of the whole, as well as in the nature of the individual, and can be recognized as such in him to whom it is addressed; only where the ideal speaks as the organ of necessity, and, therefore, always relatively. The ideal becomes mandatory only where it supposes that the person addressed enters into the reason of the requirement with serene, childlike faith, or with clear, manly insight. It is true, in word or example, the ideal is mandatory in all these cases, but always only with reference to the spirit and inner life, never with reference to outer form.

In good education, then, in genuine instruction, in true training, necessity should call forth freedom; law, self-determination; external compulsion, inner free will; external hate, inner love. Where hatred brings forth hatred;

law, dishonesty, and crime; compulsion, slavery; necessity, servitude; where oppression destroys and debases; where severity and harshness give rise to stubbornness and deceit — all education is abortive. In order to avoid the latter and to secure the former, all prescription should be adapted to the pupil's nature and needs, and secure his co-operation. This is the case when all education in instruction and training, in spite of its necessarily categorical character, bears in all details and ramifications the irrefutable and irresistible impress that the one who makes the demand is himself strictly and unavoidably subject to an eternally ruling law, to an unavoidable external necessity, and that, therefore, all despotism is banished.

All true education in training and instruction should, therefore, at every moment, in every demand and regulation, be simultaneously double-sided — giving and taking, uniting and dividing, prescribing and following, active and passive, positive yet giving scope, firm and yielding; and the pupil should be similarly conditioned: but between the two, between educator and pupil, between request and obedience, there should invisibly rule a third something, to which educator and pupil are equally subject. This third something is the *right,* the *best,* necessarily conditioned and expressed without arbitrariness in the circumstances. The calm recognition, the clear knowledge, and the serene, cheerful obedience to the rule of this third something is the particular feature that should be constantly and clearly manifest in the bearing and conduct of the educator and teacher, and often firmly and sternly emphasized by him. The child, the pupil, has a very keen feeling, a very clear apprehension, and rarely fails to distinguish, whether what the educator, the teacher, or the father says or requests is personal or arbitrary, or whether it is expressed by him as a general law and necessity.

This obedience, this trustful yielding to an unchangeable third principle to which pupil and teacher are equally subject, should appear even in the smallest details of every demand of the educator and teacher. Hence, the general formula of instruction is: *Do this and observe what follows in this particular case from thy action, and to what knowledge it leads thee.* Similarly, the precept for life in general and for everyone is: *Exhibit only thy spiritual essence, thy life, in the external, and by means of the external in thy actions, and observe the requirements of thy inner being and its nature.*

Jesus himself charges man in and with this precept to acknowledge the divinity of his mission and of his inner life, as well as the truth of his teaching; and this is, therefore, the precept that opens the way to the knowledge of all life in its origin and nature, as well as of all truth.

28

HORACE MANN

(1796–1859)

A *native of Franklin, Massachusetts, Horace Mann was destined to do his major work in his native state. He occupies a signal place in American education due to his significant work in reorganizing the system of public instruction in Massachusetts and advocating better free schools throughout the country. He studied at Brown University, graduating in 1819. He prepared for law and built up a successful practice. Entering politics, he was elected to the State Senate, where he served from 1827–1837, the last two years as president. In 1837 he accepted an appointment as secretary of the newly established State Board of Education. Under his leadership the school year was minimized at six months, teachers' salaries were doubled, normal schools were established, and high school instruction extended. He was interested in German educational practices and adapted many European ideas to the American scene. After leaving the state position, he ran for Congress, being elected to succeed John Quincy Adams. He ended his career as president of Antioch College, Yellow Springs, Ohio, where he remained until his death.*

Horace Mann's annual reports as secretary of the State Board of Education in Massachusetts exerted wide in-

*fluence and have become educational classics of a sort.
He was personally a deeply religious man and felt strongly
that religion should be integral to the life of the community's schools, though he was opposed to having sec-
tarian teaching of any kind in them. His interpretations
are important to examine with reference to a historical
view of the rise of present-day tensions concerning the
place of religion — or the possibility of it — in the nation's
schools.*

HORACE MANN . . .

American Free Schools

The Pilgrim Fathers, amid all their privations and dangers, conceived the magnificent idea, not only of a universal, but of a free education for the whole people. To find the time and the means to reduce this grand conception to practice, they stinted themselves, amid all their poverty, to a still scantier pittance; amid all their toils, they imposed upon themselves still more burdensome labors; and, amid all their perils, they braced still greater dangers. Two divine ideas filled their great hearts — their duty to God and to posterity. For the one they built the church, for the other they opened the school. Religion and knowledge — two attributes of the same glorious and eternal truth, and that truth the only one on which immortal or mortal happiness can be securely founded!

It is impossible for us adequately to conceive the boldness of the measure which aimed at a universal education through the establishment of free schools. As a fact, it had no precedent in the world's history; and, as a theory, it could have been refuted and silenced by a more formi-

Mann, Horace, *Tenth Annual Report* in the office of Secretary, Massachusetts State Board of Education. Boston, 1846.

dable array of argument and experience than was ever marshaled against any other institution of human origin. But time has ratified its soundness. Two centuries of successful operation now proclaim it to be as wise as it was courageous, and as beneficent as it was disinterested. Every community in the civilized world awards it the meed of praise; and states at home and nations abroad, in the order of their intelligence, are copying the bright example. What we call the enlightened nations of Christendom are approaching, by slow degrees, to the moral elevation which our ancestors reached at a single bound. . . .

In later times, and since the achievement of American independence, the universal and ever-repeated argument in favor of free schools has been that the general intelligence which they are capable of diffusing, and which can be imparted by no other human instrumentality, is indispensable to the continuance of a republican government. This argument, it is obvious, assumes, as a postulatum, the superiority of a republican over all other forms of government; and, as a people, we religiously believe in the soundness both of the assumption and of the argument founded upon it. But, if this be all, then a sincere monarchist, or a defender of arbitrary power, or a believer in the divine right of kings, would oppose free schools for the identical reasons we offer in their behalf. . . .

Again, the expediency of free schools is sometimes advocated on grounds of political economy. An educated people is always a more industrious and productive people. Intelligence is a primary ingredient in the wealth of nations. . . . The moralist, too, takes up the argument of the economist. He demonstrates that vice and crime are not only prodigals and spendthrifts of their own, but de-

frauders and plunderers of the means of others, that they
would seize upon all the gains of honest industry, and
exhaust the bounties of Heaven itself without satisfying
their rapacity; and that often in the history of the whole
world generations might have been trained to industry
and virtue by the wealth which one enemy to his race has
destroyed.

And yet, notwithstanding these views have been presented a thousand times with irrefutable logic, and with
a divine eloquence of truth which it would seem that nothing but combined stolidity and depravity could resist,
there is not at the present time with the exception of
the States of New England and a few small communities
elsewhere, a country or a state in Christendom which
maintains a system of free schools for the education of its
children. . . .

I believe that this amazing dereliction from duty, especially in our own country, originates more in the false
notions which men entertain *respecting the nature of their
right to property* than in anything else. In the district
school meeting, in the town meeting, in legislative halls,
everywhere, the advocates for a more generous education
could carry their respective audiences with them in behalf
of increased privileges for our children, were it not in-
stinctively foreseen that increased privileges must be followed by increased taxation. Against this obstacle, argument falls dead. The rich man who has no children declares
that the exaction of a contribution from him to educate
the children of his neighbor is an invasion of his rights of
property. The man who has reared and educated a family
of children denounces it as a double tax when he is called
upon to assist in educating the children of others also; or,
if he has reared his own children without educating them,

he thinks it peculiarly oppressive to be obliged to do for others what he refrained from doing even for himself. Another, having children, but disdaining to educate them with the common mass, withdraws them from the public school, puts them under what he calls " selector influences," and then thinks it a grievance to be obliged to support a school which he condemns. Or, if these different parties so far yield to the force of traditional sentiment and usage, and to the public opinion around them, as to consent to do something for the cause, they soon reach the limit of expense at which their admitted obligation terminates.

It seems not irrelevant, therefore, in this connection, and for the purpose of strengthening the foundation on which our free-school system reposes, to inquire into the nature of a man's right to the property he possesses, and to satisfy ourselves respecting the question whether any man has such an indefeasible title to his estates or such an absolute ownership of them as renders it unjust in the government to assess upon him his share of the expenses of educating the children of the community up to such a point as the nature of the institutions under which he lives, and the well-being of society, require. . . .

I bring my argument on this point, then, to a close; and I present a test of its validity, which, as it seems to me, defies denial or evasion.

In obedience to the laws of God and to the laws of all civilized communities, society is bound to protect the natural life of children; and this natural life cannot be protected without the appropriation and use of a portion of the property which society possesses. We prohibit infanticide under penalty of death. We practice a refinement in this particular. The life of an infant is inviolable; and he who feloniously takes it, even before birth, is as subject to the extreme penalty of the law as though he had struck down manhood in its vigor, or taken away a mother by violence from the sanctuary of home where she blesses her offspring. But why preserve the natural life of a child, why preserve unborn embryos of life, if we do not intend to watch over and to protect them, and to expand their subsequent existence into usefulness and happiness? As individuals, or as an organized community, we have no natural right, we can derive no authority or countenance from reason, we can cite no attribute or purpose of the divine nature, for giving birth to any human being, and then inflicting upon that being the curse of ignorance, of poverty, and of vice, with all their attendant calamities. We are brought, then, to this startling but inevitable alternative — the natural life of an infant should be extinguished as soon as it is born, or the means should be provided to save that life from being a curse to its possessor; and, therefore, every state is morally bound to enact a code of laws legalizing and enforcing infanticide or a code of laws establishing free schools.

The three following propositions, then, describe the broad and enduring foundation on which the common-school system of Massachusetts reposes:

The successive generations of men, taken collectively, constitute one great commonwealth.

The property of this commonwealth is pledged for the education of all its youth, up to such a point as will save them from poverty and vice, and prepare them for the adequate performance of their social and civil duties.

The successive holders of this property are trustees,

bound to the faithful execution of their trust by the most sacred obligations; and embezzlement and pillage from children and descendants have not less of criminality, and have more of meanness, than the same offenses when perpetrated against contemporaries.

29

HORACE BUSHNELL
(1802–1876)

The posthumous fame of Horace Bushnell has exceeded
his distinction during his own lifetime, though even then
he was definitely a figure to be reckoned with. His views
concerning Christian nurture were often cited by religious
educators in the early part of the twentieth century, sometimes not in full perspective. He was born in Bantam, Connecticut. Graduating from Yale in 1827, he taught school
at Norwich, Connecticut, served on the staff of a New
York newspaper, studied law, and served as an instructor
at Yale. Then he enrolled in the Yale Divinity School and
was ordained to the Congregational ministry in 1833, serving as pastor of the North Church, Hartford, until he resigned because of illness in 1861. Being of a liberal turn of
mind, he opposed certain of the more inflexible aspects of
traditional Calvinism, although he was far from being as
" liberal " in the late nineteenth- or early twentieth-century
sense as he has sometimes been represented to have been.
Among his other achievements was a share in establishing
the school that eventually became the University of California, while he was in that region in quest of health in
1856.

For his pivotal work, Christian Nurture (1847), and his
influence on subsequent American Christian education,

Bushnell would have to be included in any anthology dealing with basic writings in this field. In addition to that work he wrote The True Wealth and the Weal of Nations *(1837)*, God in Christ *(1849)*, Sermons for the New Life *(1858)*, Work and Play *(1864)*, The Moral Uses of Dark Things *(1868)*, Forgiveness and Law *(1874)*, Building Eras in Religion *(1881 — published posthumously). See Theodore T. Munger,* Horace Bushnell, Preacher and Theologian *(Houghton Mifflin and Co., 1899); A. J. William Myers,* Horace Bushnell and Religious Education *(Manthorne and Burack, Inc., 1937); Barbara M. Cross,* Horace Bushnell, Minister to a Changing America *(University of Chicago Press, 1958).*

HORACE BUSHNELL . . .

What Christian Nurture Is

" Bring them up in the nurture and admonition of the Lord." (Eph. 6:4.)

There is then some kind of nurture which is of the Lord, deriving a quality and a power from him, and communicating the same. Being instituted by him, it will of necessity have a method and a character peculiar to itself, or rather to him. It will be the Lord's way of education, having aims appropriate to him, and, if realized in its full intent, terminating in results impossible to be reached by any merely human method.

What then is the true idea of Christian or divine nurture, as distinguished from that which is not Christian? What is its aim? What its method of working? What its powers and instruments? What its contemplated results? Few questions have greater moment; and it is one of the pleasant signs of the times, that the subject involved is beginning to attract new interest and excite a spirit of inquiry which heretofore has not prevailed in our churches. . . .

Bushnell, Horace, *Christian Nurture* (Centenary Edition, with Introduction by Luther A. Weigle), Chapter I, pp. 3–23, *passim.* Yale University Press, 1947. Used by permission.

Assuming then the question above stated, What is the true idea of Christian education? — I answer in the following proposition, which it will be the aim of my argument to establish; viz.,

That the child is to grow up a Christian, and never know himself as being otherwise.

In other words, the aim, effort, and expectation should be, not, as is commonly assumed, that the child is to grow up in sin, to be converted after he comes to a mature age; but that he is to open on the world as one that is spiritually renewed, not remembering the time when he went through a technical experience, but seeming rather to have loved what is good from his earliest years. I do not affirm that every child may, in fact and without exception, be so trained that he certainly will grow up a Christian. . . .

This doctrine is not a novelty, now rashly and for the first time propounded, as some of you may be tempted to suppose. I shall show you, before I have done with the argument, that it is as old as the Christian church, and prevails extensively at the present day in other parts of the world. Neither let your own experience raise a prejudice against it. If you have endeavored to realize the very truth I here affirm, but find that your children do not exhibit the character you have looked for; if they seem to be intractable to religious influences, and sometimes to display an apparent aversion to the very subject of religion itself, you are not of course to conclude that the doctrine I here maintain is untrue or impracticable. You may be unreasonable in your expectations of your children.

Possibly, there may be seeds of holy principle in them, which you do not discover. A child acts out his present feelings, the feelings of the moment, without qualification or disguise. And how many times, would you all appear,

if you were to do the same? Will you expect of them to
be better, and more constant and consistent, than yourselves; or will you rather expect them to be children, human children still, living a mixed life, trying out the good
and evil of the world, and preparing, as older Christians
do, when they have taken a lesson of sorrow and emptiness,
to turn again to the true good?

Perhaps they will go through a rough mental struggle,
at some future day, and seem, to others and to themselves,
there to have entered on a Christian life. And yet it may
be true that there was still some root of right principle
established in their childhood, which is here only quickened and developed, as when Christians of a mature age
are revived in their piety, after a period of spiritual lethargy; for it is conceivable that regenerate character may
exist, long before it is fully and formally developed.

But suppose there is really no trace or seed of holy principle in your children, has there been no fault of piety and
constancy in your church? No want of Christian sensibility and love to God? No carnal spirit visible to them and
to all, and imparting its noxious and poisonous quality to
the Christian atmosphere in which they have had their
nurture? For it is not for you alone to realize all that is included in the idea of Christian education. It belongs to
the church of God, according to the degree of its social
power over you and in you and around your children, to
bear a part of the responsibility with you.

Then, again, have you nothing to blame in yourselves?
No lack of faithfulness? No indiscretion of manner or of
temper? No mistake of duty, which, with a better and more
cultivated piety, you would have been able to avoid? Have
you been so nearly even with your privilege and duty, that
you can find no relief but to lay some charge upon God,

or comfort yourselves in the conviction that he has appointed the failure you deplore? When God marks out a plan of education, or sets up an aim to direct its efforts, you will see, at once, that he could not base it on a want of piety in you, or on any imperfections that flow from a want of piety. It must be a plan measured by himself and the fullness of his own gracious intention.

Besides, you must not assume that we, in this age, are the best Christians that have ever lived, or most likely to produce all the fruits of piety. An atmosphere so pleasing to our vanity is more easily made than verified, but vanity is the weakest as it is the cheapest of all arguments. We have some good points, in which we compare favorably with other Christians, and Christians of other times, but our style of piety is sadly deficient, in many respects, and that to such a degree that we have little cause for self-congratulation. With all our activity and boldness of movement, there is a certain hardness and rudeness, a want of sensibility to things that do not lie in action, which can not be too much deplored, or too soon rectified. We hold a piety of conquest rather than of love — a kind of public piety, that is strenuous and fiery on great occasions, but wants the beauty of holiness, wants constancy, singleness of aim, loveliness, purity, richness, blamelessness, and — if I may add another term not so immediately religious, but one that carries, by association, a thousand religious qualities — wants domesticity of character; wants them, I mean, not as compared with the perfect standard of Christ, but as compared with other examples of piety that have been given in former times, and others that are given now.

For some reason, we do not make a Christian atmosphere about us — do not produce the conviction that we are liv-

ing unto God. There is a marvelous want of savor in our
piety. It is a flower of autumn, colored as highly as it need
be to the eye, but destitute of fragrance. It is too much to
hope that, with such an instrument, we can fulfill the true
idea of Christian education. Any such hope were even
presumptuous. At the same time, there is not so ready a
way of removing the deficiencies just described, as to re-
call our churches to their duties in domestic life; those
humble, daily, hourly duties, where the spirit we breathe
shall be a perpetual element of power and love, bathing
the life of childhood. . . .

There is, then, as the subject appears to us —

1. No absurdity in supposing that children are to grow
up in Christ. On the other hand, if there is no absurdity,
there is a very clear moral incongruity in setting up a contrary supposition, to be the aim of a system of Christian
education. There could not be a worse or more baleful
implication given to a child, than that he is to reject God
and all holy principle, till he has come to a mature age.
What authority have you from the Scriptures to tell your
child, or, by any sign, to show him, that you do not expect
him truly to love and obey God, till after he has spent
whole years in hatred and wrong? What authority to make
him feel that he is the most unprivileged of all human beings, capable of sin, but incapable of repentance; old
enough to resist all good, but too young to receive any
good whatever? It is reasonable to suppose that you have
some express authority for a lesson so manifestly cruel and
hurtful, else you would shudder to give it. I ask you for
the chapter and verse out of which it is derived. Meantime, wherein would it be less incongruous for you to teach
your child that he is to lie and steal, and go the whole
round of the vices, and then, after he comes to mature

age, reform his conduct by the rules of virtue? Perhaps you
do not give your child to expect that he is to grow up in
sin; you only expect that he will yourself. That is scarcely
better: for that which is your expectation, will assuredly be
his; and what is more, any attempt to maintain a discipline
at war with your own secret expectations, will only make
a hollow and worthless figment of that which should be an
open, earnest reality. You will never practically aim at
what you practically despair of, and if you do not practically aim to unite your child to God, you will aim at something less; that is, something unchristian, wrong, sinful. . . .

2. It is to be expected that Christian education will
radically differ from that which is not Christian. Now, it
is the very character and mark of all unchristian education, that it brings up the child for future conversion. No
effort is made, save to form a habit of outward virtue, and,
if God please to convert the family to something higher
and better, after they come to the age of maturity, it is
well. Is then Christian education, or the nurture of the
Lord, no way different from this? Or is it rather to be supposed that it will have a higher aim and a more sacred
character?

And, since it is the distinction of Christian parents, that
they are themselves in the nurture of the Lord, since
Christ and the Divine Love, communicated through him,
are become the food of their life, what will they so naturally seek as to have their children partakers with them,
heirs together with them, in the grace of life?

3. It is a fact that all Christian parents would like to
see their children grow up in piety; and the better Christians they are, the more earnestly they desire it, and, the
more lovely and constant the Christian spirit they mani-

fest, the more likely it is, in general, that their children will early display the Christian character. This is current opinion. But why should a Christian parent, the deeper his piety and the more closely he is drawn to God, be led to desire, the more earnestly, what, in God's view, is even absurd or impossible? And, if it be generally seen that the children of such are more likely to become Christians early, what forbids the hope that, if they were riper still in their piety, living a more single and Christlike life, and more cultivated in their views of family nurture, they might see their children grow up always in piety toward God? Or, if they may not always see it as clearly as they desire, might they not still be able to implant some holy principle, which shall be the seed of a Christian character in their children, though not developed fully and visibly till a later period in life?

4. Assuming the corruption of human nature, when should we think it wisest to undertake or expect a remedy? When evil is young and pliant to good, or when it is confirmed by years of sinful habit? And when, in fact, is the human heart found to be so ductile to the motives of religion, as in the simple, ingenuous age of childhood? How easy is it then, as compared with the stubbornness of adult years, to make all wrong seem odious, all good lovely and desirable. If not discouraged by some ill-temper which bruises all the gentle sensibilities, or repelled by some technical view of religious character which puts it beyond his age, how ready is the child to be taken by good, as it were beforehand, and yield his ductile nature to the truth and Spirit of God, and to a fixed prejudice against all that God forbids. . . .

There are many who assume the radical goodness of human nature, and the work of Christian education is, in their view, only to educate or educe the good that is in us. Let no one be disturbed by the suspicion of a coincidence between what I have here said and such a theory. The natural pravity of man is plainly asserted in the Scriptures, and, if it were not, the familiar laws of physiology would require us to believe what amounts to the same thing. And if neither Scripture nor physiology taught us the doctrine, if the child was born as clear of natural prejudice or damage as Adam before his sin, spiritual education, or, what is the same, probation, that which trains a being for a stable, intelligent virtue hereafter, would still involve an experiment of evil, therefore a fall and a bondage under the laws of evil; so that, view the matter as we will, there is no so unreasonable assumption, none so wide of all just philosophy, as that which proposes to form a child to virtue, by simply educing or drawing out what is in him.

The growth of Christian virtue is no vegetable process, no mere onward development. It involves a struggle with evil, a fall, and a rescue. The soul becomes established in holy virtue, as a free exercise, only as it is passed round the corner of fall and redemption, ascending thus unto God through a double experience, in which it learns the bitterness of evil and the worth of good, fighting its way out of one, and achieving the other as a victory. The child, therefore, may as well begin life under a law of hereditary damage, as to plunge himself into evil by his own experiment, which he will as naturally do from the simple impulse of curiosity, or the instinct of knowledge, as from any noxious quality in his mold derived by descent. For it is not sin which he derives from his parents; at least, not sin in any sense which imports blame, but only some prejudice to the perfect harmony of this mold, some kind of pravity or obliquity which inclines him to evil. These suggestions are offered, not as necessary to be received in every particular, but simply to show that the scheme of education proposed is not to be identified with another, which assumes the radical goodness of human nature, and according to which, if it be true, Christian education is insignificant.

5. It is implied in all our religious philosophy, that if a child ever does anything in a right spirit, ever loves anything because it is good and right, it involves the dawn of a new life. This we cannot deny or doubt without bringing in question our whole scheme of doctrine. Is it then incredible that some really good feeling should be called into exercise in a child? In all the discipline of the house, quickened as it should be by the Spirit of God, is it true that he can never once be brought to submit to parental authority lovingly and because it is right? Must we even hold the absurdity of the Scripture counsel — " Children, obey your parents in the Lord, for this is right "? When we speak thus of a love for what is right and good, we must of course discriminate between the mere excitement of a natural sensibility to pleasure in the contemplation of what is good (of which the worst minds are more or less capable) and a practicable subordination of the soul to its power, a practicable embrace of its law. The child must not only be touched with some gentle emotions toward what is right, but he must love it with a fixed love, love it for the sake of its principle, receive it as a vital and formative power. . . .

6. Children have been so trained as never to remember the time when they began to be religious. Baxter was, at one time, greatly troubled concerning himself, because he could recollect no time when there was a gracious

change in his character. But he discovered, at length, that " education is as properly a means of grace as preaching," and thus found the sweeter comfort in his love to God, that he learned to love him so early. The European churches, generally, regard Christian piety more as a habit of life, formed under the training of childhood, and less as a marked spiritual change in experience. In Germany, for example, the church includes all the people, and it is remarkable that, under a scheme so loose, and with so much of pernicious error taught in the pulpit, there is yet so much of a deep religious feeling, so much of lovely and simple character, and a savor of Christian piety so generally prevalent in the community. So true is this, that the German people are every day spoken of as a people religious by nature; no other way being observed of accounting for the strong religious bent they manifest. Whereas it is due, beyond any reasonable question, to the fact that children are placed under a form of treatment which expects them to be religious, and are not discouraged by the demand of an experience above their years. . . .

Once more, if we narrowly examine the relation of parent and child, we shall not fail to discover something like a law of organic connection, as regards character, subsisting between them. Such a connection as makes it easy to believe, and natural to expect, that the faith of the one will be propagated to the other. Perhaps I should rather say, such a connection as induced the conviction that the character of one is actually included in that of the other, as a seed is formed in the capsule; and being there matured, by a nutriment derived from the stem, is gradually separated from it. It is a singular fact that many believe substantially the same thing in regard to evil character, but have no thought of any such possibility in regard to good.

There has been much speculation, of late, as to whether
a child is born in depravity, or whether the depraved character is superinduced afterward. But, like many other
great questions, it determines much less than is commonly
supposed; for, according to the most proper view of the
subject, a child is really not born till he emerges from the
infantile state, and never before that time can he be said
to receive a separate and properly individual nature. . . .

The tendency of all our modern speculations is to an
extreme individualism, and we carry our doctrines of free
will so far as to make little or nothing of organic laws;
not observing that character may be, to a great extent, only
the free development of exercises previously wrought in
us, or extended to us, when other wills had us within their
sphere. We have much to say about the beginning of moral
agency, and we seem to fancy that there is some definite
moment when a child becomes a moral agent, passing out
of a condition where he is a moral nullity, and where no
moral agency touches his being. Whereas he is rather to be
regarded, at the first, as lying within the moral agency of
the parent, and passing out, by degrees, through a course
of mixed agency, to a proper independency and self-pos-
session. . . . The separation is gradual. . . .

And this is the very idea of Christian education, that
it begins with nurture or cultivation. And the intention is
that the Christian life and spirit of the parents, which are
in and by the Spirit of God, shall flow into the mind of
the child, to blend with his incipient and half-formed exercises; that they shall thus beget their own good within
him — their thoughts, opinions, faith, and love, which
are to become a little more, and yet a little more, his own
separate exercise, but still the same in character. The contrary assumption, that virtue must be the product of

separate and absolutely independent choice, is pure assumption. . . .

All society is organic — the church, the state, the school, the family; and there is a spirit in each of these organisms, peculiar to itself and more or less hostile, more or less favorable to religious character, and to some extent, at least, sovereign over the individual man. . . . We possess only a mixed individuality all our life long. A pure, separate, individual man, living *wholly* within and from himself, is a mere fiction. No such person ever existed or ever can. I need not say that this view of an organic connection of character subsisting between parent and child lays a basis for notions of Christian education far different from those which now prevail, under the cover of a merely fictitious and mischievous individualism.

Perhaps it may be necessary to add, that, in the strong language I have used concerning the organic connection of character between the parent and the child, it is not designed to assert a power in the parent to renew the child, or that the child can be renewed by any agency of the Spirit less immediate than that which renews the parent himself. . . . So, if there be an organic power of character in the parent, such as that of which I have spoken, it is not a complete power in itself, but only such a power as demands the realizing presence of the spirit of God, both in the parent and the child, to give it effect. As Paul said, " I have begotten you through the gospel," so we may say of the parent, who, having a living gospel enveloped in his life, brings it into organic connection with the soul of childhood. But the declaration excludes the necessity of a divine influence, not more in one case than the other.

Such are some of the considerations that offer themselves, viewing our subject on the human side, or as it appears in the light of human evidence — all concurring to produce the conviction that it is the only true idea of Christian education that a child is to grow up in the life of the parent and be a Christian in principle from his earliest years.

30

JOHN DEWEY

(1859–1952)

John Dewey was born at Burlington, Vermont, and died at New York City. His schooling took place at the University of Vermont and Johns Hopkins University. Eventually, due to his eminence as philosopher and educator, he was to be honored with degrees from Peking National University, the University of Oslo, and the University of Paris, as well as from many American institutions. He taught at the University of Michigan (with one year out, at the University of Minnesota), from 1884 to 1894. At the University of Chicago, to which President William Rainey Harper invited him, he was involved in an experimental school which did pioneer work in newer methodology, from 1894 to 1906. He then went to Columbia University for the remainder of his professorial career.

Dewey's practical pedagogy has deeply influenced the schools of the United States, and his influence has penetrated many other countries as well. He is chiefly memorable for his development of the instrumentalist philosophy and for his insistence that the child be placed at the center of the curriculum rather than subject matter in itself.

The religious education movement of the first half of the twentieth century was deeply influenced by Dewey's methodology; likewise, through his followers, by his philo-

*sophical positions. Dewey was not interested in the es-
pousal of a particular religion, but urged what he called
" the religious " as an essential ingredient of the fully developed personality. This distinction is developed in his
book,* A Common Faith (*1934*). *We see the pattern already
emerging in* My Pedagogic Creed.

Other writings by Dewey include the following: School
and Society (*1899*), Studies in Logical Theory (*1903*),
How We Think (*1909*), Interest and Effort in Education
(*1913*), Democracy and Education (*1916*), Reconstruction
in Philosophy (*1920*), The Quest for Certainty: A Study
of the Relation of Knowledge and Action (*1929*), Art as
Experience (*1934*), Freedom and Culture (*1939*), Education Today (*1946*), Problems of Man (*1946*). *For a study
of Dewey's thought, see Manford G. Gutzke,* John Dewey's
Thought and Its Implication for Christian Education
(King's Crown Press, 1956).

JOHN DEWEY . . .

My Pedagogic Creed

Article I. What Education Is

I believe that all education proceeds by the participation of the individual in the social consciousness of the race. This process begins unconsciously almost at birth, and is continually shaping the individual's powers, saturating his consciousness, forming his habits, training his ideas, and arousing his feelings and emotions. Through this unconscious education, the individual gradually comes to share in the intellectual and moral resources which humanity has succeeded in getting together. He becomes an inheritor of the funded capital of civilization. The most formal and technical education in the world cannot safely depart from this general process. It can only organize it; or differentiate it in some particular direction.

I believe that the only true education comes through the stimulation of the child's powers by the demands of the social situations in which he finds himself. Through these

Dewey, John, " My Pedagogic Creed " in *My Pedagogic Creed by Professor John Dewey and The Demands of Sociology Upon Pedagogy.* A. Flanagan Company, n.d. (This work was issued in 1898.) Article IV, " The Nature of Method," is omitted *in toto* here.

demands he is stimulated to act as a member of a unity, to emerge from his original narrowness of action and feeling, and to conceive of himself from the standpoint of the welfare of the group to which he belongs. Through the responses which others make to his own activities he comes to know what these mean in social terms. The value which they have is reflected back into them. For instance, through the response which is made to the child's instinctive babblings the child comes to know what those babblings mean; they are transformed into articulate language, and thus the child is introduced into the consolidated wealth of ideas and emotions which are now summed up in language.

I believe that this educational process has two sides — one psychological and one sociological; and that neither can be subordinated to the other or neglected without evil results following. Of these two sides, the psychological is the basis. The child's own instincts and powers furnish the material and give the starting point for all education. Save as the efforts of the educator connect with some activity which the child is carrying on of his own initiative independent of the educator, education becomes reduced to a pressure from without. It may, indeed, give certain external results, but cannot truly be called educative. Without insight into the psychological structure and activities of the individual, the educative process will, therefore, be haphazard and arbitrary. If it chances to coincide with the child's activity, it will get a leverage; if it does not, it will result in friction, or disintegration, or arrest of the child's nature.

I believe that knowledge of social conditions, of the present state of civilization, is necessary to properly interpret the child's powers. The child has his own instincts and tendencies, but we do not know what these mean until we can translate them into their social equivalents. We must be able to carry them back into a social past and see them as the inheritance of precious race activities. We must also be able to project them into the future to see what their outcome and end will be. In the illustration just used, it is the ability to see in the child's babblings the promise and potency of a future social intercourse and conversation which enables one to deal in the proper way with that instinct.

I believe that the psychological and social sides are organically related, and that education cannot be regarded as a compromise between the two, or a superimposition of one upon the other. We are told that the psychological definition of education is barren and formal — that it gives us only the idea of a development of all the mental powers without giving us any idea of the use to which these powers are put. On the other hand, it is urged that the social definition of education, as getting adjusted to civilization, makes of it a forced and external process, and results in subordinating the freedom of the individual to a preconceived social and political status.

I believe each of these objections is true when urged against one side isolated from the other. In order to know what a power really is we must know what its end, use, or function is; and this we cannot know save as we conceive of the individual as active in social relationships. But, on the other hand, the only possible adjustment which we can give to the child under existing conditions, is that which arises through putting him in complete possession of all his powers. With the advent of democracy and modern industrial conditions, it is impossible to foretell definitely just what civilization will be twenty years from now. Hence it is impossible to prepare the child for any precise set of conditions. To prepare him for the future life means to give him command of himself; it means to train him that he will have the full and ready use of all his capacities; that his eye and ear and hand may be tools ready to command, that his judgment may be capable of grasping the conditions under which it has to work, and the executive forces be trained to act economically and efficiently. It is impossible to reach this sort of adjustment save as constant regard is had to the individual's own powers, tastes, and interests — say, that is, as education is continually converted into psychological terms.

In sum, I believe that the individual who is to be educated is a social individual, and that society is an organic union of individuals. If we eliminate the social factor from the child, we are left only with an abstraction; if we eliminate the individual factor from society, we are left only with an inert and lifeless mass. Education, therefore, must begin with a psychological insight into the child's capacities, interests, and habits. It must be controlled at every point by reference to these same considerations. These powers, interests, and habits must be continually interpreted — we must know what they mean. They must be translated into terms of their social equivalents — into terms of what they are capable of in the way of social service.

Article II. What the School Is

I believe that the school is primarily a social institution. Education being a social process, the school is simply that form of community life in which all those agencies are con-

centrated that will be most effective in bringing the child
to share in the inherited resources of the race, and to use
his own powers for social ends.

I believe that education, therefore, is a process of living
and not a preparation for future living.

I believe that the school must represent present life —
life as real and vital to the child as that which he carries
on in the home, in the neighborhood, or on the playground.

I believe that education which does not occur through
forms of life, forms that are worth living for their own sake,
is always a poor substitute for the genuine reality, and
tends to cramp and to deaden.

I believe that the school, as an institution, should sim-
plify existing social life; should reduce it, as it were, to
an embryonic form. Existing life is so complex that the
child cannot be brought into contact with it without either
confusion or distraction; he is either overwhelmed by the
multiplicity of activities which are going on, so that he
loses his own power of orderly reaction, or he is so stimulated by these various activities that his powers are pre-
maturely called into play, and he becomes either unduly
specialized or else disintegrated.

I believe that, as such simplified social life, the school
life should grow gradually out of the home life; that it
should take up and continue the activities with which the
child is already familiar in the home.

I believe that it should exhibit these activities to the
child, and reproduce them in such ways that the child
will gradually learn the meaning of them, and be capable
of playing his own part in relation to them.

I believe that this is a psychological necessity, because
it is the only way of securing continuity in the child's
growth, the only way of giving a background of past ex-

perience to the new ideas given in school.

I believe it is also a social necessity, because the home is the form of social life in which the child has been nurtured and in connection with which he has had his moral training. It is the business of the school to deepen and extend his sense of the values bound up in his home life.

I believe that much of present education fails because it neglects this fundamental principle of the school as a form of community life. It conceives the school as a place where certain information is to be given, where certain lessons are to be learned, or where certain habits are to be formed. The value of these is conceived as lying largely in the remote future; the child must do these things for the sake of something else he is to do; they are mere preparations. As a result they do not become a part of the life experience of the child and so are not truly educative.

I believe that the moral education centers upon this conception of the school as a mode of social life, that the best and deepest moral training is precisely that which one gets through having to enter into proper relations with others in a unity of work and thought. The present educational systems, so far as they destroy or neglect this unity, render it difficult or impossible to get any genuine, regular moral training.

I believe that the child should be stimulated and controlled in his work through the life of the community.

I believe that under existing conditions far too much of the stimulus and control proceeds from the teacher, because of neglect of the idea of the school as a form of social life.

I believe that the teacher's place and work in the school is to be interpreted from this same basis. The teacher is not in the school to impose certain ideas or to form certain habits in the child, but is there as a member of the community to select the influences which shall affect the child and to assist him in properly responding to these influences.

I believe that the discipline of the school should proceed from the life of the school as a whole and not directly from the teacher.

I believe that the teacher's business is simply to determine, on the basis of larger experience and riper wisdom, how the discipline of life shall come to the child.

I believe that all questions of the grading of the child and his promotion should be determined by reference to the same standard. Examinations are of use only so far as they test the child's fitness for social life and reveal the place in which he can be of the most service and where he can receive the most help.

ARTICLE III. THE SUBJECT MATTER OF EDUCATION

. . . I believe that there is, therefore, no succession of studies in the ideal school curriculum. If education is life, all life has, from the outset, a scientific aspect; an aspect of art and culture; and an aspect of communication. It cannot, therefore, be true that the proper studies for one grade are mere reading and writing, and that at a later grade, reading, or literature, or science, may be introduced. The progress is not in the succession of studies, but in the development of new attitudes toward, and new interests in, experience.

I believe, finally, that education must be conceived as a continuing reconstruction of experience; that the process and the goal of education are one and the same thing.

I believe that to set up any end outside of education, as furnishing its goal and standard, is to deprive the educational process of much of its meaning, and tends to make us rely upon false and external stimuli in dealing with the child. . . .

ARTICLE V. THE SCHOOL AND SOCIAL PROGRESS

. . . I believe that education thus conceived marks the most perfect and intimate union of science and art conceivable in human experience.

I believe that the art of thus giving shape to human powers and adapting them to social service is the supreme art; one calling into its service the best of artists; that no insight, tact, executive power is too great for such service. . . .

I believe that when science and art thus join hands the most commanding motive for human action will be reached; the most genuine springs of human conduct aroused, and the best service that human nature is capable of guaranteed.

I believe, finally, that the teacher is engaged, not simply in the training of individuals, but in the formation of the proper social life.

I believe that every teacher should realize the dignity of his calling; that he is a social servant set apart for the maintenance of proper social order and the securing of the right social growth.

I believe that in this way the teacher always is the prophet of the true God and the usherer in of the true Kingdom of God.

The Nature of Method

THE TRAITS OF INDIVIDUAL METHOD

. . . The specific elements of an individual's method or way of attack upon a problem are found ultimately in his native tendencies and his acquired habits and interests. The method of one will vary from that of another (and *properly* vary) as his original instinctive capacities vary, as his past experiences and his preferences vary. Those who have already studied these matters are in possession of information which will help teachers in understanding the responses different pupils make, and help them in guiding these responses to greater efficiency. Child study, psychology, and a knowledge of social environment supplement the personal acquaintance gained by the teacher. But methods remain the personal concern, approach, and attack of an individual, and no catalogue can ever exhaust their diversity of form and tint.

Some attitudes may be named, however, which are central in effective intellectual ways of dealing with subject matter. Among the most important are directness, open-mindedness, single-mindedness (or whole-heartedness), and responsibility.

1. It is easier to indicate what is meant by directness through negative terms than in positive ones. Self-consciousness, embarrassment, and constraint are its menacing foes. They indicate that a person is not immediately con-

Dewey, John, *Democracy and Education:* An Introduction to the Philosophy of Education, pp. 203–211, *passim.* The Macmillan Company, 1926. Used by permission.

cerned with subject matter. Something has come between which deflects concern to side issues. A self-conscious person is partly thinking about his problem and partly about what others think of his performances. Diverted energy means loss of power and confusion of ideas. . . .

Confidence is a good name for what is intended by the term directness. It should not be confused, however, with *self*-confidence which may be a form of self-consciousness — or of " cheek." Confidence is not a name for what one thinks or feels about his attitude; it is not reflex. It denotes the straightforwardness with which one goes at what he has to do. It denotes not *conscious* trust in the efficacy of one's powers but unconscious faith in the possibilities of the situation. . . . Whatever methods of a teacher call a pupil's attention off from what he has to do and transfer it to his own attitude toward what he is doing impair directness of concern and action. Persisted in, the pupil acquires a permanent tendency to fumble, to gaze about aimlessly, to look for some clew of action besides that which the subject matter supplies. Dependence upon extraneous suggestions and directions, a state of foggy confusion, take the place of that sureness with which children (and grown-up people who have not been sophisticated by " education ") confront the situations of life.

2. Open-mindedness. Partiality is, as we have seen, an accompaniment of the existence of interest, since this means sharing, partaking, taking sides in some movement. All the more reason, therefore, for an attitude of mind which actively welcomes suggestions and relevant information from all sides. . . . The worst thing about stubbornness of mind, about prejudices, is that they arrest development; they shut the mind off from new stimuli. Open-mindedness means retention of the childlike atti-

tude; closed-mindedness means premature intellectual old age. . . .

Open-mindedness is not the same as empty-mindedness. To hang out a sign saying " Come right in; there is no one at home " is not the equivalent of hospitality. But there is a kind of passivity, willingness to let experiences accumulate and sink in and ripen, which is an essential of development. Results (external answers or solutions) may be hurried; processes may not be forced. They take their own time to mature. Were all instructors to realize that the quality of mental process, not the production of correct answers, is the measure of educative growth something hardly less than a revolution in teaching would be worked.

3. Single-mindedness. . . . What the word is here intended to convey is *completeness* of interest, unity of purpose; the absence of suppressed but effectual ulterior aims for which the professed aim is but a mask. It is equivalent to mental integrity. Absorption, engrossment, full concern with subject matter for its own sake, nurture it. Divided interest and evasion destroy it. . . .

School conditions favorable to this division of mind between avowed, public, and socially responsible undertakings, and private, ill-regulated, and suppressed indulgences of thought are not hard to find. What is sometimes called " stern discipline," i.e., external coercive pressure, has this tendency. Motivation through rewards extraneous to the thing to be done has a like effect. Everything that makes schooling merely preparatory works in this direction. Ends being beyond the pupil's present grasp, other agencies have to be found to procure immediate attention to assigned tasks. Some responses are secured, but desires and affections not enlisted must find other outlets. . . . What do teachers imagine is happening to thought and emotion when the latter get no outlet in the things of immediate activity? Were they merely kept in temporary abeyance, or even only calloused, it would not be a matter of so much moment. But they are not abolished; they are not suspended; they are not suppressed — save with reference to the task in question. They follow their own chaotic and undisciplined course. What is native, spontaneous, and vital in mental reaction goes unused and untested, and the habits formed are such that these qualities become less and less available for public and avowed ends.

4. Responsibility. By responsibility as an element in intellectual attitude is meant the disposition to consider in advance the probable consequences of any projected step and deliberately to accept them; to accept them in the sense of taking them into account, acknowledging them in action, not yielding a mere verbal assent. . . .

Intellectual *thoroughness* is thus another name for the attitude we are considering. There is a kind of thoroughness which is almost purely physical; the kind that signifies mechanical and exhausting drill upon all the details of a subject. Intellectual thoroughness is *seeing a thing through*. It depends upon a unity of purpose in which details are subordinated, not upon presenting a multitude of disconnected details. It is manifested in the firmness with which the full meaning of the purpose is developed, not in attention, however "conscientious" it may be, to the steps of action externally imposed and directed.

SUMMARY

Method is a statement of the way the subject matter of an experience develops most effectively and fruitfully. It is derived, accordingly, from observation of the course of experiences where there is no conscious distinction of personal attitude and manner from material dealt with. The assumption that method is something separate is connected with the notion of the isolation of mind and self from the world of things. It makes instruction and learning formal, mechanical, constrained. While methods are individualized, certain features of the normal course of an experience to its fruition may be discriminated, because of the fund of wisdom derived from prior experiences and because of general similarities in the materials dealt with from time to time. Expressed in terms of the attitude of the individual the traits of good method are straightforwardness, flexible intellectual interest or open-minded will to learn, integrity of purpose, and acceptance of responsibility for the consequences of one's activity including thought.

31

GEORGE ALBERT COE
(1862–1951)

George Albert Coe was born in 1862. After studies in Boston University School of Theology, he began his teaching career at the University of Southern California. Awarded a traveling fellowship from Boston University in 1890, he spent a year in Germany. In 1893 he was appointed to the philosophy department in Northwestern University, and in 1909 to Union Theological Seminary, New York, as professor of religious education. In 1922 he resigned from Union and accepted a professorship in Teachers College, Columbia University, where he stayed until his retirement five years later.

Much influenced by John Dewey, Coe exercised tremendous influence in the whole " liberal" period of the religious education movement. He was active in the Religious Education Association from its founding in 1903. He advocated a scientific approach to the religious life and a constant reconstruction of values. In the years of his formal retirement he continued writing actively. He was to live until 1951, meanwhile seeing on the horizon considerable shifts in emphasis in the very movement he had fostered and lamenting publicly the growing influence of neo-orthodox positions. In a very real sense Coe's professional career can be said to have included both the zenith

*and the beginning of the decline of the distinctive causes
to which he devoted his keen mind.*

*In addition to many articles in learned journals, Coe
wrote the following books:* The Spiritual Life: Studies in
the Science of Religion (*1900*), The Religion of a Mature
Mind (*1902*), Education in Religion and Morals (*1904*),
The Psychology of Religion (*1916*), A Social Theory of
Religious Education (*1917*), Law and Freedom in the
School (*1924*), What Ails Our Youth? (*1924*), The Motives of Men (*1928*), What Is Christian Education?
(*1929*), Educating for Citizenship (*1932*), What Is Religion Doing to Our Consciences? (*1943*). *See* Religious
Education, *Vol. XLVII, No. 2, March–April, 1952, dedicated in memoriam to Coe, for evaluative and biographical
material.*

GEORGE ALBERT COE . . .

The Starting Point of a Solution

RELIGION CHANGES IN THE ACT OF TEACHING IT

At what point shall we begin the attempt to rethink the nature of Christian education? Perhaps the simplest procedure that moves within the concrete, and does not wander off into abstract definitions, is this: Imagining a teacher and a pupil together, each responding to the other, to ask what this relationship between the two is. What is it to be a teacher, and what is it to be a pupil, where Christian education is going on?

A distinction between the two individuals comes at once to the surface. I do not refer to the fact that usually one is considerably older than the other, for sometimes this age relation is reversed. The important difference is that, whereas the teacher acts in a representative capacity, speaking for the church, or for God, or for a cause or a curriculum, the pupil represents nobody but himself. Let us examine this contrast and some consequences of it.

The teacher certainly is an agent or an instrument, but is he nothing more than this? Is he a lamp that grows in-

Coe, George A., *What Is Christian Education?* Chapter II, pp. 23–24, and " Coda," p. 296. Charles Scribner's Sons, 1929.

candescent and warm only when and because someone else presses a button? Is he merely an animated tool? Everybody, Catholic and Protestant alike, will answer that what the teacher himself is, his individual personality, what he is by virtue of his own choices, efforts, and habits, is a vital factor in the teacher-pupil relationship.

For Catholics this answer might conceivably call attention to a rather odd difference in standpoint within their church. According to the Roman doctrine, in the sacrifice of the mass, which is regarded as the central channel through which the saving grace of God flows into the church, the character of the officiating priest is nonessential. He may be a bad Catholic and a bad man, he may be drunk or trifling at the time, but if he has been properly ordained, and if he says mass according to the prescribed formula, the full value of the sacrifice is realized. On the other hand, a bad Catholic or bad man, or one drunk or trifling at the time, even if he had been ordained, and even if he spoke Catholic doctrine and ideals without a flaw, could not be a good teacher of the Catholic religion. Why this discrepancy between the minimal requirement for mediating God to a congregation and the minimal qualifications of a teacher who is to stand in the presence of a child? I shall leave the answer to any Catholic who may be interested in the question.

Probably Catholics and Protestants would give the same reason for their insistence upon truly Christian character and earnestness in the teacher, namely, that what the teacher is mingles itself inextricably with what he says, so that response of the pupil is a response to the teacher as well as to the curriculum that he uses, the church that commissions him, and the God on whose behalf the church speaks through him.

In fact, that which we can be most certain of whenever we undertake to teach is some interplay between the teacher and the pupil, with some resulting modification of the pupil's personality. This, indeed, is psychologically inevitable, and it has far-reaching implications.

The first of these implications will now be stated, but others will be postponed for a time. The personality principle implies that Christian education, as well as the Christian teacher, is not a mere tool or instrument of our religion, but the actual fulfillment, or attempt at fulfillment, of the ends of our religion in the teacher-and-learner relationship.

Something like this has been said many times, but whether the full meaning and consequence of it have been perceived may be doubted. For it signifies that what is most personal and free in each of the persons concerned can be educational in the most Christian sense. The pupil, as we have remarked, speaks for nobody but himself. The teacher, in turn, though he is a messenger and transmitter, is such by his own conviction and voluntary loyalty. This loyalty of his adds impressiveness to the message and to the authority back of it, making concrete, near, and warm what otherwise would not seem so close. Moreover, the teacher adjusts himself to the pupil, varying the form of words, the emphasis and angle of thought, and the type of attitude, to suit the age, the experience, and the individuality of the other. Thus, into the relationship there is injected a meaning to which the teacher's own individuality clings and must cling, and likewise a meaning to which the pupil's individuality clings.

Consider, now, that personality is a sensitive, changing thing, and that no two personalities are exactly alike. Any two Christians are Christians in at least slightly different ways, probably in ways that are not slight. Pupils, likewise, are individual and different from one another; their spiritual responses, though couched in identical words, are not exactly the same. Here, then, are two necessarily variable elements. Though we reduce the variation to the lowest possible point, we do not quite extinguish it.

These variations or shadings in religion, taking place in the acts of teaching and learning it, have received entirely inadequate consideration. One probable reason is that, like biological variations, they are usually slight and therefore apparently not important.

In fact, they are not always slight, but even when they are they have a way of accumulating that is not unimportant. Religions can change their complexion almost insensibly along with the other changes in their adherents and pupils. A church population, Protestant or Catholic, that makes the transition from weakness to power, from poverty to wealth, or from crudity to culture, drifts into changed religious attitudes. It does so by accumulating such slight individual variations as have been described.

Christian education participated in these variations not only because the teacher's convictions reflect them, but also because he is, and is known by the pupil to be, a representative of his church. Through the teacher the church as a whole says, " Follow us "; or, if it says, " Follow Jesus," the pupil assumes, in the absence of specific information to the contrary, that following Jesus consists in what his professed disciples do. Thus the prevailing habits of Christians, which are changing habits, supply an interpretative background to anything that teacher or textbook or sermon or the Bible says, and to any worship or other activity that is included in the church program.

This background meaning shifts because ideas and conduct shift. General formulas of approval and disapproval may remain the same while particular acts, attitudes, and notions exchange places to any extent in the scale that reaches from what is praised, through what is permitted, to what is condemned. Practices in which the religious society acquiesces become standards, at least standards of the religiously permissible. One can see this from the short history of the motorcar, or from the history of race relations during the last hundred years. The atrophy of a custom — family prayers, for example — is reflected in a changed sense of duty, though there be no change in the formulas of piety. Even sudden and profound spiritual displacements can occur, as in the Great War, without formal acknowledgment. It is then the emotional situation that does the effective teaching. The same curriculum material may have been taught in 1913, 1918, and 1928, but how different the kinds of Christianity that it represented to the pupil! All this " not-in-the-curriculum " meaning is mediated to the pupil by the personal presence of the teacher.

What shall the Christian teacher do about this kind of inescapable fact? He will, of course, endeavor to hand on to his pupil the best thing in the religious inheritance, and over and above what he intentionally hands on he will almost automatically transmit much more. Education always is transmission; no one need fear that it ever will cease to be this. But the other factor, likewise inevitable, is minimized by Catholics and fumbled by Protestants. It is true that Protestants sentimentalize over the importance of " the teacher's personality "; they sometimes even substitute winsomeness for sound work within the curriculum. But never, I think, has it been recognized that precisely in the personal relations between teacher and pupil the re-

ligion of the churches undergoes modification either slowly
or rapidly, and never has this process of modification been
taken purposefully in hand and given deliberate direction.

The concept that now emerges is that of the possibility
of a church that, through its educational system, exercises
voluntary selection among possible changes in its religion
some of which are bound to occur. Changes unforeseen
and not fully voluntary will continue to take place — the
complexity of the details and the unpredictable factors
in personality assure this — but mere drift can be reduced,
it can be recognized as such and therefore modified far
earlier than is now the case, and there can be conscious
and controlled development, growth, in the qualities of
our religion.

THE CHRISTIAN TEACHER'S DILEMMA

Almost invariably the assumption has prevailed that the
work of the Christian teacher is to transmit a religion, and
that the contribution of the teacher's personality is simply
and solely that of a reinforcement of the transmission process. We now see that this " simply and solely " is a psychological impossibility. When teachers of religion become
psychologically awake and thoroughly realistic, they will
perceive that they must take a voluntary attitude toward
a flow in religion that cannot in any case be wholly prevented. They will be face to face with a practical dilemma:
Shall the personality factor in teaching be so used as to
secure the maximum of conformity and the minimum of
change, or so as to produce attitudes of freedom in the
presence of conditions that might lead to change? There
will dawn upon the mind the possibility of religious crea-
tiveness through Christian education, whereupon the relation of transmission to creation within the educative

process will have to be worked out. Practically everything that remains to be said in this volume concerns this practical dilemma and its relation on the one hand to existing defects in religious education, and on the other hand to the achievement of something new and better but still Christian. Therefore some pages will now be devoted to a preliminary illumination of the alternatives between which we shall have to choose.

It is not within our power to determine whether education shall be both transmission from the past and response to the present — it is bound to be in some measure each of these — but we can select one or the other of them as the primary function, and we can make either of them contributory to the other. Accordingly, the Christian teacher's practical dilemma takes this form: Shall the primary purpose of Christian education be to hand on a religion, or to create a new world?

A dim inkling that education is not mere transmission pervades the schooling of both the state and the church. For no school endeavors to perpetuate, whole and unchanged, any culture whatever. When we teach literature we select the specimens according to our own taste, not according to the taste of our ancestors. When we teach history or biography we ourselves determine what shall be foreground and what background. And when we come to morals, again we select. We do it rather drastically, too, for we never tell the young the whole truth about the conduct of the present adult generation, nor about the standards that it in practice accepts. By maintaining discreet silence concerning parts of our civilization, we hope to save the coming generation from civilization as we ourselves practice it.

Wherever the schools do not avow this policy they come

perilously near the edge of duplicity. The schools of the state scarcely ever tell the whole truth about how the government is run and what it has done; instead, they cover up or slur over the blunders and the wrongs committed by our nation, causing pupils to believe that our better national qualities are more commanding than they ever have been. Thus, professing to transmit a political culture, the schools idealize it by a process of selection that really implies condemnation as well as praise, the need of reconstruction as well as of transmission.

An almost identical educational policy prevails in the schools of the church. No Sunday school, church college, or theological seminary paints an impartially realistic picture of the state of our religion, or with some exceptions in theological schools — of any past state of it. No church, however holy it thinks itself, goes the whole length of complete self-revelation. When God, incarnated in children, peers about our ecclesiastical garden, every denomination resorts to fig leaves.

This selective function of education, normal and proper though it be, is seldom fully avowed by school administrators; it is seldom thorough, and the implication that education should squarely accept the duty of social criticism and reconstruction is scarcely ever accepted. No, the dominant concern is that the rising generation should not get too far away from precedents, should not become too unlike us.

As it is not within our power to determine whether education shall be both transmission from the past and response to the present, so it is beyond our scope to permit or forbid selection among the possible responses to the present. Selection takes place anyhow, whether consciously or unconsciously, whether by successive yieldings to circumstances or by a continuous plan. The one thing that we can do is to make deliberate choices, and consolidate them into a policy, instead of drifting, or being only partly steered by others, dead or alive, while we vainly imagine that we are wholly guided by them. If we should conclude that our job as teachers is not, first and foremost, to hand on something that already exists, but to enter creatively into the flow of present experience, a part of our problem would then take this form: Is there anything creative in the religion that has been handed down to us, any principle that provides for a self-transcending and self-transforming process within the historic faith itself? If so, this principle might conceivably approve itself as a guide to original, unprescribed, and unprecedented responses to our present world, which is itself unprecedented, and we should then have a creative education that is nevertheless Christian. Let us look at this concept a little more closely.

The Concept of a Creative Education That Is Christian

That God is now, as through all history, creating a spiritual or moral order of righteousness and good will is a very old item in Christian thinking. At least, words like these are old. But the concept of continuous creation, it appears, has been hard to grasp; the nearest that most minds come to it is the notion of a quantitative increase of something that is qualitatively finished and complete. The growth of the Kingdom of God has been conceived as " more of the same " — more geographic areas covered, more members in the church, more resources at command, more faithfulness in doing duties that the saints long ago performed to the full. Growth, in the sense of qualitative change, the coming into being of something unprecedented and

unpredictable from the past, involving possibly the super-
seding of some ancient good — this notion of the inexhaust-
ible vitality of the divine has not been common.

Oddly enough, however, it has been many times declared that imitation, even of the Master, does not suffice.
He was unmarried, and at the crucial period of his life
he lived outside of the family; apparently he had no settled place of abode, and it is not clear that he made any
economic contribution to his own support. In short, he
did not have our particular problems to meet, and to imitate his conduct is no solution of them. Therefore, instead
of imitating him, we are to adopt his spirit, his ends and
principles of action, and by applying them in our situations
develop modes of conduct of our very own.

The growth of social consciousness and conscience
within the Christian churches during the last thirty and
more years has brought to the surface a most interesting
phase of this idea. The Gospels give us no direct guidance
concerning capital and labor, property, the profit system,
corporations, government ownership, social insurance, international law, and so on, though these are the sphere of
severest moral strains of our time. Nevertheless, no one
doubts that in Jesus' approach to life there is something
that does bear upon this whole area of modern social struggle, and that if we take this approach we shall produce
unprecedented modes of social life and unprecedented
good. How our modern mass life can become Christian we
simply do not know and cannot know except by experi-
mentation; we must create the good life or we shall miss
it. Already we see that the old sorts of goodness, the Christian life of other generations, are inadequate and sometimes obstructive, and it dawns upon us that *we* cannot be
Christian unless we take upon ourselves the burdens and

the risks of re-creating in some measure our Christianity itself.

This re-creation, these phases of religious living that Jesus never thought of, can yet be Christian in the sense of carrying forward something that Jesus started or something to which he gave impetus; and his mode of approach to life (as distinct from the particular things he did, and the particular connections in his thought) is universally valid because it is the way of perpetual discovery and perpetual creation. It may be — I shall show that this is the fact — that we cannot maintain vital continuity with Jesus unless we do take his road of discovery and creation. It is quite possible — indeed, the preceding chapter gave examples of this — to attempt a kind of continuity that is self-defeating. The churches have broken away from Jesus time and again at the very points where they thought they were exalting him. I do not see how we can ever really outgrow him; the issue for us is whether we will be creators with him, evoking the unprecedented by our own thinking, experimenting, daring, and suffering. Reconstruction, continuous reconstruction, is of the essence of the divine work in and through the human.

Of course we cannot reconstruct anything unless we are acquainted with it; we cannot take a creative part in the moral order without intelligence as to its present and its past. But the focal point of true education is not acquaintance with the past, it is the building forth of a future different from the present and from the past. Moreover, creative education implies that the nature and the degree of this difference are to be determined within and by means of the educative processes; they cannot be dictated or imposed; they cannot be discovered by exegesis of any historical document.

This, in a preliminary and schematic way, is what is meant by creative education that is likewise Christian. Looked at from the standpoint of the learner's experience, what has been said means that learning to be a Christian should be, essentially and primarily, an experience of free creativity. Looked at from the standpoint of the teacher, it means fellowship of teacher and pupil in forming and executing purposes that are unprecedented as well as those that follow precedent. From the standpoint of the church, it means ecclesiastical self-reconstruction in and through fresh approaches to the surrounding world.

Of course any such idea of education bristles with questions, and it is provocative of so many doubts that no one need fear that it will be precipitately adopted. We can afford to examine it in a leisurely spirit. It will be well to look, first of all, at the alternative. How, as a matter of fact, is the transmission theory of Christian education working? What should we have to give up if we shifted to the theory of creativity? In the next chapter I shall endeavor to present a realistic picture of actual conditions that show in some detail what our alternatives are. After that we shall be ready for exposition of the specific nature of the creative principle, already within our historic religion, that might control Christian education.

CODA

What, Then, Is Christian Education?

It is the systematic, critical examination and reconstruction of relations between persons, guided by Jesus' assumption that persons are of infinite worth, and by the hypothesis of the existence of God, the Great Valuer of Persons.

BIBLIOGRAPHY

General Works on Historical Backgrounds of Education

Adamson, John William, *Pioneers of Modern Education*. Cambridge University Press, Cambridge, 1921.

Brubacher, John S., *A History of the Problems of Education*. McGraw-Hill Book Co., Inc., 1947.

Butts, R. Freeman, *A Cultural History of Western Education* (2d ed.). McGraw-Hill Book Co., Inc., 1955.

Castle, E. B., *Moral Education in Christian Times*. George Allen and Unwin, Ltd., London, 1958.

Cole, Luella, *A History of Education: Socrates to Montessori*. Rinehart & Company, Inc., 1950.

Cubberley, Ellwood P., *The History of Education*. Houghton Mifflin Company, 1920.

—— *Readings in the History of Education*. Houghton Mifflin Company, 1920.

Drane, Augusta Theodosia, *Christian Schools and Scholars; or Sketches of Education from the Christian Era to the Council of Trent* (new ed., ed. by Walter Gumbley). Benziger Brothers, 1924.

Duggan, Stephen, *A Student's Textbook in the History of Education* (3d ed.). Appleton-Century-Crofts, Inc., 1948.

Eby, Frederick, *Early Protestant Educators*. McGraw-Hill Book Co., Inc., 1931.

Eby, Frederick, and Arrowood, Charles F., *The History and*

Philosophy of Education, Ancient and Medieval. Prentice-Hall, Inc., 1940.

Good, H. G., *A History of Western Education.* The Macmillan Company, 1947.

Graves, Frank P., *A History of Education.* The Macmillan Company, 1910.

Haarhof, Theodore Johannes, *Schools of Gaul: A Study of Pagan and Christian Education in the Last Century of the Western Empire.* Oxford University Press, 1920.

Hodgson, Geraldine, *Primitive Christian Education.* T. & T. Clark, Edinburgh, 1906.

Jarman, T. L., *Landmarks in the History of Education.* The Cresset Press, London, 1951.

Kinloch, T. F., *Pioneers of Religious Education.* Oxford University Press, Inc., 1939.

Knight, Edgar W., *Readings in American Educational History.* Appleton-Century-Crofts, Inc., 1951.

Marique, Pierre J., *History of Christian Education* (3 vols.). Fordham University Press, 1924, 1926, 1932.

Melvin, A. Gordon, *Education, a History.* The John Day Co., Inc., 1946.

Monroe, Paul, *Source Book of the History of Education.* The Macmillan Company, 1901.

Moore, E. C., *The Story of Instruction: The Church, the Renaissance, and the Reformation.* The Macmillan Company, 1938.

Noble, Stuart G., *A History of American Education* (rev. ed.). Rinehart & Company, Inc., 1954.

Painter, F. V. N., *Great Pedagogical Essays.* American Book Company, 1905.

Rashdall, Hastings, *The Universities of Europe in the Middle Ages* (new ed., 3 vols., ed. by F. M. Powicke and A. B. Emden). Oxford University Press, 1936.

Rusk, Robert R., *The Doctrines of the Great Educators* (2d ed.). Macmillan and Company, Ltd., London, 1954.

Sherrill, Lewis Joseph, *The Rise of Christian Education.* The Macmillan Company, 1944.

Thut, I. N., *The Story of Education: Philosophical and Historical Foundations.* McGraw-Hill Book Co., 1957.

Ulich, Robert, *History of Educational Thought*. American Book
    Company, 1943.
—— *Three Thousand Years of Educational Wisdom*. Harvard
    University Press, 1947.
Woodward, William Harrison, *Studies in Education During the
    Age of the Renaissance, 1400–1600*. Cambridge University
    Press, Cambridge, 1924.

Works Illustrative of Trends and Developments in Christian Education Since George Albert Coe

Elliott, Harrison S., *Can Religious Education Be Christian?*
The Macmillan Company, 1940.

Smith, H. Shelton, *Faith and Nurture*. Charles Scribner's Sons, 1941.

Vieth, Paul H., ed., *The Church and Christian Education*. The Bethany Press, 1947.

Miller, Randolph Crump, *The Clue to Christian Education*. Charles Scribner's Sons, 1952.

Smart, James D., *The Teaching Ministry of the Church*. The Westminster Press, 1954.

Sherrill, Lewis Joseph, *The Gift of Power*. The Macmillan Company, 1955.

Cully, Iris V., *The Dynamics of Christian Education*. The Westminster Press, 1958.

Wyckoff, D. Campbell, *The Gospel and Christian Education*. The Westminster Press, 1959.

This list of significant works in recent years is given in "Theology and Christian Education: An Editorial," by James Blair Miller, in *Encounter*, Autumn, 1958, pp. 379 f. See also "Two Decades of Thinking Concerning Christian Nurture," by Kendig Brubaker Cully, in *Religious Education*, Vol. LIV, No. 6 (Nov.–Dec., 1959), pp. 481–489.

INDEX

Acacius, 32
Actuality, 108
Address to Origen, 27–31
Adeodatus, 63
Aelius Donatus, 41
Aesop, 212
Agathus, 240
Agriculture, 200, 253
Alcuin, 83–87, 88, 93
Alexander, 146
Alexander V, Pope, 119
Ambrose, 62
American Free Schools, 289–294
Andrews, Bishop, 191
Andros, Sir Edmund, 229
Aquinas, Thomas, 102–118
Aratus, 201
Architecture, 200
Areopagitica, 192
Arians, 32
Aristotle, 200, 202
Arithmetic, 95, 98, 158, 200, 257
Arts, 53, 196
Asceticism, 42, 49, 150, 224

Ascham, Roger, 170–176, 191
Astronomy, 96, 100
Augustine, Aurelius, 62–73, 106 ff.
Aurelian, 25
Ave Maria, 131

Baptism, 21, 33, 37, 39, 79 f., 165
Baugulf, Abbot, 89
Belief, 66
Biblical theology, 11
Boethius, 109
Bond, R., 191
Books, 187, 227, 247
Boys, 51 ff., 91 f.
Brief Essay to Direct and Excite Family Religion, 231–237
Brunner, Emil, 253
Bushnell, Horace, 295–309
Bust of Eaton, 190

Calvin, John, 62, 162–169
Castelvetro, 203

Catechesis, 36 ff., 64 ff., 164 ff., 224, 228

Catechetical Lectures, 32, 33–40

Catechetical school, Alexandria, 15, 25

Catechism of the Church of Geneva, 164–168

Catechisms, 32, 162, 164 ff., 214, 218 ff.

Catechizing of the Uninstructed, 64–73

Catechumens, 36 ff., 74, 79 f.

Cathedral schools, 138

Cato, 200

Celibacy, 129

Celsus, 200

Character, 181 f., 308

Charlemagne, 83, 88–92

Charles II, King, 185

Charondas, 202

Children, 19 ff., 43 ff., 121 ff., 137 ff., 171, 181 ff., 187 ff., 233 ff., 241, 255 ff., 281, 293, 298 ff., 313 ff.

Christ the Educator, 17–24

Christian Discipline, etc., 240–249

Christian Nurture, 295 ff.

Christmas, 259

Chrysostom, John, 49–61

Church, 35, 38, 40, 74 ff., 337 f.

Cicero, 42, 182, 202 f.

Clarke, Edward, 206

Clement of Alexandria, 10, 15–24

Coe, George Albert, 10 f., 325–338

Cognition, 109 ff.

Colleges, 265, 334

Columella, 200

Comenius, John Amos, 177–184

Community life, 317

Conduct of the Schools, 218–223

Confession, 129 ff.

Confirmation, 165, 168, 266, 272

Congregational Library, 230

Conidas, 191

Conscience, 241

Constitutions of the Holy Apostles, 74–80

Conversion, 299 f.

Cooper, 187

Counseling, 121 ff.

Crafts, 255 f.

Cranmer, Archbishop, 234

Creeds, 92, 212, 214

Cromwell, Oliver, 192

Cully, Iris V., 342

Culture, 20, 93, 192

Curriculum, 266, 310, 318 ff.

Cyril of Jerusalem, 32–40

Damasus I, Pope, 41

de la Salle, Jean Baptiste, 216–223

Deeds, 17

Demosthenes, 203

Denominations, 272

Deogratias, Brother, 64

Dewey, John, 10, 310–324, 325

Dialectic, 29 ff., 96 ff.

Didactic writings, 239

Dionysius, 201

Discipline, 52, 78, 173 ff., 187 ff., 225 f., 253, 260 f., 322 f.
Discipline of self, 35, 284 f.
Discovery, 117 f.
Disputation, 103
Doctrine, 95, 166, 246, 293
Dominic, 105
Donatus, 146
Dress, 44, 60 f.

Early centuries, 15–80
Easter, 100, 259
Ecumenical movement, 11
Education, 20, 22, 193 ff., 207 ff., 267 ff., 278, 312 ff., 327 ff.
Education of Man, 277–286
Education of the Clergy, 95–101
Education, universal, 136, 289 ff.
Educational Proclamations, 89–92
Eighteenth century and beyond, 253–338
Elizabeth I, Queen, 170
Elliott, Harrison S., 342
England, 173 f., 199, 202
Eraste, 247
Ethics, 201, 260 ff., 335 ff.
Eugenio, 240 ff.
Eusebius, 25
Exhortation, 64
Exhortation to the Greeks, 15
Experience, 20, 267 f.

Faith, 108, 152
Faith, the, 17, 19, 63 f., 66, 78

Families, 231 ff., 273 f.
Fathers, 51 ff., 98, 225, 241 ff., 273
Felix of Urgel, 83
Festival days, 100
Francke, August Hermann, 224–228
Francke Institutions, 224
Freedom, 284
Freethinkers, 247
Friendship, 28 f., 48, 193
Froebel, Friedrich, 275–286
Fuller, Thomas, 185–191

Galileo, 192
Gaudentius, 48
Geometry, 96, 99, 200
German, 140, 148
Germany, 137 f., 287, 306
Gerold, 160
Gerson, Jean, 119–132
Girls, 43 ff.
Good, the, 96
Good Schoolmaster, The, 186–191
Gospel, 139 ff., 154
Grace, 35, 38, 140, 176
Grammar, 96 f., 199
Great Didactic, 179–184
Greek language, 19 f., 144, 148, 195 f., 200 f., 272
Greek thought, 15
Gregory Thaumaturgus, 25–31
Grimes, Howard, 63
Guidance, 124
Guilt, 109 f.

Habits, 17 f., 35, 46, 270
Harper, William Rainey, 310

Hartgrave of Burnley School,
    191
Hartlib, Samuel, 193
Hartopp, Sir John, 238
Health, 17 f., 117 f.
Hearing, 56 f., 72
Hebrew, 143, 148, 202
Herbart, Johann Friedrich,
    265–274
Herbartian method, 265
Heresy, 69
Hermogenes, 203
Hesiod, 201
History, 10, 77, 95, 202, 288,
    337
Holy Spirit, 34, 36, 39 f., 96,
    144, 152 f., 303, 307
Homer, 15
Hooper, 234
Hope, 36
Horace, 203
How to Study, 104 f.
Hugh of St. Victor, 119
Hus, John, 119
Hymns, 238

Idealism, 265
Ignorance, 21, 27, 63, 109 f.,
    141 ff., 212, 221
Incarnation, 80
Indoctrination, 201 f.
*Institutes of the Christian Re-
    ligion*, 162
Instruction, 18, 38, 68, 118,
    233 f., 280
Instrumentalism, 310
Intention, 34
Interest, 322

Isidore of Seville, 94
Italian, 199, 202

Jerome, 41–48, 87
Jesus Christ, 22, 36, 40, 122 ff.,
    150, 153, 155, 160, 165,
    232 ff., 242, 283, 286, 330,
    336 f.
John, Brother, 104
Justinian, 202

Kant, Immanuel, 265
Kingdom of God, 319, 335
Knowledge, 15, 18 f., 95, 98,
    106 ff.

La Chatolais, 206
Laertius, 202
Langethal, Heinrich, 275
Language, 27, 140 ff., 195
Latin, 140, 148, 166, 170 f.,
    190, 195 f., 200 ff.
Law, 77, 160, 202, 270, 277 ff.
Lectures, 32, 36, 65 ff., 199
Leo X, Pope, 135
Leonard and Gertrude, 255–
    264
Letter to Charlemagne, 85–87
Letter to Pacatula, 43–48
Liberal arts, 93 ff., 143
Liberal movement, 276, 325
Locke, John, 205–215
Longinus, 203
Lord's Prayer, 92, 131, 212,
    214
Lucretius, 201
Luther, Martin, 135–149, 150
Lycurgus, 202

Man, 179 ff.
Manichaean movement, 62
Manilius, 201
Mann, Horace, 287–294
Marriage, 60, 79
Mather, Cotton, 229–237
Mather, Increase, 229
Maurus, Rabanus, 93–101
Mazzonei, 203
Medicine, 95, 201, 205
Meetings, 236
Mela, 200
Melanchthon, 136, 150
Memorization, 46, 212
Memory, 175, 242
Method, 320 ff.
Middendorf, Wilhelm, 275
Middle centuries, 83–132
Miller, James Blair, 342
Miller, Randolph Crump, 342
Milton, John, 192–204
Ministers, 35, 71, 95 ff., 121 ff.,
    255 ff.
Miscellanies, 15
Monasticism, 89, 91, 138 ff.
Monica, 62
Mothers, 45, 51, 57, 60, 188 f.,
    247 f., 273
Mulcaster, 191
Music, 92, 96, 99 f., 228
Mysteries, 36, 74, 90, 154
Myth, 273

Names, 57
Nature, 153, 201, 257, 282 f.
Navigation, 200
Neo-orthodoxy, 11, 325
Nicander, 201

Nominalism, 119
Nurture, 297 ff.

Obedience, 45, 286
Of the Upbringing and Edu-
    cation of Youth, etc., 152–
    161
On Education, 193–204
On Leading Children to
    Christ, 121–132
Oratory, 70 ff.
Origen, 25 ff.
Orpheus, 201
Outlines of Educational Doc-
    trine, 267–274
Ovid, 123

Pantaenus, 15
Parental responsibility, 45, 49,
    51–61, 78 f., 241 ff.
Parents, 157, 241 ff.
Passion (of Christ), 80
Passions, 17 f.
Past, the, 9, 48
Paulinus, 41
Pedagogy, theory of, 15,
    267 ff., 279 ff.
Pepin the Short, 88
Pericles, 152
Personality, 329 ff.
Persuasion, 17 f., 31
Pestalozzi, Heinrich, 10, 206,
    253–264, 265
Peterson, Houston, 25
Phalereus, 203
Philosophy, 27 f., 59, 100,
    196 f., 265, 268, 271, 310 f.
Pilgrim Fathers, 289

Pittacus, 179
Plato, 15, 202 f., 272
Play, 44, 156 ff., 174 f.
Pliny, 42, 200
Plutarch, 199, 202
Poetry, 203
Politics, 60, 202, 287
Potentiality, 108
Prayer, 39, 53, 104, 228
Procatechesis, 32
Progress, social, 319
Property, 291 ff., 336
Protestantism, 328, 331
Providence, 153
Psychology, 265, 268, 313 f.
Psychology, depth, 11
Punishment, 241 f.
Pupil concern, 26, 224
Pupils, 222 f., 327 ff.
Pythagoras, 100

Questions, 115 f., 218 f.

Reading, 91, 212 ff.
Reason, 20, 27 f., 97, 105 ff., 129, 180, 244
Rebirth, 21
Reconstruction, 337
Reformation and after, 135–249
Regeneration, 37, 39
Religious Education Association, 325
Renaissance, 136
Repentance, 33, 242
Responsibility, 323
Resurrection, 80
Reverence, 208
Rewards, 44, 242, 270

Rhetoric, 62, 96
Right Way for Parents to Bring Up Their Children, 51–61
Roman Catholic doctrine, 328
Rousseau, Jean Jacques, 206, 253

Sacraments, 68, 140, 266, 272, 328
Sacrifice, 45, 154, 231 f.
Salvation, 23
Scapula, 187
Scholasticism, 119
Schoolmaster, The, 172–176
Schools, 91, 97, 126, 136 ff., 172 ff., 186 ff., 253, 288 ff., 315 ff.
Science, 97 ff., 224, 243, 269
Scriptures, 19, 35 f., 57 f., 67 ff., 74, 76 f., 90, 95 ff., 147 f., 202 f., 213 f., 224, 228, 233, 243 ff., 255, 272, 301 ff., 330, 336
Seeing, 59 f.
Self-control, 43
Seminaries, 334
Seneca, 42, 124, 200
Sermons, 37
Sex relations, 45
Shaftesbury, Earl of, 205
Sherrill, Lewis Joseph, 342
Sin, 20 f., 33, 39, 47, 124, 246, 304
Siricius, Pope, 41
Smart, James D., 342
Smith, H. Shelton, 342
Social situations, 312 ff.
Socrates, 156, 172 f., 199, 272

Socratic method, 30
Solinus, 200
Solon, 202
Some Thoughts Concerning Education, 207–215
Son of God, 33
Speech, 52, 55 f., 65 ff., 90, 95, 97, 104, 204, 247 f., 256 ff.
Spencer, Herbert, 11
Spinoza, Baruch, 274
Starting Point of a Solution, The, 327–338
State, 142 ff.
Stoics, 15
Storytelling, 56 f.
Study, 40, 102, 104 f., 245
Summa Theologica, 102
Sunday observance, 273
Sunday school, 334
Symbols, 106 f., 167

Tasso, 203
Taxation, 291 ff.
Teacher, The, 105–118
Teacher-pupil relationships, 15, 121 ff., 171, 218 ff., 225 ff.
Teachers, 25, 46, 59, 67, 105 ff., 172 ff., 185 ff., 218 ff., 244 ff., 255 ff., 317, 325 ff., 332 ff.
Teaching, 40, 105 ff., 172 ff., 185 ff., 195 ff., 218 ff., 224, 255 ff.
Teaching, Art of, 28 ff., 185 ff.
Teaching plan, 227 f.
Temptation, 39, 70, 130
Ten Commandments, 212, 214
Terence, 126
Theocritus, 201

Thoughts on Teaching, 225–228
To the Councilmen of All Cities, etc., 137–149
Touch, 59
Transmission, 334 f.
Trent, Council of, 41
Truth, 96, 159, 211 f., 227, 286

Udal, Nicholas, 189
Ulich, Robert, 119
United States of America, 11, 290 ff.
Unity, Divine, 276 ff.
Universities, 138 ff.

Varro, 200
Victorines, 119
Victorinus, 41
Vieth, Paul H., 342
Virgil, 201
Virginity, 52
Virtue, 18, 117 f., 155, 161, 176, 209, 243 ff., 269 ff., 304
Vitruvius, 200
Vocations, 78, 145 f., 188, 224
von Bora, Katharine, 135
Vulgate, 41

Watts, Isaac, 238–249
What Christian Nurture Is, 297–309
What Is Christian Education? 327–338
Whitaker, Dr., 191
William, King, 205
William of Paris, 128
Wisdom, 20, 59 f., 83, 96, 175 f., 211 f., 262

Word of God, 18 ff., 29, 147, 152

Xenophon, 202

Words, 27, 31, 95

Youth, 152 ff., 240 ff.

Worthington, John, 214

Writing, 90, 96, 204, 228

Zaleucus, 202

Wyckoff, D. Campbell, 342

Zwingli, Ulrich, 150–161